Nazareth College Library
Nazareth, Michigan 49074

D1003101

Y OF
E OF FLINT

Sophisms on Meaning and Truth

CENTURY PHILOSOPHY SOURCEBOOKS

JUSTUS BUCHLER AND STERLING P. LAMPRECHT, *Editors*

John Buridan: SOPHISMS ON MEANING AND TRUTH

Translated and with an introduction by
Theodore Kermit Scott
Purdue University

NEW YORK
APPLETON - CENTURY - CROFTS
Division of Meredith Publishing Company

Copyright © 1966 by
MEREDITH PUBLISHING COMPANY

All rights reserved. This book, or parts thereof, must not be used or reproduced in any manner without written permission. For information address the publisher, Appleton-Century-Crofts, Division of Meredith Publishing Company, 440 Park Avenue South, New York, N.Y. 10016.

696-1
Library of Congress Card Number: 66-26800

PRINTED IN THE UNITED STATES OF AMERICA
E 15395

165
B917

TO MY FATHER
AND IN MEMORY OF MY MOTHER

Gift
4-5-67

Nazareth College Library
Nazareth, Michigan 49074

46608

PREFACE

Despite the considerable efforts of historians of medieval philosophy, and sometimes because of them, the philosophical winds that have prevailed since the seventeenth century still carry most students from Peripateticus to Cartesius, with scarcely a sighting of intermediate ports of call. Like *medieval* itself, *scholastic* is too often a pejorative, implying at best the heroic futility of mind ensnared by dogma and at worst (and more typically) the barren niggling of dialectic without content. And even those who have discovered the power of the great theologico-philosophical syntheses of the thirteenth century have mixed their praise with lamentations over the post-Thomistic "collapse" of reason.

This translation of John Buridan's *Sophismata* is undertaken in the belief that seeing for oneself is the most effective antidote for preconception. Here is a work, by one of the greatest of the later scholastics, which carries no theological freight and so cannot be accused on that count. But whether it will escape the charge of quibbling pretension is not so easy to know. Those who equate stylistic formality with rigidity of mind and who confuse care for detail with nitpicking will not find a vindication of scholasticism in Buridan. But insight and analytic power have their value for some, and they will find in him not historical curiosities, but exciting new answers to old and persistent questions. There can be no higher recommendation.

I wish to thank my colleague, Mr. Milton Fisk, for a number of helpful suggestions on the Introduction, and Professor Ernest A. Moody for allowing me to draw so often on his vast knowledge and deep understanding of later medieval philosophy. Professor Paul O. Kristeller read an initial draft of the translation, and whatever value it has is due largely to his many corrections and suggestions. The shortcomings that remain are, of course, mine. Very special gratitude goes to my teacher and friend, Professor James J. Walsh, who not only read the entire manuscript with great care, but who also first introduced me to medieval thought and to Buridan. And finally, I thank my wife for the drudgery patiently undergone and for the encouragement that brought the work to completion.

T. K. S.

CONTENTS

Sophisms on Meaning and Truth

INTRODUCTION

I. Life, Influence, and Writings

John Buridan was born at Bethune in the diocese of Arras shortly before 1300.[1] As a young man, he was a member of the College of the Cardinal Lemoine in Paris and later studied and taught in the College of Navarre. He then joined the Faculty of Arts of the University of Paris, where he enjoyed a long and distinguished career, being appointed Rector of the University in 1328 and again in 1340. Popular as a mediator of political and jurisdictional disputes, he also retained the constant favor of ecclesiastical authorities and received at least three separate benefices. He traveled at least once to the seat of the papacy at Avignon, pausing en route to ascend Mount Ventoux to make astronomical observations. He died about 1358.

The magnitude of Buridan's influence during the two centuries following his death is hard for a modern reader to comprehend. He completely dominated later medieval philosophy at Paris, and as late as 1516, George Lockert wrote that he still ruled the study of physics.[2] His students, such as Albert of Saxony, who was the first Rector of the University of Vienna, and Marsilius of Inghen, who was Rector at Heidelberg, early carried his writings and ideas to Eastern Europe, where they remained central well into the sixteenth century.[3] In 1398,

[1] For a complete account of Buridan's life and writings, see E. Faral, "Jean Buridan: Maître ès Arts de L'Université de Paris," *Historie littéraire de la France*, XXXVIII (1949), 462–605. And by the same author, "Jean Buridan. Notes sur les manuscrits, les éditions et le contenu de ses ouvrages," *Archives d'histoire doctrinale et littéraire du moyen âge*, XV (1946), 1–55.

[2] See H. Elie, "Quelques Maîtres de l'Université de Paris vers l'an 1500," *Archives d'histoire doctrinale et littéraire du moyen âge*, XXV–XXVI (1950–1951), 198–199.

[3] On this aspect of Buridan's influence, see G. Ritter, *Studien zur Spätscholastik, I: Marsilius von Inghen und die Ockhamistische Schule in Deutschland*, Vol. XXII, No. 4 (1921) of *Sitzungsberichte der Heidelberger Akademie der*

only shortly after his death, his *Sum of Dialectic* was inscribed on the program of authors to be read in the Faculty of Arts at Cologne. And in 1425, the masters of Cologne defended a return to the study of Albert the Great and Thomas Aquinas, by replying to a group of objecting princes that the realism of Thomas and Albert was quite respectable and had even been dominant at some universities "before the age of Buridan." [4] Through followers such as John Major, his influence spread beyond the continent, and in fifteenth-century Scotland, the two dominant schools of thought were known as the *via Alberti* and the *via Buridani.* [5]

It is not easy to know how widely read he was after the sixteenth century, but it is certain that Buridan did not quite fall into the oblivion reserved for most later scholastics. His *Questions on the Nicomachean Ethics* was published in 1637 at Oxford, his *Questions on the Politics* in 1640, and most remarkably, his *Sum of Dialectic* was published not only in 1637, but in 1740 as well. There is as yet no record of such late editions of his works on the continent, but he was apparently not forgotten, since Schopenhauer mentions him several times as a well-known scholastic and describes in some detail an edition of the *Sophismata* that he owned and had read carefully. [6]

Like many scholastics, Buridan wrote widely, and his works cover most areas of philosophical interest, except theology, which was officially closed to him as a Master of Arts. Not including his logical works, his most important ideas are developed in questions and commentaries on Aristotle. He wrote commentaries on the *Physics, On the Heavens, On Generation and Corruption, Meteorology*, and the short physical treatises or *parva naturalia.* And there are both commentary

---

Wissenschaften: Philosophisch-historische Klasse. Also Ritter, *Studien zur Spätscholastik, II: Via Antiqua und Via Moderna auf den Deutschen Universitäten des XV. Jahrhunderts*, Vol. XIII, No. 7 (1922) of the same series.

[4] The reply to the princes is printed in F. Ehrle, "Franziskanische Studien," *Der Sentenzenkommentar Peters von Candia des Pisaner Papstes Alexander V: Ein Beitrag zur Scheidung der Schulen in der Scholastik des Vierzehnten Jahrhunderts und zur Geschichte des Wegestreites* (Supplement IX; Münster in Westfallen, 1925), 283–284.

[5] H. Rashdall, *Universities of Europe in the Middle Ages* (3 vols.: new edition by F. M. Powicke and A. B. Emden; Oxford, 1936), Vol. I, 496.

[6] See A. Schopenhauer, "Die Beiden Grundprobleme der Ethik," *Sämtliche Werke,* Vol. 4, ed. J. Frauenstädt and A. Hübscher (Wiesbaden, 1950), pp. 58–59.

and questions on the *Metaphysics* and questions on both the *Nicomachean Ethics* and the *Politics*.

His logical writings include the work here translated and two others. His *Sum of Dialectic* is an introduction to logic, consisting of eight tracts and including the traditional analysis of terms, syllogistic inference, and the dialectical topics or "places," as well as a final tract on definition and demonstration. The collection of sophisms below was intended as a ninth tract of this work. Another important logical study, the *Consequences*, discusses rules governing simple consequences and both assertoric and modal syllogisms.

The present work is entitled simply *Sophismata* and is known to exist in two manuscripts (Erfurt Ampl. F302, fols. 155–191, and a brief fragment in Erfurt Ampl. F305, fol. 98) and five early printed editions (Paris, c. 1489, 1491, 1493, c. 1496/1500, and 1500).[7] The most satisfactory of these almost identical editions is that of c. 1496/1500, published by Antoine Denidel and Nicolus de La Barre, and the translation is of an edition I have prepared based on that *incunabulum* and the two available manuscripts. That edition has not been published.

II. Sophisms in Medieval Philosophy

Buridan's collection of topically arranged sophisms was one of the first by an individual author. But the sophism was a standard tool of university training, and lists of them had been compiled for pedagogical purposes by groups of scholars for almost a hundred years before Buridan.[8]

[7] A bit of manuscript in the Vienna Bibliothek der Dominikaner, Cod. 160/130, fols. 56v–60r, which bears the title *Sophismata Buridani*, is not part of this work and is not, so far as I can determine, part of any of the other known works of Buridan.

[8] On the *sophismata* tradition, see M. Grabmann, *Bearbeitungen und Auslegungen der Aristotelischen Logik aus der Zeit von Peter Abaelard bis Petrus Hispanus*, No. 5 (1937) of *Abhandlungen der Preussischen Akademie der Wissenshaften*; M. Grabmann, *Die Geschichte der Scholastischen Methode* (2 vols., Freiburg, 1909–1911); M. Grabmann, *Mittelalterliches Geistesleben: Abhandlungen zur Geschichte der Scholastik und Mystik* (3 vols., Munich, 1926–1956); M. Grabmann, "Die Sophismataliteratur des 12. und 13. Jahrhunderts mit Textausgabe eines Sophisma des Boetius von Dacien," *Beiträge zur Geschichte der Philosophie und Theologie des Mittelalters: Texte und Untersuchungen*, Vol. XXXVI, No. 1 (1940); P. Mandonnet, *Siger de Brabant et l'averroisme latin au*

The word *sophisma* was used by the Sophists to characterize the conclusion of any sophistical argument, but its more special medieval use probably stems from the Stoics, who employed it in their discussions of Aristotle's *On Sophistical Refutations* to designate the conclusion of an apparently well-constructed syllogism, which is nonetheless false or obscure. The first significant treatment of sophisms in the Middle Ages is probably that found in the *Ars Disserendi* of Adam of Balsham, who wrote in the early twelfth century at about the time Aristotle's *Topics* and *On Sophistical Refutations* were recovered.[9] But Adam only discusses ways in which words may be used sophistically and does not actually list examples of sophisms. Such lists first appear in the later twelfth century, when dialectic came to be considered that part of logic which deals with the art of disputation and response and the *disputatio* as an advanced exercise in dialectic became a standard part of university training.

Classroom instruction in medieval universities settled rather quickly into three basic forms. The *expositio* was a lecture, or reading and commentary, on some classical or early medieval text. The *quaestio* and the *disputatio*, on the other hand, both involved student participation and were highly stylized colloquies for the discussion of philosophical and theological issues. In the beginning, such discussions were all known as *quaestiones disputatae*, but with the rejuvenation of dialectic as a study valuable in itself, the *disputatio*, as a purely dialectical exercise employing many kinds of problems from logic, physics, ethics, metaphysics or theology, was separated from the *quaestio*, which was confined, for the most part, to discussions of issues raised by some important text.[10] The format for the two remained about the same, however, and in both cases a proposition was

XIIIme siècle, VI (1911) and VII (1908) of *Les Philosophes belges;* K. Michalski, "Les Criticisme et le scepticisme dans la philosophie du XIVe siècle," *Bulletin de l'Académie polonaise des sciences et des lettres* (Cracow, 1925); L. Minio-Paluello, "The 'Ars Disserendi' of Adam of Balsham 'Parvipontanus'," *Mediaeval and Renaissance Studies*, III (1954), 116–169; A. Niglis, *Siger von Courtrai, Beiträge zu Seiner Würdigung* (Freiburg, 1903); G. Wallerand, ed. "Les Œuvres de Siger de Courtrai: Etude critique et textes inedits," *Les Philosophes belges* VIII (1913).

[9] Adam's work has been edited by L. Minio-Paluello as No. 1 of *Twelfth Century Logic: Texts and Studies* (Rome, 1956).

[10] Neither of these should be confused with the *quaestiones quodlibetales*, which were not classroom discussions, but exercises open to the public.

presented for discussion by the Master. One party then argued for the truth of the proposition, another against it, and finally the definitive solution of the teacher was given. The course of the discussion was usually recorded either by the teacher or by one of the students, and these published records are our most important source for the thought of almost all the later scholastics.

Since the *disputatio* did not rely on a classical text, it became necessary to compile and publish lengthy lists of propositions for the use of students in preparing for the exercises. These problem sentences or sophisms thus became the literary bearer of the art of disputation. By the middle of the thirteenth century, there had evolved three kinds of these propositions—*insolubilia, impossibilia,* and *sophismata.* An insoluble was a proposition arrived at by apparently valid forms of reasoning, which nonetheless implies its own contradictory. An impossible was a proposition whose contradictory is evident, so that it cannot be demonstrated, and the exercise employing impossibles then consisted in attempting to demonstrate the impossible, so that it was intended to give practice in the use and recognition of paralogisms. The sophisms designated simply *sophismata* were characterized more broadly as propositions seeming to follow from well-established rules, which yet are somehow unacceptable or present special problems. They were used primarily, but not exclusively, for the testing and application of logical rules.

As is evident in Buridan's work, by the fourteenth century, the sophism had taken on major philosophical importance and its scope had been restricted, by and large, to a consideration of logical and semantical questions. The *impossibilia,* as merely formal exercises, are ignored by Buridan, and the insolubles are retained only as sophisms of a special sort. This is because the development of the logical *summa* as an introduction to logic freed the sophisms from more menial duties and allowed them to serve as tests of logical rules and as devices for extending the application of basic principles expounded in the *summae.* And since logic was understood very broadly as including questions of meaning and truth, as well as structure and inference, Buridan's sophisms are anything but a mere dialectical exercise and are arranged so as to constitute an advanced treatise in the theory of language.

Among the more important thirteenth-century collections of

sophisms by individual authors are those of Robert Kilwardby,[11] those of Siger of Courtrai, [12] and the impossibles of Siger of Brabant.[13] In the fourteenth century, Albert of Saxony compiled what was perhaps the largest collection, containing some two hundred sophisms. [14] And William Heytesbury and Richard Kilmington also collected groups that are of particular importance.[15]

III. Buridan's Work in the Scholastic Tradition

Leaving aside the great theologico-philosophical issues familiar to all who have read the older histories of medieval philosophy, surely the most persistent purely philosophical debate in the Middle Ages was over a group of questions that came to be known, collectively, as the problem of universals. [16] From the time of Boethius' commentary on the *Isagoge* of Porphyry in the early sixth century, the problem held an unparalleled fascination for almost every philosopher.

The classificatory gains of talk about genera and species of things and the indispensability of general terms in both natural and scientific language were felt to be facts sufficiently obvious to warrant the question whether there is a corresponding "generality" in things talked about. Are there really kinds or sorts of things, in addition to the singular things themselves, and if so, what mode of existence do these universals have? Are they really distinct from individuals or somehow "inherent" in them? If they are distinct from individuals, how are they related to them? And if they are not distinct, how is it that the mind is able to grasp the universal in abstraction from its individual

[11] A manuscript at Erfurt Ampl. Q328, fols. 1–73.

[12] G. Wallerand, *op. cit.*, pp. 129–165.

[13] C. Baeumker, "Die Impossibilia des Siger von Bragant: Eine Philosophische Streitschrift aus dem XIII. Jahrhundert zum Ersten Male Vollständig Herausgegeben und Besprochen," *Beiträge zur Geschichte der Philosophie des Mittelalters,* Vol. IV, No. 6 (1898).

[14] *Sophismata Alberti de Saxonia Nuper Emendata* (Paris, 1495).

[15] Both of these groups have been edited by C. Wilson, *William Heytesbury: Medieval Logic and the Rise of Mathematical Physics* (Madison, Wisconsin, 1956), pp. 153–168.

[16] The best brief history of the problem is in J. Weinberg, *A Short History of Medieval Philosophy* (Princeton, N.J., 1964), pp. 58–60, 72–73, 78–91, 243–253.

instances? *Realists,* who answered the first of these questions by affirming the existence of universals, were then arrayed against *nominalists,* who rejected universals.[17]

That the debate was accorded such weight from its inception, and particularly during the eleventh and twelfth centuries, must be explained by the attraction of its subtlety to men who were establishing, for the first time in the Middle Ages, a rigorous standard for philosophical thinking, and by the early recognition that an answer to the question of universals was not without theological significance.[18] Because from a strictly philosophical perspective, neither party was able to establish very clear theoretical gains offered by its position, so that during these early years, it is hard to see the dispute as more than a dialectical exercise. All parties adopted as axiomatic both the existence of singular entities in the world and the existence of a language employing general terms that is about that world. The battle was then joined over the question which of these facts was to be granted primacy. The realists' most formidable weapon was the spectre of skepticism, the claim that since knowledge depends upon general ideas of fixed signification and since univocity of signification requires a corresponding unity in what is signified, knowledge cannot exist without some real generality as its object. The nominalists typically replied that the realist gained knowledge but lost the world. For if universals are real, then singulars are merely instances of these universals and so have no independent existence.

Substantive philosophical gains from the dispute were slight before the thirteenth century. But it is interesting to note, as a psychological fact of importance for understanding later developments, that in the most famous round of the debate, William of Champeaux lost to his pupil, Peter Abelard, not only because of Abelard's superior dialectical skill, but because of their basic agreement on ontological priorities. William, a realist, was defeated by the nominalist Abelard largely because both of them found the existence of singular things more compelling than the fact of general knowledge, and it was William's

[17] On the history of the terms "realist" and "nominalist," see Ehrle, *op. cit.*, pp. 106–112.

[18] See for example, Anselm's condemnation of nominalism in his *Monologium* (Ch. XVII in particular) as not only false, but impious. An English translation is available in Anselm, *Basic Writings*, tr. S. N. Deane (La Salle, Illinois, 1962).

admission that his "indifferentist" theory of universals failed to preserve the integrity of the concrete singular that cost him not only the debate, but his academic career as well.

The dispute finally found its *raison d'etre* in the thirteenth century, when the translations of the bulk of Aristotle's philosophy and the acceptance of it as a unified system of thought suggested to the medievals, for the first time, the possibility that the human mind, unaided by divine illumination, might attain a considerable degree of certain knowledge of the universe. And in particular, Aristotle's natural philosophy offered hope of a complete science of nature, so that it became a matter of first importance to ferret out all his scattered remarks on the nature of knowledge and to fit them into a consistent system. But it was soon found that at least part of this task lent new significance to the old problem of universals.

According to Aristotle, being is composed of individual substances and their accidents, and a science is a collection of demonstrative syllogisms which conclude in truths about these beings, by proceeding from indemonstrable premisses, arrived at by "induction" from experience, to conclusions which predicate accidents of their subjects.[19] But at the same time, he insists that scientific knowledge is of the universal and necessary, not of the contingent and particular. [20] These two opinions, when read in the light of the long medieval tradition, proved difficult to reconcile. How could there be a science of the natural world of contingent, individual substances, which nonetheless had as its objects things both universal and necessary?

Working under the influence of the dominant Augustinian-Platonic tradition, newly reinforced by neo-platonic interpretations of Aristotle by Moslem thinkers, medieval philosophers almost uniformly agreed that if science is to be of the universal and necessary, there must be some sort of universal and necessary being in the world. On the other hand, not only Aristotelian philosophy, but the Christian emphasis on the integrity and personal immortality of the human soul, demanded that the ontological autonomy of the individual substance be preserved. In the face of such a dilemma, diverse interpretations are to be expected. But in fact, although there were disagree-

[19] See Aristotle, *Metaphysics* IV. 2. 1003b 5–35; *Metaphysics* V. 8; *Posterior Analytics* I. 1–2.

[20] See *Posterior Analytics* I. 8; *Nicomachean Ethics* VI. 6.

ments on details, scholastic philosophers, possessed of a common intellectual heritage, moved rather quickly toward a general consensus. The opinion agreed upon has been dubbed "moderate realism" by the historians. On this view, there are no real universals independent of the individual substances that populate the world, excepting perhaps the ideas of the divine mind. But since science employs universal concepts, these must have some foundation in reality. So it was held that although substances are numerically distinct, several of them may possess a Common Nature, and that although this Nature is incapable of independent existence, it is yet real and can be abstracted by the mind from its individuated instances, on the basis of experience of the individuals to which it belongs.

This opinion, adopted in some form by Avicenna, Averroes, Thomas Aquinas, Duns Scotus, and others, claims both the independence of the individual substance and a real basis for universal knowledge, so that it apparently meets both of Aristotle's requirements. But it was still faced with a difficulty that had plagued realists since Plato, that of explaining how a Nature that is in itself common or general is contracted so that it exists only in individuals. Or to put it another way, if many individuals share the same Nature, what justification is there for supposing them to have independent existence at all? What is needed is an account of the way in which the Common Nature is contracted to the individual, so that it becomes the nature of just *that* individual; and it is not too much to say that the prime preoccupation of late thirteenth-century philosophy was the search for an adequate and believable "principal of individuation."

When viewed from this historical perspective, the third decade of the fourteenth century must be accounted a major watershed in the history of philosophy. For it was at this time that William of Ockham, in his Oxford lectures on the *Sentences* of Peter Lombard, launched his decisive attack on the entire tradition of moderate realism.[21] Ockham's principal target was Duns Scotus, but the implications of his criticism extended beyond Scotus and even beyond the problem of universals as such. Before the century was out, many philosophers clearly saw that Ockham's "nominalism" was much more than merely a new ontology. There had, after all, been nominalists before, so that a

[21] The best account of Ockham's contribution is E. A. Moody, *The Logic of William of Ockham* (New York, 1935).

simple rejection of universals would hardly have shaken the philosophical world. It was recognized that in spite of Ockham's personal devotion to the tradition of scholastic philosophy and theology, the nature of his attack on the realists implied not merely that they had reached the wrong conclusions, but that they had asked the wrong questions. Whether he knew it or not, Ockham had called for a "new way" of doing philosophy, a *via moderna* to replace the *via antiqua* then firmly established in the schools.[22]

But if a philosophical revolution was Ockham's achievement, it was most surely not his intent. The honorific title of Venerable Inceptor, by which he came to be known, derived from his academic rank, not from any new beginnings deliberately undertaken. Indeed his was the call of a conservative for a return to the true Aristotle. His objections were not to what was old fashioned, but to what was current, to the men he often called the *moderni*.

Ockham thought that whereas Aristotle himself had begun with the ordinary world of individual substances and had sought a science that would yield general and certain knowledge of such a world, his modern interpreters, their modes of thought encrusted with the Platonism of the age, had confused and reversed his program. Conflating the realms of language and reality, which Aristotle had so carefully separated, they had assimilated general knowledge to universal being. And in so doing, they had not only made impossible the Aristotelian goal of a science of the world of particulars, but had also made the very existence of ordinary things the major philosophical problem. If one begins, as had these "moderns," with the assumption that knowledge is only of the universal Common Nature, not of singular substances, the most remarkable intellectual gyrations are required to establish that there *are* any singulars at all. Their error lay in allowing the forms of scientific language to dictate their ontological decisions, for the truth of propositions can be judged only in the light of prior knowledge of what there is.

Philosophy is a discipline of interpretation, not a science of discovery, so that it is not surprising that Ockham's revolution brought a

[22] The account of knowledge engendered by philosophical nominalism had consequences for theology which, though of every great importance, will not be considered here. See H. Obermann, *The Harvest of Medieval Theology* (Cambridge, Mass., 1964).

new point of view, not new facts, particularly since his opponents were as steeped in Aristotle as he was himself. In fact, the whole transformation was due to the rigor with which Ockham upheld a single distinction that had been too often ignored, the distinction between ideas and their objects. The principle underlying Ockhamism is just that thought is one thing and its objects something else. Once the implications of this principle are realized, the proper interpretation of Aristotle is clear. Knowledge is a product of cognitive activity and so belongs to the realm of thought. But knowledge has as its objects things not of that realm. Knowledge is universal, so universality also belongs to the realm of thought, to concepts of the mind. But the objects conceived by those concepts are neither mental nor universal. They are just the concrete substances and accidents that are the objects of knowledge. So man has knowledge of universal concepts and also of the objects conceived, but those objects are the ordinary things of the world that are the subjects of science. This is, Ockham thought, the self-evident import of Aristotle's philosophy, and once it is accepted, the whole doctrine of Common Natures, with its problem of individuation, can and must be abandoned.

The effect of this point of view is to change the function of the philosopher. He need no longer waste his energies on aimless speculations as to what sorts of things there might be in the world. What there is in the world is just what we come to know by studying the world, i.e., the objects of science. The philosopher's job is to analyze and explicate the means by which we *do in fact* have general knowledge of a world of singulars. And the task has a double aspect: (1) to account for the genesis of knowledge, by explaining how it is that the mind comes to possess universal concepts from its starting point in intuitive awareness of singular things; (2) beginning with the fact of general concepts, to explain just how a concept can be a univocal idea of many singulars. The first part of the program called for a general epistemological theory of the process of coming to know, and we shall have occasion to refer briefly to this theory in what follows. But for an understanding of the work of Buridan here translated, the second part of the program is much more important and deserves some additional attention.

A rigorous answer to the question of the relation of concepts to extra-mental reality was made possible by the recognition of an intimate relation between thinking and talking. In Buridan's phrase, "one can speak of what one understands" (Ch. VIII, Soph. 7).[23] Paralleling every relation among concepts, there is a corresponding relation among words in a spoken (or written) language. Thus the question of the relation of concepts to reality becomes the question of the relation of language to reality.

Since the concept of many singular things is the means of knowing, the basic unit of meaning in any corresponding language must be the term, understood as signifying many singulars. That is, every language rests on a base of words which, when considered in isolation, may be understood to refer to some concrete thing or things. Such a word is the categorematic term, which may be characterized as being the sort of word that can serve as subject or predicate in a categorical proposition about the external world.

The decision to ground discourse in the term enabled Ockham and his followers to make use of a well-developed methodological tool, the so-called "terminist" logic. A distinctively medieval creation, this logic had developed out of a long logico-grammatical tradition and was apparently first codified in the *Summulae Logicales* of Peter of Spain in the thirteenth century.[24] The terminist logic itself was neutral as to the reality of universals, but involved a commitment to the term as the only independently significant element of language. Its primary feature was a complex machinery for an analysis of what were known as the "properties of terms." This was actually a misleading label, since these "properties" not only established the meaning and reference of terms taken individually, but explicated the relationships in propositions among categorematic terms and between categorematic and syncategorematic words, in addition to providing the essential material for an elaboration of truth-conditions for all propositions.

A central feature of Ockham's philosophy is his use of this received logical tradition to explain the relation of language to the world. In particular, he was concerned to provide the formal con-

[23] All references in the text will be to the work translated below.

[24] *Petri Hispani Summulae Logicales*, ed. I. M. Bochenski (Torino, 1947); the most important tract has been translated by J. P. Mullally, *The Summulae Logicales of Peter of Spain* (Notre Dame, Indiana, 1945).

ditions of the possibility of a real science of the actual world of singular substances and their accidents, which nonetheless makes use of a language heavily dependent on general terms.

What Ockham had begun, Buridan continued, but with an even clearer realization of ends in view. While Buridan never acknowledges his debt to Ockham, it is obvious not only in his handling of specific issues, but also in his whole philosophic attitude. If Ockham initiated a new way of doing philosophy, Buridan is already a man of the new way. If Ockham was the evangel of a new creed, Buridan is inescapably its stolid practitioner. He cites Aristotle with approval, and at times with disapproval, but he seldom interprets him against the realists. He is a nominalist (a much more radical one than Ockham), but he is less concerned to defend nominalism than to use it. Elaboration of philosophical overviews is replaced by care for important philosophical detail. While hardly a twentieth-century pragmatic analyst, he is, to a surprising degree, willing to leave it to science to tell men both what there is and how it is. Specific issues arising from the nature of science and its objects most often command his attention. He wants to develop a philosophy of science that makes clear the presuppositions and procedures of science. Where science is inconsistent, he attempts to make it consistent. And finally, he attempts to reconstruct all language on the model of scientific language, in order to make clear the commitments and nature of ordinary talk about the world.[25]

This last is the undertaking of the present work. Whereas the *Sum of Dialectic* is an introduction to his logic and theory of language, this collection of sophisms is designed to raise and meet objections to that theory. What emerges is a strictly nominalistic language that is to serve both the ends of ordinary discourse about the world and those of demonstrative science. Buridan is a medieval man, not a modern one, and the science he defends is not modern experimental science. But whatever one's views on the possibilities of Aristotelian science, the theory of language here presented is both impressive and provocative.

[25] But as a possible exception to this, see the Proemium to his *Questions on the Nicomachean Ethics,* where he suggests the need for a different sort of language, a "moral logic," for the practical sciences.

IV. The Ontology of Buridanian Nominalism

The nominalistic tradition in later medieval thought is characterized by an agreement to countenance the being of a good many more words than things. But the rejection of a Common Nature for every common noun reflects not so much a mere preference for a less densely populated universe as a conviction that Common Natures had owed their ontological status to an outmoded way of doing philosophy. The propensity of earlier philosophers to allow the grammatical forms of natural language to dictate their ontological commitments had consequences more dire than a simply uncomfortable proliferation of entities. It spent the bulk of their energies on problems that never should have arisen in the first place, such as the problem of individuation. And most importantly, it made impossible a science of the ordinary particulars of everyday experience and so violated both the spirit of Aristotle and the proper end of philosophy. In calling for a recognition of the ontic priority of these particulars, the nominalist is thus proposing a "new way" for philosophers to proceed. They are no longer to begin by speculating on the implications of the forms of ordinary language and to end by deciding what sorts of things science *might* be about. Rather they are to begin by recognizing the obvious existence of a world of individuals and the fact that science *is* about those individuals and their attributes. Their task is then to develop a theory of language that can consistently account for such a science about such a world.

This is the general program of medieval nominalism and on it there seems to have been widespread agreement. But this was agreement in principle among independent thinkers, so that it was matched by considerable variance as to details. Buridan's most important philosophical disputes were almost all with his fellow nominalists, rather than with realists. And the disputes can almost always be traced to differences in ontology among the nominalists themselves. So because Buridan's theory of language is intelligible only in the light of his peculiar brand of nominalism, it is of some importance to understand in advance just what he thinks there is.

Generally speaking, Buridan admits only one sort of entity, the concrete individual, although apparently not all such individuals are capable of isolated existence.[26] His ontology is grounded in, but not quite restricted to, physical things and their parts, in addition, of course, to the angels and God. Concepts exist but only as singular ideas in individual minds, and they are never shared.[27] More explicitly, he rejects not only universals, but all sorts of abstract objects, including at least one abstract particular. The extent of his nominalism can be more precisely gauged, however, by reviewing how he stands with regard to some entities found in most realistic universes—propositions, attributes, relations, and classes.[28]

A. *Propositions*

For any medieval logician, a proposition (*propositio*) is what is now ordinarily called a sentence, as opposed to what is expressed by a sentence. But Buridan goes farther than this and identifies the proposition with a sentence token, a single utterance or inscription.[29] He allows neither classes of these sentences nor what is now known as a sentence type.[30]

He gives considerable attention to the rejection of any abstract entity as the significate or "meaning" of a proposition. Some of Buridan's contemporaries, among them his colleague, Gregory of

[26] The distinction between concrete and abstract entities is not clear, and not much will be dependent on it here. Buridan's universe includes not only visuo-tactual solids, but the angels and God. It also contains thunder, shadows, and rainbows. What is does *not* contain is much more interesting and will be given in some detail.

[27] When he says that two men have the same concept (as for instance, in the conclusions of Chapter VI), it is quite clear that he means only that the concepts are similar, not that they are numerically identical.

[28] To conserve space, I have not considered his position as regards numbers, which also belong to a realistic ontology. But many of his remarks make it clear that he follows Ockham (and Aristotle) in rejecting numbers as entities apart from things numbered. For a good statement of the position, see Ockham, *Summa Logicae: Pars Prima*, ed. P. Boehner (St. Bonaventure, N.Y., 1957), Ch. 44; *cf.*, Moody, *The Logic of William of Ockham*, pp. 143–156.

[29] Henceforth, "proposition" will be used in Buridan's sense, unless otherwise indicated.

[30] On rare occasions, he can be caught talking as though there were types, as in saying that two men utter the same proposition or that a term is used by several men or on different occasions. In such cases, the nature of the proposition is never at stake. And when it matters, he is remarkably consistent. Note, for example, the eighth sophism of Chapter VIII, where Socrates, Plato, and Robert are said to utter three propositions, not one.

Rimini, held that such a significate must be allowed.[31] Taking as a point of departure some remarks by Aristotle in his *Categories*,[32] Gregory decided that every proposition signifies a complex entity, known variously as an enunciable (*enuntiabile*), as the significate of the whole proposition (*significatum totale propositionis*) or, more commonly, as a complex signifiable (*complexe significabile*). It was ordinarily designated by either an infinitive or a gerundive expression, so that a proposition such as "A man is an animal" was said to signify man-being-animal (*i.e.*, that-man-is-an-animal). The signifiable was characterized as real, but not as existent, as abstract, therefore, but also as particular rather than universal, and as eternal. It was held to be the immediate object of scientific knowledge, although it could be described only through the proposition signifying it.[33]

Buridan rejects the complex signifiable as a reified logical construction. A proposition is, of course, a complex of terms and so signifies things in a complex manner, and we sometimes put this by saying that it signifies things to be somehow or other (Ch. I, solution of Soph. 3). But that is just a way of saying *how* it signifies, not *what* it signifies; and strictly speaking, only what exists can be signified, and only concrete singulars exist. A proposition signifies just the thing or things signified by its categorematic terms (Ch. I, Concl. 8 and solution of Soph. 3). The substantive phrase "man-being-animal" can be taken as designating either the inscription "A man is an animal" or the man or men who are, in fact, animals (Ch. I, solution of Soph. 5 and Ch. III, Remark 2). And if it is said "John knows that a man is an animal" or "John knows a man to be an animal," then what John is being said to know is, in the first instance, an inscription similar to "A man is an animal," and beyond that he is being said to have knowledge of whatever the terms of that inscription designate.[34]

One consequence of this view, which is further explored in the

[31] See *Gregorii Ariminensis Super Primum et Secundum Sententiarum* (Venice, 1522; reprinted by The Franciscan Institute, St. Bonaventure, N.Y., 1955), Prol., Q. I, art. 1.

[32] Aristotle, *Categories* 10. 12b 6–15.

[33] The complex signifiable does not originate with Gregory. It is found in exactly the same form in Abelard, "Logica 'Ingredientibus'," *Peter Abaelards Philosophische Schriften*, ed. B. Geyer (Münster, 1919), pp. 365–366, and it may be traceable to Augustine. Gregory himself was General of the Augustinian Order and cites Augustine about as often as Aristotle.

[34] See the discussion of connotation below.

fourth chapter (Soph. 9–15) is that no two men can be said to know the same thing, unless they are aware of the same inscription or utterance. If Socrates knows the proposition "John loves Mary" and Plato knows the proposition "Mary is loved by John," Buridan allows both that Socrates and Plato know that John loves Mary and that Socrates and Plato do not know the same thing. He uses this distinction to account for those contexts recently called referentially opaque.[35]

Furthermore, a proposition in this sense is merely a physical entity and may be destroyed (Ch. VIII, Soph. 1). And since truth is a property only of such propositions, Buridan is able to use their possible non-existence in his resolution of certain paradoxes. For on account of it, what a proposition asserts may be the case and yet the proposition not be true, if it does not exist.[36]

But this account will not quite stand without some provisos, since not every inscription or utterance qualifies as a proposition. The word-group must be meaningful, and Buridan accounts for this by saying that corresponding to every spoken proposition, there is a mental proposition; or as he puts it, every spoken proposition signifies a mental proposition (Ch. I, solution of Soph. 1).[37] Yet he apparently does not want to say either that a proposition is simply an inscription (or sound)-plus-mental-proposition, for he also claims that the *same* proposition may be true for one man and false for another, if they speak different languages, *i.e.*, if the proposition signifies different mental propositions (Ch. VI, Concl. 1). So a proposition is an inscription or utterance that signifies some mental proposition or other, but no one in particular.[38] And since almost any mark or sound *may* signify a mental proposition for somebody or other, he puts emphasis on the proper construction of spoken or written language as providing a common base for signification. So he says that nothing ought to be allowed to count as a proposition in the strictest sense, unless it has

[35] See W. V. Quine, *Word and Object* (Cambridge, Mass., 1960), pp. 144–151. *Cf.*, the discussion of connotation below.

[36] See the discussion of insolubles below.

[37] The mental proposition is a single mental event (although, presumably, it can be stored in the mind over a period), so the admission of it does not affect Buridan's nominalism. See the discussion of signification below.

[38] Whether an inscription is a proposition at all if it belongs to no language, or if no one is considering it, is not specified. Presumably it is not, although it makes no practical difference.

the correct form, *i.e.*, unless it has a subject and predicate joined by a copula or is reducible to such a proposition or is a compound of several such propositions joined by logical connectives (Ch. VI, Soph. 3).

B. Attributes

As a Christian, Buridan accepts on faith both substances and attributes, since their existence and separability is required by the sacrament of Holy Communion. But even from a philosophical point of view, there is good reason to suppose that he admits attributes. An Aristotelian science is a procedure for investigating the attributes of the subject-genus of the science, so that it is natural to root it in an ontology admitting both substances and attributes. Certainly their existence seems to be presupposed by the discussion of connotative terms in Chapter IV, since a connotative term is often said to stand for some individual and to connote a quality of that individual. So it seems clear that attributes are admitted.

But attributes are not abstract and shared by a number of individuals (Ch. IV, Soph. 8). They are parts of individuals and so are concrete singulars (Ch. IV, solution of Soph. 1).[39] John's whiteness is not identical with Peter's whiteness—it comes into being (not earlier, and maybe later, than John), ceases to be, changes in intensity, etc. The entities designated by abstract terms in the category of quality are not themselves abstract, but exist in space and time. John and Peter are both called white because they possess equal, or at least similar, qualities. [40]

Buridan's position is apt to be rejected out of hand as involving an infinite regress.[41] The argument is that the claim that qualities are not general, but are only similar, calls for an explanation of

[39] On some of the ramifications of such a position, see G. Küng, "Concrete and Abstract Properties," *Notre Dame Journal of Formal Logic,* V (1964), 31–36.

[40] Which properties there are is decided pre-linguistically, as are all ontological questions. So the number of properties is not equal to the number of abstract nouns. Sight is a property, but blindness is not (Ch. IV, Remark 2), so the concept of blindness conceives just the property of sight, but in a certain way (roughly, as not being possessed). The idea that things can be conceived in a certain way, without thereby affecting the content of the concept, is the epistemological basis for the doctrine of connotation. See also the discussion of signification below.

[41] *Cf.*, C. A. Baylis, "Universals, Communicable Knowledge, and Metaphysics," *Journal of Philosophy,* XLVIII (1951), 636–644.

"similar qualities." If it is said to mean only that distinct things are designated by the same or similar terms, then this new use of "same" or "similar" must be explained. If "similar terms" is said to mean only tokens of the same or similar shape, then "same shape" must be explained. And so ad infinitum.

Buridan does not discuss the possibility of such a regress, most likely because it poses no threat to him. Because in fact, a regress develops only if one supposes either that the use of the same or similar terms can be used to *explain* similar properties or, as is more common, that the claim that there are similar properties can be used to *explain* the use of general terms. But the novelty of the medieval nominalists' program lies just in their refusal to attempt such explanations. On the other hand, such explanations were a central feature of the program of medieval realists. The belief of the realist that he could explain the use of general terms and so arrive at a general theory of naming, was typical of the confusion of his enterprise. Because he confounded the realms of thought and being, the realist supposed that by inventing new words, he was discovering new beings, which could be used to explain the nature of language. But in fact, language and being are distinct. New words have to be explained by using old words, and the nature of language can be explained only by employing the language. Which is just to say that it cannot be explained at all. Buridan just takes it as obvious (and as required by the demonstrative science by which man knows his world) that only singulars exist, that they are similar and that general terms designate similar things. No one of these facts is used to explain any of the others. It is evident that we do know individuals, that we do recognize them as similar, and that we do talk about them with general terms. Or taking it from the other side, we call John and Peter white because they are white, and when one of us says they are white, another usually understands just what is being said.

This can all be clarified some by distinguishing between accounting for the use of a term and explaining a fact. To the question "Why do you call both John and Peter white?" the reply "Because they are similar in color" or "Because they possess similar color qualities" may be quite satisfactory. If the questioner was unsure how to use the word "white" (or in Buridanian language, if he was unsure what concept was signified by the spoken term "white"), he may now understand that it is to be used in talking about pale-hued things like Peter and John. And by the same token, there are occasions on which the question "Why do you say that Peter and John possess similar qualities?" (*i.e.*, "Why do you say that one of John's qualities is similar to one of Peter's?"), can be well answered by "Because they are both white." In both cases, an unfamiliar locution is rendered familiar, and Buridan's assertion of the obvious existence of similar qualities reflects the fact that interchanges such as these succeed more often than not.

On the other hand, to the distinctively philosophical question "Why are we able to use general terms?" the answer "Because there are similar qualities" will not do. What is now called for is not clarification of an unfamiliar expression, but rather a general *explanation* of naming. And since an explanation is complete only if the terms of its explanans are themselves clear, one must also explain what is meant by "similar qualities," which requires reference to same or similar tokens, and so introduces a regress.

Since an explanation of similar qualities must make use of tokens that are themselves the same or similar or (if that fails) of pointings to objects that are similar, a Buridanian ontology cannot be justified on the ground of its ability to account for the use of general terms. But the point is that neither can a realist ontology be justified on that ground. And this merely reflects the fact that a decision as to the existence of universals is made independently of a theory of signification because a realist, who explains general terms by means of shared qualities, can indicate what is meant by sharing a quality only by either pointing (at exactly what a nominalist points at) or by using tokens which themselves share a quality. That is, a quality is just what is shared by individuals designated by the same term, and to say that Peter and John possess whiteness is just to say that they are both white.

Medieval realism flourished so long and engaged so many able minds primarily because of the ingenuity of philosophers in inventing new words to cloak their inability to get beyond words to things. And what is most appealing about Buridan (and Ockham before him) is that he rejects the traditional attempt to give a general explanation of naming. He simply assumes on independent grounds the existence of both similar singulars and general terms and then goes about the philosophically important business of analyzing the forms of language by which those singulars are known by the mediation of those terms.

C. Relations

Not much attention is paid to relations in this work, but the eighth sophism of Chapter IV shows that they are to be renounced along with enunciables. Relational terms designate only singular substances and their accidents. In the proposition "Socrates and Plato are similar," the term "similar" stands only for Socrates and Plato, not for a relation.[42] And in the proposition "Socrates' whiteness is his similarity to Plato," the terms "whiteness" and "similarity" stand for the same thing, a concrete quality possessed by Socrates.[43]

Buridan accounts for the relational character of some propositions by holding that terms in the category of relation are connotative. They stand for one substance or quality and connote another or some others. That is, a relational term signifies (in a broad sense) an ordered pair (or triad, etc.) of concrete singulars, but there are no relations in addition to these singulars. In the proposition "Socrates is similar to Plato," the term "similar" stands for Socrates and connotes Plato as possessing an attribute designated by a term which also designates an attribute possessed by Socrates. And a substantive term such as "similarity" signifies all the ordered pairs of attributes whose possessors' names could fill the blanks of the predicable "———is similar to ———," in order to obtain a true proposition.

D. Classes

Classes go the way of all abstract entities. General nouns are referential just as are proper names, but general nouns are not proper names, and in no case do they stand for classes (Ch. III, Soph. 3 and 4 and their solutions). The reference of a general term, whether abstract or concrete, is in every case distributive, not collective, and the only referents are singulars (Ch. I, Concl. 3–6).

A portion of Buridan's theory of supposition, discussed below, constitutes a theory of quantification, which is in some ways analogous, to, but by no means identical with, the quantification theory of mod-

[42] Actually, the term "similar" in that proposition stands not only for Socrates and Plato, but for all similar things. See the doctrine of supposition as discussed below.

[43] Again, "similarity" really stands not just for a property possessed by Socrates, but for all presently existing properties that are similar to any other properties, and the term "whiteness" stands for all presently existing concrete properties of whiteness. See the discussion of supposition below.

ern logic. One important difference is that the terminists made no use of variables, and quantification is over general terms.[44] But this requires no commitment to classes. Commitment waits upon a decision as to the referents of general terms, just as it does upon a decision as to the possible values of the variables of modern logic. And Buridan makes explicit the distributive reference of the terms.

V. Buridan's Theory of Language

Terminist logicians characterized logic as a rational science and contrasted it with the real sciences, such as physics and psychology. This means that logic is concerned with language, not with the objects signified by language. This was often put by saying that logic is a science of second intentions, in that it is a science of language (and of concepts, insofar as they are considered mental signs), as opposed to sciences of first intentions, which make use of language but are *of* the objects of extra-linguistic reality. Since it consists of talk about talk and not of talk about things, logic is neither a real science nor a speculative discipline, *i.e.*, it is neither physics nor metaphysics. Its concern is with the formal structure of language, particularly scientific language.[45]

But this requires qualification, because while terminist logic, like modern formal logic, investigated the formal structures of language—the logical syntax of language, the formal role of quantifying words, truth-functional combinations of propositions, the conditions of validity for consequences, and methods of formal proof—it also provided within itself an interpretation of these structures. Its core and starting-point was a study of the so-called "properties of terms," and this study was built around concepts belonging more properly to semantics than to formal logic as such. The properties of signification, supposition, ampliation, and connotation belong to bits of language *in relation to extra-mental reality*, and this means that no terminist logician could

[44] Although not aware of the gains afforded by the use of variables, Buridan is, of course, familiar with their use as simply place-markers. See for example, the second sophism of Chapter VI.

[45] *Cf.*, E. A. Moody, *Truth and Consequence in Mediaeval Logic* (Amsterdam, 1953), pp. 13–16. Neither is the terminist logic an analysis of ordinary language. It is designed to bring language into line with science, and while it stays as close to ordinary language as possible, rearrangement is undertaken whenever necessary to accomplish desired purposes.

be ontologically neutral. To say that terminist logic was neither a speculative discipline nor a real science is to say that it made no attempt to prove or demonstrate the existence or nature of external realities. But in order to provide an analysis of the properties of terms, an ontology had to be *assumed* by any logician, since an explanation of the relation of language to the world required some notion of what sorts of things constitute the world.

The eight groups of sophisms here translated are almost exclusively concerned with the semantical aspect of terminist logic. Unlike the first eight tracts of the *Sum of Dialectic,* which are a general introduction to logic, and the *Consequences,* which investigates the formal conditions of validity, this ninth tract is concerned with the connection of language with its users and with a world of concrete singulars; and its aim is to defend a strictly nominalistic theory of language. Because of this, the work is best introduced by means of a characterization of the properties of terms on which it is based. So this section is divided into considerations of signification, supposition, ampliation (as an extension of supposition) and connotation. And due to the special problems they pose, a final section is devoted to some of the "insolubles" of Chapter VIII.

A. *Signification*

The guiding principle of Buridan's philosophy and the principle that most nearly expresses its spirit is that *being is prior to all rational constructions.* For the doctrine of signification, this means that only what is can be signified, that the objects of signification are determined by a pre-linguistic recognition of what there is, not by ways of speaking. Given Buridan's ontology, it follows that the only significates are individual substances and their accidents. And although this will need some elaboration, it is well to state in the beginning that just as there is only one sort of significate, the individual, so there is only one relation of signifying that holds between language and its significates, that of a categorematic term standing for or naming one or more individual substances or accidents. And to say that a term is significant is, in the last analysis, to say that it can be used to refer to some such individuals.

Significant language rests on a base of simple concepts and the terms corresponding to them. Knowledge of the world begins in direct intuition of concrete individuals. Then by a process of abstraction (the details of which we ignore here), the mind is able to separate consideration of the things intuited from consideration of their accidental spatio-temporal existence and so arrive at a general concept.[46] For example, after experience of one or more dogs, a man is able, by this process of abstraction, to form a general concept of dog. Such a concept, which is the immediate term of a cognitive process beginning in experience, is called simple, in that it is derived directly from experience and does not result from any combination of concepts.

This concept is said to be a concept of many particulars, so that the concept of dog is a concept of all dogs. This is not to say, of course, that a man who has a concept of dog is thinking simultaneously of all dogs, because it is said to be a concept of absolutely *all* dogs—whether present, past, or future—of many of which a man could not be aware. It is to say, rather, that he understands what it is for something to be a dog, so that he would recognize absolutely any dog as a dog. But a concept is a concept only of individuals, in the sense that if a man understands at all, he must understand something, and since only being can be understood, the objects of his understanding must be just the individuals that populate the universe (Ch. I, Concl. 3).

It is then said that terms are instituted to correspond to such simple concepts and to signify the individuals conceived by them (Ch. I, Concl. 9). So the basic unit of signification in a language is the categorematic term corresponding to a simple concept and capable of being used to refer to whatever that concept conceives.[47] And because a concept corresponds to every such term, the concept is sometimes said to be a natural sign of those things of which the term is a conventional sign, thus introducing the notion of a mental language that exactly parallels written and spoken languages.

In order to account for more complex units of language, Buridan brings in the possibility of combining simple concepts to form com-

[46] There are also ideas or simple concepts of only a single individual (*e.g.*, the idea of Socrates), and their epistemological status places them lower in the "order of abstraction." But for present purposes, the difference can be ignored, because the function of the concept is as a mental term, and that function is fulfilled by singular ideas as well.

[47] That Buridan would not blink at admitting the proposition "There is something which is signified, and it does not exist" is but a single example of how little he is bothered by existential commitment. This will appear again in the doctrine of ampliation.

plex concepts (Ch. I, Concl. 7–8). Such a complex concept is a linking of simple concepts, so that what is conceived by the complex concept is just what is conceived by the simple concepts taken individually, no more and no less. But although the linking of concepts does not affect their content, they may be linked in many different ways. And in the corresponding spoken or written language, syncategorematic words are instituted by convention to reflect these ways of combining concepts. So the linguistic unit corresponding to a complex concept consists of the categorematic terms corresponding to the simple concepts, combined with syncategorematic words in a certain way to mirror the way in which the simple concepts are combined.[48] Since the linking of simple concepts does not affect what is conceived by them, it follows that syncategorematic words have no effect on the extra-mental signification of any linguistic complex in which they occur (Ch. I, solution of Soph. 3). Hence, every such linguistic complex signifies outside the mind just the things that are signified by its categorematic terms (Ch. II, Concl. 3).

The most obvious example of a complex concept is the mental proposition, and a mental proposition is said to correspond to every spoken or written proposition, so that every proposition of the language is said to signify a mental proposition and to signify whatever

[48] The psychological question how the mind relates concepts is unimportant for the theory of language, since corresponding to every mental complex, there is a linguistic complex that reflects that manner of conceiving. One need not worry what it means to say that a mental proposition conceives things "universally" or "negatively" or in some other way. It is only important that the corresponding spoken or written propositions, containing syncategorematic words such as "every" and "not," be analyzed in such a way that the *syncategoremata* affect only the structure of the analyzed propositions and not the extra-mental things signified by the categorematic terms. And this sort of analysis is provided by the divisions of personal supposition discussed below.

In fact, since an operation on spoken or written terms corresponds to every relation among concepts, the nature of the concept is in general of little interest. A good deal of confusion about just what the nominalist logicians thought the nature of the concept to be is due to the fact that they were little concerned about the nature of the concept. The concept is posited to serve two purposes: (a) to provide the genetic condition for the possibility of general knowledge of singular things; and (b) to provide the formal condition for significant language by explaining the signification of singulars by general terms. To accomplish the first, one need only regard the concept as the term of a cognitive process by which many singulars are conceived. To accomplish the second, the concept need be only a sign of many. The nominalists say just enough about the concept to achieve these ends.

is conceived by the concepts of that mental proposition (Ch. II, Concl. 1 and Concl. 5–7). But since what is conceived by the mental proposition is just all and only what is conceived by its simple concepts, the corresponding spoken or written proposition signifies, outside the mind, only the entities to which its categorematic terms can refer. This means that the two propositions "Every man is an animal" and "No man is an animal" correspond to different mental propositions, but since each of these propositions combines the same two categorematic terms, "man" and "animal" (albeit in different ways), those linguistic propositions signify exactly the same things, namely, all men and all animals—present, past, and future. So a proposition signifies just what is signified by its categorematic terms, and their signification is unaffected by their propositional context.

A proposition is a complex expression corresponding to a complex concept. But words are conventional and there is no reason why a complex of words need correspond to a complex concept. Man can, if he wishes, invent a single term to correspond to one of his complex concepts (Ch. I, Concl. 11). And in that case, although the word functions in propositions as a categorematic term, its signification is not necessarily any entities to which it can refer (Ch. I, Concl. 5). For example, on the basis of his experience, a man may form simple concepts of animal, head, lion, body, goat, tail, and serpent. And since he can manipulate concepts in any way he wants, he may combine those concepts into a complex concept. That complex concept then conceives all animals, all heads, all lions, all bodies, all goats, all tails, and all serpents, in a certain way. To signify that concept and those entities, he may then form a linguistic complex such as "animal with the head of a lion, the body of a goat, and the tail of a serpent," which combines the categorematic terms corresponding to those simple concepts with *syncategoremata* that reflect the way in which the simple concepts are linked. But since words are conventional, he may also substitute for that complex expression the simple word "chimera." In this case, the word "chimera," which appears to be a simple categorematic term, can be used to refer to nothing. Yet it is significant, because the categorematic terms of that complex expression for which it was substituted (and which is said to be its "nominal definition" (Ch. I, Concl 11)) *can* be used to refer to extra-mental entities.

Since a simple word may be used to correspond to a complex

concept and to signify all that is conceived by that concept, it is not possible to determine whether a concept is simple or complex by a mere examination of its linguistic correlate. It may seem obvious enough that "chimera" must signify a complex concept, since it is a significant word and yet could not possibly refer to anything, since chimeras cannot possibly exist. But it is worth noting that virtually *any* word *may* correspond to a complex concept. For concepts belong only to individual minds and a man can have a simple concept only of what he has experienced. So if a man has had no contact with elephants, then he cannot have a simple concept of elephant. And if he is able to use the term "elephant" properly, that can only be because he has learned what an elephant is from a description that employs terms that correspond to concepts of things he has experienced and so conceived simply. In this case, "elephant" signifies for him just what is signified by the terms of that description, so that it may signify a great many non-elephantine things.[49] So even among men who use the same language, the same terms are not simple.[50]

In sum, then, it should be understood that although some linguistic units correspond to several concepts which conceive many things in different ways, all extra-mental signification in Buridan is of one kind, that of a categorematic term signifying some individual entities, in the sense that it can be used to refer to them. There are syntactical ways of combining these terms, but there are no "ways" in which a term signifies what it signifies, and the signification of a term, understood as atemporal reference, is unaffected by its contexts, as are the things that it signifies.[51]

[49] As an interesting sidelight, note that if that description contains the term "animal," for example, so that the man does have a simple concept of animal, then since that term signifies *all* animals and that concept conceives all animals, it can be said that the man, by using that term "animal" and having that concept of animal, signifies and conceives elephants, among other animals. For this reason, Buridan puts great emphasis not merely on the *things* that are known and signified by a man, but on the terms and concepts *by which* what is known is known. On this point, see the discussion of connotation below.

[50] Professor Moody points out that there is an exception to this in the case of the demonstrative sciences, which are founded on a number of primitive concepts assumed to be simple for all who understand the language of science.

[51] Growing out of the same dialectical and grammatical tradition as the terminist logic, there had developed, by Buridan's time, a flourishing study known as "speculative grammar." Claiming independence from the grammar of any natural language, this was an investigation of the functions of words in any

It cannot be overemphasized that Buridan recognizes only *one* kind of extra-mental signification—designation by a term of things conceived by a simple concept.[52] In particular, there is no special kind of signification associated with propositions as opposed to terms. His insistence on this point is the basis for his repeated warnings about the improper use of a traditional notion of truth.

From Aristotle's famous definition of truth in the *Metaphysics*,[53] medieval logicians had derived the following "definition": "A proposition is true if howsoever it signifies the case to be, so it is (*qualitercumque significat esse, ita est*)." Those familiar with contemporary struggles to define truth will appreciate the appeal this simple statement, with its astute adverbial twist, must have had. In fact, Buridan quite clearly thinks its importance had been overplayed by some of his fellows.

His objections are not to the definition itself, but to misapplications of it. He is willing to have it used as a shorthand way of characterizing either truth or a true proposition. But it is really no more than a conveniently obscure way of saying that some one of a complex set of truth-conditions is fulfilled by some proposition (Ch. II, Concl. 14), since strictly speaking, truth is nothing but a true proposition. Two specific sorts of mistakes must be avoided: in the first place, the definition must not be interpreted as allowing either a special

---

language. Leaders of the movement were Siger of Courtrai, Michael of Marbais, and Thomas of Erfurt (long confused with Duns Scotus). On the doctrine of signification, they held that although different parts of speech (nouns, verbs, adjectives, etc.) may signify the same entities, they have different "modes of signifying"; and corresponding to these they posited analogous "modes of being."

Buridan rejects, of course, any modes of being in addition to the substances and accidents that have being (*Cf.*, Ch. I, Concl. 2). But his scattered references to the platonizing grammarians indicate no especially hostile attitute toward them. And really very little has been done toward determining the influence these traditions exercised on each other, beyond noting that Pierre d'Ailly, a nominalist of the later fourteenth century, attacked the modes of signifying, while John Gerson in the fifteenth century, who is sometimes accounted an Ockhamist, was more sympathetic. There must have been some interplay and it deserves investigation. For an informed summary of the grammatical tradition and some bibliography, see M. Grabmann, "Die Entwicklung der Mittelalterlichen Sprachlogik," *Philosophisches Jahrbuch*, XXXV (1922), 121–135, 199–214.

[52] To see how easily the point may be missed, see A. N. Prior, "Some Problems of Self-Reference in John Buridan," *Proceedings of the British Academy*, XLVIII (1962), 281–296. The following is designed to forestall Prior's sort of misreading.

[53] Aristotle, *Metaphysics* IV. 7. 1011b 25–28.

kind of signification (*e.g.*, a "signifying that" or "signifying somehow") associated with propositions or a special kind of entity signified by propositions; and secondly, the definition must not be assumed to provide a test for the truth of any proposition.

As to the first point, there is his conviction that there is only one sort of signifying, that of a term signifying some substances or accidents. Considered as a unit, the proposition signifies nothing except a mental proposition. Its terms are the only units of signification, and their signification is unaffected by their presence in a proposition. Also he rejects the position of Gregory of Rimini, mentioned above, according to which propositions signify in the same way as terms, but signify different sorts of things. There are no complex entities as significates of propositions. When it is said that "A is B" signifies or asserts that A is B, we are not to suppose that that-A-is-B (or A-being-B) is something in addition to A and B. To say that "A is B" signifies A-being-B is to say either that it signifies the mental proposition corresponding to that spoken proposition or that it signifies an A that is, in fact, B (Ch. II, Concl. 3). The proposition "A man is white" signifies man-being-white, in that it signifies a mental proposition, and beyond that, it signifies a white man (if there are any), along with all other men and all other white things. And if there neither has been nor is nor will be a white man, then man-being-white is not signified by any proposition, since only being can be signified.

A good deal of the second chapter is devoted to stressing the second point, that the definition of truth cannot provide a test for truth. In particular, it cannot be understood to mean that a proposition is true if what it signifies exists (Ch. II, Concl. 1–2), for that must mean either that a corresponding mental proposition exists, in which case every proposition is true, or that what it signifies outside the mind exists, in which case many obviously true propositions of past and future tenses must be regarded as false. For a test for truth, one must look to supposition, not signification (Ch. II, Concl. 8).

B. Supposition

The theory of supposition is the core of terminist logic. [54] Signifi-

[54] The use of the term *suppositio* stems from the use of the verb *suppono* ("to place under" or "to stand in place of") made by both classical and medieval grammarians. The habit of grammarians of using the notion of standing for primarily in connection with pronouns helps explain the adaptation, for considerations of pronominal reference are inseparable from considerations of occasions

cation is a function of terms and concepts taken in isolation, but supposition is a function of the predication of terms and concepts.[55] In at least one of its aspects, supposition differs from signification as using a term differs from knowing how to use it. It is treated as a property of terms, but only as they occur in propositions, and it is used both as the basis for a theory of truth and as a tool for the purely syntactical analysis of propositions.

It is this double function of supposition that has led astray most attempts to give a general characterization of the theory. It is in fact, not one theory, but two, and they require separate treatments.[56] The first, which can be called simply the doctrine of supposition proper, is a set of rules governing the reference of terms in propositions and is the basis of a theory of truth. The second, which I call the doctrine of modes of supposition, has no effect on the reference of terms, but is a set of rules for the syntactical analysis of propositions containing quantifying words and is thus the quantification theory of terminist logic.

(1) *The Doctrine of Supposition Proper:* Buridan writes that supposition is "the taking of a term in a proposition to stand for some thing or things, in such a way that if that thing or those things are indicated by the pronoun 'this' or 'these', or the equivalent, then that term is truly affirmed of this pronoun by mediation of the copula of the proposition" (Ch. III, Remark 1). This is a good definition of "supposition" as it is used in the first doctrine. Unlike the signification of a term, which is unaffected by the use made of the term, its supposition is wholly determined by its propositional context. For example, the term "man" signifies all men—present, past, and future—but in the proposition "A man is a barber," its supposition is confined to presently existing men (the things at which one can point

---

and contexts of use, which is just what distinguishes supposition from signification in terminist logic. For a brief account of the history of the use of the term and of the doctrine, see Mullally, *op. cit.*, pp. xlvi–xlvii.

[55] As in the case of signification, the supposition of a concept always matches that of the corresponding term, so that discussion can be confined to the supposition of terms.

[56] Whether Buridan is himself fully aware of the distinction is uncertain. In his only general definition of "supposition," at Chapter III, Remark 1, he takes account of only one of the theories. But he does separate the two in practice, devoting the first six sophisms of Chapter III to the first and the last four to the second.

and say "These are men"), while in the proposition "A man was a barber," it stands for (*supponit pro*) both presently existing men and those who have existed in the past. More obviously, in the proposition "Man is an animal," the term "man" stands for (at least some of) the things it signifies, whereas in the proposition "Man is a noun," it stands for none of its significates, but rather stands autonymously for itself and other similar tokens.

It will be noticed that in the first two propositions given as examples above, the difference in the supposition of the term "man" is merely one of the *number* of things for which the term stands. Differences of this kind are accounted for by reference to the notion of ampliation and restriction of supposition, which will be discussed shortly. On the other hand, the difference in the supposition of the term "man" in the latter two propositions is more radical, since the term does not stand for any of the same things in the two propositions, and indeed stands for entirely different *sorts* of things. In the first case, the term stands for men, while in the second, it stands for signs.

Buridan marks this latter kind of difference by dividing supposition into two fundamental types—*personal* supposition and *material* suposition (Ch. III, Remark 2). A term is said to stand personally (or significatively), if it is taken to stand for the thing or things that it signifies. It is said to stand materially, if it stands for itself and other signs, considered purely as signs. Thus in the proposition "A man is an animal," the subject and predicate terms stand significatively for men and animals respectively. But in the propositions "Man is a noun" and "Man is a species," the term 'man' has material supposition.[57] Material supposition serves (roughly) the

[57] This last example is of interest as reflecting Buridan's rejection of a third type of supposition—simple supposition—that was apparently admitted by every other terminist logician. The early terminists, who were realistically inclined, held that a term has simple supposition if it is taken to stand for a universal nature, and there were two characteristic positions for terms having this type. Since they understood predication as the attributing of a general attribute to a group of individuals, the predicate term in most categorical propositions was said to have simple supposition. And in some propositions *about* universals, such as "Man is a species," the subject term was taken in simple supposition.

When Ockham rejected real universality, he also rejected the first use of simple supposition and held that the predicate term in a categorical proposition has the same supposition (ordinarily personal) as the subject term. But impressed as he was with the concept as the new seat of universality, he wanted to disfunction served in contemporary discussions by the enclosing of a term or phrase in single quotation marks, and for purposes of clarity, I have employed this device throughout the translation.[58]

But even if similar tokens in different propositions stand for the same sorts of things, their suppositions may differ, since one may stand for more of those things than the other. One reason for this is that Buridan (like other terminists) regards the copula of the proposition as tensed, so that terms belonging to propositions of different tenses always differ in supposition.[59] But more generally, the presence of almost any temporal or modal word in a proposition is said either to "ampliate" or to "restrict" the supposition of at least one of its terms (see all of Ch. V). The following rules cover most of the cases of ampliation and restriction:

---

tinguish this concept from a mere language sign. So he maintained that in propositions about universal concepts, such as "Man is a species," the subject has simple supposition, while in a proposition about language signs, such as "Man is a noun," the subject has material supposition.

In Tract IV of the *Sum of Dialectic*, Buridan rejects simple supposition as a vestige of abandoned realism, and replaces it with an extended use of material supposition. His reason is that the concept is nothing but a sign, from the point of view of logic, and nothing is gained by a distinction between linguistic and mental signs. Besides an ironic use of Ockham's Razor, this must be seen as part of a general program against what Buridan regards as undue reification of the concept by Ockham, and it moves him even nearer a purely inscriptionist semantics.

[58] There is the significant difference that whereas enclosing a term in single quotation marks indicates the use of a *new* term, which is the name of the original term, Buridan's material supposition makes use of the *same* term to refer to itself. In fact, it is likely that had they been more acutely attuned to possible hierarchies of type, the terminists would not have distinguished personal and material supposition as they did. For since every term corresponds to a concept, it would seem that a term corresponding to a concept of a non-linguistic entity must differ from one corresponding to a concept of a term. So it seems that rather than a new kind of supposition, there is really a new term with the same kind. This is most obvious in Buridan's contention that whole phrases (*e.g.*, "man being animal") and even propositions may stand materially (Ch. II, Concl. 3), because if a phrase or proposition is taken materially, it is a new sort of sign—a name—having no internal logical structure.

[59] The exception is again in the case of propositions of demonstrative science. Such propositions are usually categoricals of present tense, and yet they are necessary, so their truth cannot depend on the accidents of current existence. Buridan attributes a different sort of supposition—natural supposition—to the terms of such propositions (*Cf.*, *Sum of Dialectic*, Tract IV), so that regardless of the tense of the proposition, the terms are taken to stand for all their significates atemporally. See note 74 below.

(a) A term occurring before the verb in a categorical proposition of past tense is ampliated to stand for past things as well as present things. Thus in the proposition "Some man was bald," the term "man" stands for both presently existing men and those who have existed in the past, so that the proposition is "exponible" as "Something which is a man or was a man was bald."

(b) A term occurring before the verb in a categorical of future tense is ampliated to stand for future things as well as present things. The proposition "A man will run" is exponible as "Something which is a man or will be a man will run."

(c) A term occurring after the verb in a categorical of some tense other than the present stands only for things existing for the time of the verb and not also for present things. Thus in the examples of (a) and (b), the predicates "bald" and "run" (*i.e.*, "running thing") stand only for past hairless things and future runners respectively.

(d) A term occurring either before or after the verb "can" or either before or after the copula of a proposition stating a possibility is ampliated to stand for possible things, whether or not they exist or have existed. So in the propositions "A man can be an angel" and "A man is possibly an angel," the term "man" stands for all possible men and the term "angel" for all possible angels.[60]

(e) If a term is placed before or after the copula in a proposition of necessity, it stands for all possible things, just as in rule (d).

(f) A term, whether it occurs before the verb or after the verb, is ampliated to stand for past and future things, if it is taken with a verb associated with an act of the intellective soul, *i.e.*, verbs such as "to know," "to signify," "to understand," and "to opine." Hence, it is true that a man is known by me if Aristotle (who no longer exists) or Antichrist (who does not yet exist) is known by me.[61]

(g) Gerunds and participles ampliate the subject of a proposition just as verbs do. Thus participles ending in "-ble," such as "generable," "corruptible," and "knowable" ampliate the subject to stand for all possible things. Participles such as "dead," "corrupted," and "generated" ampliate supposition to all past things. And something analogous can be said of future participles.

[60] This is true only of possibility *de dicto*, or in the composite sense, in which possibility is predicated of the entire proposition. If there is an assertion of possibility which affects only a single extreme, then only that is so ampliated. In the proposition "A man is a possible angel," only the predicate stands for all possible angels. The subject stands for presently existing men alone.

[61] That knowledge is independent of temporal accidents and that science is of all things of all times is an axiom of central importance for Buridan.

(h) Temporal words such as "today," "tomorrow," and "next week" restrict the supposition of words with which they are associated to the specific time period they designate.

These are only a few of the rules that could be given, but perhaps they suffice to indicate the nature and complexity of the doctrine.[62]

The doctrine of supposition so developed is the basis for Buridan's rules for the truth of categorical propositions (Ch. II, Concl. 9–14). Every affirmative categorical proposition is said to be a statement of (at least partial) identity between the *supposita* of the subject and predicate terms, or to be analyzable into such a statement.[63] And a negative proposition is said to assert a corresponding non-identity of reference. Since an affirmative proposition asserts an identity of reference, it is trivially false if one of its terms stands for nothing, and under the same condition, a negative proposition is trivially true.[64]

Beyond this, there are specific rules for the truth of each sort of proposition, but these need not be repeated, since the third chapter discusses them in detail. But instead of developing this entire theory of truth, it might be helpful to summarize how Buridan adapts the idea of truth in general to his nominalism.

It will be remembered that for Buridan a proposition is a definite inscription or event of utterance. And truth is a property of such an inscription or utterance, so that unless the group of words actually

[62] This free and easy talk about the extension of supposition to non-existents will sound queer to contemporary ears. Terminist logicians simply saw no problem here. In his *Questions on the Nicomachean Ethics* (Book VI, Question 6), he states as self-evident the view that we can separate the concept of a thing from the concept of the time of its existence. Things are conceived by means of accidents, including temporal ones, and what is conceived by an accident may be thought of as independent of that accident. This is regarded as an essential condition for a science which proceeds by demonstrating accidents of the substances to which they belong. So far from being bothered by the commitments of existential quantification, Buridan insists on the preservation of facts about non-existents as a way of guaranteeing the independence of knowledge from the vagaries of existence.

[63] On the copula as signifying identity of reference, and on an opposed theory of the realist tradition, see E. A. Moody, *Truth and Consequence in Mediaeval Logic*, pp. 32–38.

[64] This existential involvement was thought to validate inferences from propositions in which a form of the term "to be" serves as copula to others in which the form of "to be" functions also as predicate. Thus in the proposition "Every man is an animal," the verb is said to occur *tertio adiacente*, and it is legitimate to move from this proposition to "Every man is," in which the verb occurs *secundo adiacente*.

exists, there is no truth (Ch. VIII, Soph. 7). But a proposition is not just a string of words. No words constitute a proposition unless they correspond to a mental proposition (Ch. VI, Soph. 2), and mental propositions are found only in individual minds. This has several consequences. In the first place, since the same set of words may signify different mental propositions for different men, the same inscription or utterance may be both true and false (Ch. VII, Soph. 7). Also since every spoken proposition is tensed, its truth depends upon the way in which its speaker chooses to divide time into present, past, and future (Ch. VII, *passim*). And finally, since an inscription may endure through time, it may signify a succession of mental propositions (Ch. VI. Soph. 6), and even if it always signifies the same one, its truth-value may change, due to the coming into being, passing away, or changing of the things for which its terms stand (Ch. VII, Soph. 2). Hence, truth is a trait of an utterance or inscription for a man at a time. [65] And "is true" is really an incomplete predicate, the complete predicate being what is obtained by filling the blanks of the predicable "is true for —— at ——" with the name of a man (or angel, or God) and the name of a segment of time.

(2) *The Doctrine of Modes of Supposition:* This second doctrine is given in terms of several subdivisions of personal supposition (Ch. III, Remark 3), and because of this, it is apt to be misunderstood. Since the doctrine of supposition so far discussed is a theory of the relation of terms to their objects, there is a tendency to suppose that these divisions of personal supposition also have to do with that relation. But this is not the case. Rather, it is a separate theory designed to explain the role of quantifying words, such as "every," "some," and "no." [66] And it does this not by further qualifying the reference of terms, but by a syntactical analysis which establishes identities of supposition (and so of truth-value) between propositions

[65] *Cf.*, Quine, *op. cit.*, p. 191.

[66] The best statement of the doctrine is in *Sum of Dialectic*, Tract IV. On the relation of this doctrine to modern quantification theory, see P. Boehner, *Medieval Logic* (Chicago, 1952), pp. 40–44, and Gareth B. Matthews, "Ockham's Supposition Theory and Modern Logic," *Philosophical Review*, LXXIII (1964), 91–99. For an informative but complete misunderstanding of the doctrine, see P. T. Geach, *Reference and Generality* (Ithaca, N.Y., 1962), Chs. 3 and 4. And for a very brief critique of Geach, which does not take account of a number of straightforwardly historical errors in his book, see my note, "Mr. Geach on Supposition," *Mind* (October, 1966).

containing quantifying words and others in which those quantifiers are eliminated.[67]

The sort of thing for which a term stands is determined completely by saying that it has personal supposition. And while it is true that the number of things for which it stands is not thus determined and requires the doctrine of ampliation for its determination, the doctrine of ampliation contains no rules for quantifying words, and such words have no effect on the reference of terms. Finally, neither do quantifying words in any way affect the way in which a term stands for things. There are no "ways of referring" in Buridan's logic. When he says that a term has distributive supposition, for example, he does not mean that there is some sort of "distributive" entity for which it stands, nor does he mean that there is some "distributive" relation of referring.[68] He means only that the proposition in which the term occurs has the same supposition as another proposition of a certain form. And he usually puts this by saying that it is "suitable to descend" from the original, quantified proposition to the other proposition, which contains no quantifiers. For this reason, the operation of the doctrine is sometimes known as the "descent to singulars."[69]

[67] Note that what is established in these cases are identities of supposition, not equivalences or identities of signification. As a matter of fact, the quantified and unquantified propositions are usually *not* equivalent, since the quantified proposition ordinarily signifies many non-existents, whereas the proposition without quantifiers signifies things that exist for the time of the verb. In the criticism of Geach mentioned in the previous note, I said that the doctrine does establish equivalences, but this has no effect on the essence of that criticism. The distinction between equivalence and sameness of supposition will be emphasized when an objection to Buridan's theory is considered below.

[68] Nor should the notion of distributive supposition be used to confound this doctrine with the doctrine of distribution, which is a modern development. The latter does indeed assimilate differences among quantified propositions to differences in reference. But although Buridan himself often speaks of a term standing distributively, his analysis is always in terms of whole propositions and their form, not of the reference of terms. His talk about distribution in Chapter IV, however, which is at times very loose, makes it easy to see how the doctrine was misunderstood, converted into the doctrine of distribution and pressed into service to explain immediate inferences. For some interesting ideas on the progressive misappropriation that led to the doctrine of distribution, see P. T. Geach, "The Doctrine of Distribution," *Mind*, LXX (1956), 67–74.

[69] The concern is ordinarily only with establishing the move from a quantified proposition to one without quantifiers, so that the converse entailment was largely ignored. But searching reveals that in every case, both Ockham and Buridan allowed this second entailment as well.

Buridan follows Ockham in dividing personal supposition into *discrete* supposition and *common* supposition. A term possesses discrete supposition only if it is either a proper name of an individual or a common noun preceded by a demonstrative pronoun. The only interest of this type of supposition for a general theory of quantification stems from the fact that the predicates of propositions are also quantified by the terminists. And propositions such as "Socrates is a man," whose subjects have discrete supposition, are treated as universal, so that all rules for universal propositions apply to these as well.

Common supposition is that possessed by a general term. It is divided into *determinate* supposition and *confused* supposition. A term is said to have determinate supposition if the proposition in which it occurs agrees in supposition with a proposition composed of a disjunction of categoricals, in each of which that term is immediately preceded by a demonstrative pronoun or is replaced by the name of each of the individuals for which it stands in personal supposition. In the proposition "A man is running," the term "man" has determinate supposition, because this proposition agrees in supposition with "This man is running or that man is running or . . . or that man is running," indicating each presently existing man. The general rule for this sort of supposition can be stated as follows: any term immediately preceded by a particular quantifier (*i.e.*, by "some," "a" or "an") [70] which is not itself preceded in the proposition by either a universal quantifier or a negation sign, has determinate supposition.

Confused supposition is of two sorts, *confused and distributive* and *merely confused*. Confused and distributive supposition is possessed by a term if the proposition in which it occurs agrees in supposition with a proposition composed of a conjunction of categoricals, in each of which that term is immediately preceded by a demonstrative pronoun or is replaced by the name of each of the individual things for which it stands in personal supposition. In the proposition "Every man is an animal," the term "man" has confused and distributive supposition, since this proposition agrees in supposition with "This man is an animal and that man is an animal and . . . and that man is an animal," indicating each presently existing man. And in the proposition "Socrates is not a barber," the term "barber" has confused and distributive supposition, since this proposition is equivalent

[70] Of course, in Latin there is no indefinite article, so the relevant rule applies in Latin to words preceded either by a particular quantifier or by none at all.

to "Socrates is not this barber and Socrates is not that barber and . . . and Socrates is not that barber." The general rule is: Any term immediately preceded by either a universal quantifier (*i.e.*, by "every," "all," "no," or the like) or by any negation sign has confused and distributive supposition.

Finally, merely confused supposition is possessed by a term if the proposition in which it occurs agrees in supposition with a proposition in which one extreme consists of a disjunction composed of occurrences of that term preceded in each case by a demonstrative pronoun or replaced by the proper names of each of the things for which it stands in personal supposition. In the proposition "Every man is an animal," the term "animal" has merely confused supposition, since this proposition agrees in supposition with "Every man is this animal or that animal or . . . or that animal." The general rule is: Any term immediately preceded by a particular quantifier, which is itself preceded in the proposition by either a universal quantifier or a negation sign, has merely confused supposition. [71]

These rules provide the machinery for an analysis of any quantified proposition. And when this doctrine is taken together with the preceding one, the foundation is laid for the whole of terminist logic. But by way of closing the discussion, I want to mention one recent objection to both these doctrines, since the objection typifies the sort of confusion that has surrounded discussions of medieval logic. [72]

The objection interprets the terminist logic as holding that a general term is merely an abbreviation for a list of proper names. But if this is the case, then every proposition is either necessarily true or necessarily false, and so the "descent to singulars" is impossible. For example, the contingent proposition "Socrates is a barber" is, if true, equivalent to the proposition "Socrates is either Socrates or Plato

[71] To this already untidy doctrine, two qualifications must be added. The first is that the rules given cover the analysis of quantifiers only if they occur in a primary way, not merely as part of an extreme (as for example, in the proposition "The man who loves every girl is a nuisance"). There are rules for these cases also, but they need not be stated here. Secondly, the rules are understood to apply only to propositions of standard form, but this includes "exponible" propositions reducible to standard form. In the proposition "Only men are animals," the term "men" has merely confused supposition, because this proposition is reducible to "Every animal is a man."

[72] See W. Kneale and M. Kneale, *The Development of Logic* (Oxford, 1962), pp. 267–268.

or . . . or Zeno" (listing all barbers), which is necessarily true. And if the proposition "Socrates is a barber" is false, it is equivalent to "Socrates is either Plato or Robert or . . . or Zeno" (listing every barber, but not Socrates), which is necessarily false. In fact, the objection goes, in saying that Socrates is a barber, I do not mean that Socrates is either Socrates or Plato or some other man. Rather, I mean that Socrates has a certain nature or property or character.

Buridan might reply to such an objection in two ways. The first reply is in the nature of a countercharge, that if there are problems here, they are not solved by introducing natures and characters. When it is said that the proposition "Socrates is a barber" attributes a character to Socrates, one need only ask what character. And although the question can be forestalled by the invention of abstract nouns (*e.g.*, "barberness"), the only possible answer ultimately is that it is the character possessed by all and only barbers, *i.e.*, by Socrates and Plato and others.

But Buridan can also avoid the objection outright. And just how it is to be met depends upon what the objection means by the statement that a general noun is an abbreviation for a list of proper names; for there are at least three obvious possibilities:

(a) It could mean that a general noun signifies the same concept in the mind as a list of proper names. But that is just false. The term "barber" signifies the concept of barber, but the names of all the barbers do not signify that concept. Rather, they signify each of the individual ideas of particular men that they name, *i.e.*, the concepts of Socrates and Plato, etc.

(b) More likely, it might mean that a general noun signifies the same extra-mental things as a list of proper names. And there is a sense in which that is true. The proposition "Socrates is a barber" does not signify all the same things as the proposition "Socrates is either Socrates or Plato or . . . or Zeno" which is reached by the "descent to singulars," for that first proposition signifies all barbers—present, past, and future—whereas the latter proposition contains the names of presently existing barbers only. But the proposition "Socrates is a barber" does signify the same things as a proposition such as "Socrates is either Socrates or Plato or . . . or Zeno," if it is understood that this latter proposition lists not only presently existing barbers, but all possible barbers. So we may assume that this is the intent of the objection. Now if equivalence is understood in the usual way, as sameness of signification, then the propositions "Socrates is a barber" and "Socrates is either Socrates or Plato or . . . or Zeno" (listing all possible barbers) are equivalent. And what the objection is stating is that if "Socrates is a barber" is true, it is necessarily true, just because it is equivalent to a necessarily true proposition. And we can examine this claim by assuming (what will be denied later) that the above proposition "Socrates is either Socrates or Plato or . . . or Zeno" is in fact necessarily true. Then if any equivalent proposition is also necessarily true, it is certainly the case that "Socrates is a barber" is necessarily true. But so are all other propositions equivalent to that one, *i.e.*, all other propositions having the same signification. This means that "Socrates is not a barber" is also necessarily true. For a proposition signifies just what is signified by its categorematic terms and the *signification* of a term, unlike its *supposition*, is unaffected by its propositional context, and "Socrates is not a barber" contains the same categorematic terms as "Socrates is a barber." Furthermore, the proposition "Socrates is all barbers" is also necessarily true, as is "Socrates is Socrates and Plato and . . . and Zeno," again listing all possible barbers. Hence, if we allow truth to be a function of signification and sameness of truth-value to be a function of equivalence, *i.e.*, sameness of signification, then it is not only the case that every true proposition containing a general term is necessarily true, but also many false propositions containing general terms are necessarily true, which is absurd. In fact, however, Buridan does not make truth a function of signification, but of supposition. And this brings us to the third possible interpretation of the objection.

(c) To say that every general term is an abbreviation for a list of proper names might mean that the general term and some list of names have the same *supposition*. And while this is not always the case, it is very often the case, so the possibility deserves attention. Again take the proposition "Socrates is a barber" and suppose it to be true. It then has the same supposition as "Socrates is either Socrates or Plato or . . . or Zeno," this time listing all *presently existing* barbers. Now truth *is* a matter of supposition, so here we are at least on the right track. Of course, it is not the case that *any* two propositions having the same supposition have the same truth-value. For the propositions "All men are barbers" and "No men are barbers" have the same supposition, namely, all presently existing men and barbers. But it is true that any proposition obtained from another by a proper "descent to singulars" has the same truth-value as the proposition from which it was obtained. And we may suppose this to be the case for the propositions "Socrates is a barber" and "Socrates is either Socrates or Plato or . . . or Zeno." So if the latter of these two is necessarily true, then so is the former. But is the proposition "Socrates is either Socrates or Plato or . . . or Zeno" necessarily true? The answer is that it is not, for truth is always truth at a time for Buridan, and no affirmative proposition is true unless its terms stand for something. Hence, the proposition "Socrates is Socrates" is false if Socrates does not currently exist, and the proposition "A chimera is a chimera" is always false (Ch. II, Concl. 10 and solution of Soph. 3). So the proposition "Socrates is either Socrates or Plato or . . . or Zeno" is not necessarily true, since it might be false. And by the same token, if Socrates does not currently exist or if he is not a barber, then the proposition "Socrates is a barber" is false and has the same supposition and truth-value as "Socrates is either Plato or Robert or . . . or Zeno" (listing all barbers, but not Socrates). But this latter proposition is not necessarily false. For Socrates might legally change his name and make it "Socrates Plato." For Buridan a necessary proposition is simply one that is eternally true. This means that necessity belongs only to true propositions about God, since he is the only necessarily existent and unchanging being. [73] No others are necessary, since the *supposita* of their terms are contingent. [74]

[73] The realist preserves necessity by introducing meanings. The question is whether he can make sense of meanings.

[74] There is again the exception of the propositions of demonstrative science, including mathematics, which are held to be necessary, since they are essential predications. Given current knowledge of Buridan's epistemology, the necessity of such propositions is not easy to account for. It may be simply that here, as so often elsewhere, he is impressed with the *fait accompli*. Propositions expressing essential predications are not demonstrated, nor are they supported by a realist ontology. But it is clear that on the basis of intuitive cognition of singulars and conceptual abstraction, men *do* agree on the "first subjects" of properties under investigation, *i.e.*, on the primitives of a science. And for this reason, they do agree on the self-evident premisses which serve as the basis of a science. The epistemological process involved is less interesting than this agreement and the use made of it in developing sciences. In fact, Buridan seems to come very near the view that the primitives are simply posits that allow maximum agreement, simplicity, and explanatory power.

It might be objected that if Socrates changes his name as above, then the proposition "Socrates is Plato" is not the same proposition with a new truth-value, but a different proposition. But this would be very inconvenient. The proposition has *not* changed in signification, for signification is atemporal, and the proposition signifies just the same things at any time, namely, any things that either are or have been or will be named "Socrates" or "Plato." So if it is a new proposition, it is so just because its supposition has changed. But since any proposition which changes in truth-value does so because its supposition changes, this means that every change in truth-value signals a new proposition, and one is left in the position of making the truth-value of a proposition logically prior to a determination of what proposition it is, which is surely not desirable.[75]

C. *Connotation*

As in the case of supposition, Buridan divides his discussion of connotation (Ch. IV) into two parts.[76] This reflects, however, not two doctrines, but two uses of a single doctrine.

The use made of the theory in the first eight sophisms of Chapter IV apparently follows, with little elaboration, Ockham's distinc-

[75] On the importance of this point and Buridan's recognition of it, see Geach, *Reference and Generality*, p. xi.

[76] The property Buridan calls *appellatio*, which has been translated by "connotation," is nearer Ockham's account of connotative terms than it is to previous doctrines of "appellation." According to Peter of Spain, for example, the only real distinction between supposition and appellation is that the appellation of a term is confined to existents, whereas supposition may extend to non-existents as well (Mullally, *op. cit.*, p. 45). Apparently arising out of some discomfort with the notion of supposition for non-existents, Peter's property of appellation is an attempt to distinguish between standing for a thing and naming it, which, of course, just adds confusion to obscurity. In his *Introductiones in logicam*, ed. M. Grabmann (Munich, 1937), 82, 6–17, William Shyreswood characterizes appellation in a new way. For him appellation is the property of predicability and belongs to a term only as predicable of something, *i.e.*, only when it occurs as predicate in a categorical proposition of standard form. In the proposition "Some man is white," the subject term stands for all men, and it would so stand if it were the subject in any other proposition, provided it were taken in personal supposition (which Shyreswood calls "formal" supposition). But the predicate term "white" stands for men only because it happens to be predicated of them in this proposition. Ockham (*op. cit.*, Ch. 63) acknowledges this use of appellation as a brand of supposition, but abandons it, since he wants to say that a term such as "white" stands for all white things, regardless of the proposition in which it occurs, so long as it is taken in personal supposition. Buridan is then reinstating the term *appellatio*, but he uses it in new ways.

tion between absolute and connotative terms.[77] According to Ockham, an absolute term is one which, in a proposition, stands for some thing or things and does not consignify or refer to any other things in an indirect or secondary way, while a connotative term, when it occurs in a proposition, not only stands for some things, but also indirectly "connotes" some other things. In the proposition "A man is white," the term "man" is absolute and stands only for (presently existing) men. But the term "white" is connotative, since it not only stands for what the subject term stands for, but also connotes whiteness as a property or number of concrete properties possessed by the objects for which it stands.[78]

Not every connotative term connotes an attribute. In the proposition "Socrates is similar to Plato," the term "similar" stands for Socrates and connotes Plato as that to which Socrates is similar. But the objects of connotation, like the objects of supposition, are limited to substances and their concrete accidents. The doctrine of connotation is meant to reinforce Buridan's ontology, not undermine it.

But while saying this, it must yet be noted that in speaking of connotation, he does make reference to the *way* in which a term connotes what it connotes (Ch. IV, Remark 2). He says that "white" connotes whiteness positively and "blind" connotes vision privatively. And he adds that from the differing ways of connoting, the different categories are taken (Ch. IV, Remark 3). I think, however, that it would be a mistake to make too much of this. He almost certainly does not want to admit that the relation of a term to what it connotes is in itself different from that of the term to what it stands for. Rather, this talk about modes of connoting should be traced to the associated concept, and one should understand only that things are

[77] Ockham, *op. cit.*, Ch. 10. *Cf.*, Moody, *The Logic of William of Ockham*, pp. 54–57.

[78] The only misgiving about identifying his view with Ockham's comes from his statement that from the different ways in which what it connoted affects what a term stands for are taken the ten categories (Ch. IV, Remark 3). This seems to imply that *all* terms are connotative, including those in the category of substance. But this is no real difference from Ockham, since it is quite clear that terms in the category of substance connote only what they stand for, whereas terms of other categories stand for one thing and connote another. If a term such as "man" connoted anything beyond its supposition, it would presumably connote humanity, but for Buridan, humanity as something other than individual men is not allowed to be at all.

conceived in different ways or because of different features (Ch. I, Concl. 6). For even if two concepts are of exactly the same things, those things must be conceived differently. If it happens that all and only men are white, for example, then the concept of man conceives just what the concept of white conceives. But the concepts differ in that one arises because note is taken of the similarity of some concrete things called men, whereas the other arises because note is taken of the similarity of some concrete attributes of things called men, namely, the attributes signified by the term "whiteness." And it is from these different ways of conceiving that terms of different categories are taken.

Buridan makes use of connotation to bolster a purely extensional theory of identity. In particular, he is able to explain, without introducing realms of "meanings," how it is that the proposition "Socrates is white" differs in significance from the proposition "Socrates is Socrates," even if Socrates is the only white object (Ch. IV, solution of Soph. 1). Interchangeability of terms with common suppositions always preserves truth-value, but it may alter significance, if one of the terms is connotative. [79]

The theory of connotation is also the basis of Buridan's account of relations, as we have seen. Relational terms are connotative, so that they stand for some things and connote other things, but there are no relations. A proposition containing a relational term is "exponible" as a multiply-quantified proposition in which no relational term occurs. The proposition "Chicken Big is the mother of Chicken Little," for example, becomes something like "There is something that is Chicken Big and something that is Chicken Little, and there was an egg such that Chicken Big laid that egg and Chicken Little hatched from that egg" (*Cf.*, Ch. IV, Remark 1). [80]

The second use of the doctrine of connotation, in Sophisms 9–15

[79] Of course, it may happen that both terms concerned are absolute, and in such a case, he seems committed to denying a difference in significance. If Socrates is the only man, then the propositions "Socrates is Socrates" and "Socrates is a man" are identical in both truth-value and extra-mental signification. The difference is only that they signify different mental propositions.

[80] There is no need to consider all the qualifications of this doctrine, due to considerations of temporal and modal words. But it might be noted how far he has departed from the doctrine of appellation of Peter of Spain. Almost all the first eight sophisms of Chapter IV depend for their solutions on the possibility of connotation of non-existents.

of Chapter IV, is a direct outgrowth of Buridan's view of the nature of knowledge and of demonstrative science in particular.[81] We have seen that he rejects abstract entities as the significates of propositions and the objects of knowledge. But he also accepts the Aristotelian claim that science is of the necessary and eternal. He then interprets this as meaning that science is immediately of necessary (*i.e.*, eternally true) propositions and so is only secondarily of the contingent things for which the terms of such propositions stand. At the same time, he insists on an objective base for knowledge and holds that to know a proposition is at the same time to have knowledge of the things for which its terms stand (Ch. IV, Soph. 13). When generalized, his position is that the object of any cognitive attitude (belief, opinion, doubt, etc.) is a proposition or phrase or term, in short, a particular bit of language. But to be cognitively related to such a group of words is at the same time to be cognitively related to their significates. All of this is easily seen to follow from both his epistemology and his theory of meaning and reference, so that any problems in connection with it affect the core of his philosophy. It is with a group of such problems that he is concerned in the last seven sophisms of Chapter IV.

The problems are all of the same sort, having to do with the question of reference in certain cognitive contexts.[82] Broadly stated, the problem arises from the fact that whereas terms referring to the same things can ordinarily be interchanged in any proposition *salva veritate*, there are certain contexts in which such an interchange seems to force a change in truth-value. For example, although the terms

[81] His most concise and revealing discussion of scientific knowledge and its objects is found in his *Questions on the Nicomachean Ethics*, Book VI, Question 6. His view derives from Ockham, but differs in certain respects. See my article, "John Buridan on the Objects of Demonstrative Science," *Speculum* (October, 1965).

[82] These problems have been much discussed in recent literature. See G. Frege, "On Sense and Nominatum," tr. H. Feigl, *Readings in Philosophical Analysis*, eds. H. Feigl and W. Sellars (New York, 1949), pp. 85–102; A. Church, "A Formulation of the Logic of Sense and Denotation," *Structure, Method, and Meaning*, eds. P. Henle, H. M. Kallen, and S. K. Langer (New York, 1951), pp. 3–24; R. Carnap, *Meaning and Necessity* (Chicago, 1947), pp. 96–144; Quine, *op. cit.*, pp. 141–156, 191–216. Buridan's contribution to the discussion was first noted by E. A. Moody, whose paper "Buridan and a Dilemma of Nominalism" was circulated among scholars in 1962 and has been published in the H. A. Wolfson *Jubilee Volume* (Jerusalem, 1965), pp. 577–596.

"the one approaching" and "your father" may stand for the same individual, there seem to be certain circumstances in which, due to your partial ignorance, the proposition "You know your father" is true, while the proposition "You know the one approaching" is false (Soph. 9). More generally, from any proposition "A is B," it is ordinarily possible to infer a proposition of the form "Something is B," and from this latter to infer a proposition of the form "C is B," where "C" is any term standing for just those things for which "A" stands in the first proposition. [83] But there are some contexts for which such moves seem illegitimate. If the astronomer Socrates is in a dungeon and so knows that some stars or other are above, but does not know which ones, then it seems illicit to infer "There is something Socrates knows to be above" from "Socrates knows some stars are above" (Ch. IV, Soph. 14), particularly since the first of these propositions implies the proposition "Socrates knows the stars of Aries are above" (assuming that they are above), which seems obviously false. On the other hand, if the term designating the object of the cognitive attitude occurs outside the cognitive context itself, these problems do not arise. If your father is the one approaching, then from "Your father is known by you" or "Your father is someone you know," there seems to be no difficulty in inferring "The one approaching is known by you" or "The one approaching is someone you know." And from "There are some stars which Socrates knows to be above," one can infer "There are some things which Socrates knows to be above," and consequently (assuming the stars of Aries are above) "The stars of Aries are known by Socrates to be above." [84]

There are two rather obvious ways of dealing with this problem. One is to maintain that terms in such contexts do not stand for the objects for which they ordinarily stand, but rather stand for some intensional entities or "meanings" peculiar to them. Interchangeability is then not allowed, because even if two terms designate the same objects extensionally, they do not have the same meanings. [85]

[83] That is, both the process of existential generalization and that of instantiation are valid.

[84] In modern literature, this is put by saying that although it seems illegitimate to allow quantifiers outside such contexts to bind variables within them, there is no problem if the variable is placed outside the context.

[85] This is the view of Walter Burleigh, a realist logician and English contemporary of Ockham, according to whom terms in such contexts have simple

Or if one chooses not to acknowledge intensional objects, he may simply regard terms in such contexts as non-referential and so again disallow interchangeability. [86]

Buridan rejects both these solutions, the first because he refuses to admit intensional objects and the second because of his insistence that in knowing a proposition, we also know the objects to which its terms refer. Hence, he wants to maintain that terms in such contexts stand for just the objects they stand for in any other proposition. And he wants to allow inferences of the kind cited above involving the astronomer. To account for the difficulties attendant upon such a position, he holds that all verbs of mental attitude and their accompanying participles, gerunds, and abstract nouns, cause terms following them to connote the "reasons" for their application (Ch. IV, Remark 7). The proposition "You know the one approaching" not only asserts that you have knowledge of some individual, but it also connotes or signifies that you know him *as* the one approaching, not in any other way. And if your father is the one approaching, then that proposition also asserts that you know your father, but it connotes that you know him not as your father, but as the one approaching.

It is not altogether clear just what these "reasons" are that are connoted. Nor is it clear whether we have here a new *kind* of connotation or simply some new *objects* of connotation. The following paragraphs are meant to interpret Buridan's position by restating it in the light of his general epistemological stand.

The proposition "Socrates knows some stars to be above," and others of similar form employing cognitive verbs, are not in standard categorical form. That is, they do not consist precisely of a subject-term and a predicate-term, joined by a copula which is some form of the verb "to be" (Ch. VI, Soph. 3). The proposition above, if put into standard form, reads "Socrates is [one] knowing some stars to be above," where the predicate is the complex term "[one]-knowing-some-

---

supposition and so stand for the universal natures they signify, rather than for the individual objects for which they stand in personal supposition. See his *De Puritate Artis Logicae: Tractatus Longior*, ed. P. Boehner (St. Bonaventure, N.Y., 1955), I, 3.

[86] Buridan mentions those who say that we have knowledge only of propositions and not of the objects designated by their terms. Whose view this is, is uncertain, but there is some evidence he may have had Ockham himself in mind. See the article cited in note 74.

stars-to-be-above," which has the same supposition as the subject-term, namely, Socrates. By the same token, a proposition such as "Some stars are known by Socrates to be above" reduces to "Some stars are [things] known by Socrates to be above," where the complex predicate "[things]-known-by-Socrates-to-be-above" stands for the same things as the subject, namely, all stars. And in both propositions, it is the complex predicate that Buridan regards as connotative.

On this basis, the theory of connotation in cognitive contexts can be understood. In a proposition such as "Socrates is [one] knowing some stars to be above," the predicate stands for Socrates and connotes, as the "reason" for his knowing, a specific proposition as that by which he knows, for knowledge is only by means of particular propositions. Exactly which proposition is so connoted is indicated by the content of the predicate. In the example given, the associated proposition is, of course, "Some stars are above." And the proposition is not true unless Socrates has knowledge of just that proposition. But of course, it is not only the proposition that is known, but also the things for which the terms of the proposition stand. So Socrates has knowledge of some specific stars, among them those that are above. This legitimizes the inference from "Socrates knows some stars to be above" to "Some things are known by Socrates to be above." And if the stars of Aries are in fact above, it can be further inferred that the stars of Aries are known by Socrates to be above. Thus Buridan does allow such inferences. But he does not allow interchangeability of terms in these contexts, in spite of the fact that he does regard such terms as referential. The reason is that since the proposition connoted by a cognitive predicate is determined by the terms constituting the predicate, to change the terms is to change the connoted proposition and so to change the significance of the entire proposition and, quite possibly, its truth-value as well. Hence, if the stars of Aries are above, one cannot conclude from "Socrates knows some stars to be above" to "Socrates knows the stars of Aries to be above." For while the terms of these two propositions stand for (at least some of) the same things, the first connotes the proposition "Some stars are above" and the second the proposition "The stars of Aries are above," so that one may be true and the other false.[87]

[87] In a move that would come practically to the same, Buridan might have required that the connoted proposition be attached as a rider to every such proposi-

In the case of a proposition such as "Some stars are known by Socrates to be above," where the term designating the objects known occurs as subject, the situation is different. For the terms of such a proposition stand for objects known, not for a knower. And although the proposition asserts that the objects are known, it is a matter of indifference by which proposition they are known. So the predicate of such a proposition is said to connote a disjunction of all possible propositions by which those objects might be known (Ch. IV, Remark 8).

Buridan concludes then that there are many occasions on which a man can be said to have knowledge of something, even if he claims not to know anything of it. Indeed, since many propositions make reference to all possible existents, a man may have knowledge of something that does not exist and whose existence he thinks impossible. For a language user, mental activity is linguistic activity, so that the objects of such activity are determined not by what we claim to know, believe, opine, etc., but by a theory of meaning and reference. And this means that not only specifically cognitive verbs, but verbs of any sort of mental activity whatever, involve connotation of propositions and their referents. He mentions some of these verbs—"to want," "to desire," "to long for," "to promise," "to owe," and "to obligate" (Ch. IV, Remark 9)—but he would undoubtedly be willing to extend the list. [88]

D. *Insolubles*

The insolubles are usually associated with semantic paradoxes, particularly the paradox known as the Liar, [89] but not all insolubles are

---

tion and so allowed interchangeability. Then the proposition "Socrates knows some stars to be above" would be regarded as an abbreviated form of "Socrates knows some stars to be above, by means of 'Some stars are above.'" He could then allow interchangeability of terms with common suppositions. Such a change in the above case would yield something like "Socrates knows the stars of Aries to be above, by means of 'Some stars are above,'" which preserves the distinction. This is all by way of emphasizing that although he does disallow interchangeability, it is only because he wants to retain the usual propositional form and at the same time make clear which proposition is connoted, not because he regards terms in these contexts as non-referential.

[88] For further examples of problem-verbs, see Quine, *op. cit.*, pp. 144–151.

[89] The paradox of the Liar is a semantic antinomy arising from a self-referential assertion of falsity. Hence, its clearest and most radical form is a

forms of the Liar. An insoluble is a sentence that raises problems difficult to solve, so that almost any problem-sentence could be so designated. But Buridan follows a tradition that restricts consideration to sentences which raise problems of reference, particularly those that are self-referential.[90] The possibility of self-reference not only challenges a theory of meaning and truth, but may be a source of practical difficulty to language users. So a solution of these problems is meant to complete the theory of language.

There are at least four groups of sophisms in Chapter VIII, and in an introduction, it would be out of place to discuss them all. But I do want to mention a few leading ideas and review two of the kinds of paradoxes developed, by way of summarizing theoretical points.

---

proposition such as "This sentence is false," understood as referring to itself. But as Buridan's discussion indicates, there are many variations on this form. In fact, with minor shifts in statement, all but four or five of the sophisms of Chapter VIII can be construed as forms of the Liar. To one of these forms, similar to Buridan's seventh sophism, the paradox owes its name, since tradition has it that Epimenides the Cretan (c. 600 B.C.) originated the discussion with his claim that all Cretans are liars, which earned him and his fellow citizens the contempt of St. Paul (*Epistle to Titus* 1:10–13). Serious discussion of the paradox seems to date from the fourth century B.C., beginning perhaps with Eubulides (c. 340 B.C.). Aristotle (*On Sophistical Refutations* 25. 180b 2–7) mentions the problem whether a man can say both what is true and what is false at once. And although his remarks are not very enlightening, his suggestion that a statement may be false absolutely but true in some respect seems to be the inspiration of many medieval resolutions of the Liar. The Stoics were apparently concerned with the paradox, but interest in it seems to have died with them, and it next appears in the twelfth century, when Aristotle's sophistics was recovered, and the brief references in works of that time (such as the *Ars Disserendi* of Adam of Balsham) reveal little insight into the nature of the problem. Even in the middle of the thirteenth century, a thinker as eminent as Albert the Great (*In Duos Libros Elenchorum*, II, 3, 3, 694b) merely repeats Aristotle's remarks. But by the end of that century, interest in the paradox was growing, and Buridan's own discussion indicates the importance assigned it by fourteenth-century logicians. And by the fifteenth century, Paul of Venice (*Logica Magna*, II, 15) was able to give formulations of the Liar, together with no fewer than fifteen known solutions. Not until the twentieth century did the paradox again receive such sophisticated attention.

[90] Since all Buridan's insolubles are based on reference, those that are paradoxes at all would today be classified as either semantic or pragmatic. Philosophers of the Middle Ages failed to recognize anything resembling what are called logical paradoxes, such as Russell's paradox about the class of all classes that are not members of themselves. Buridan skirts the edges of such a paradox in the fourth sophism of Chapter III, where he asks whether a genus is wider than the most general genus, since the most general genus is itself a genus. But his concern there is only to deny the reality of genera and to make a distinction between the supposition of the term "genus" taken personally and its supposition taken materially.

Buridan begins his last chapter by elaborating the nature of the proposition and some of its properties, to make possible a distinction (corresponding to the use-mention distinction in modern logic) between what a proposition asserts and properties (such as truth) of the proposition itself.

Once again, a proposition is not what is asserted or signified by a sentence, but is the sentence itself. Every such proposition corresponds to a mental proposition, but just as correspondence to a mental proposition does not of itself make an inscription true, so not every group of words (even if of normal propositional form), together with a mental proposition, is a genuine proposition (Soph. 5). A proposition is a group of words uttered or written by someone with some intent. And it is that *whole* group of words as intended in that way that is a true or false proposition. The importance of what is *meant* by what is said or written is particularly evident in Sophism 8, where there is an attempt to develop an inscriptional account of the contradictories and equivalents of self-reflexive propositions.

Beyond a mental proposition, a proposition also signifies "something to be the case." That is, it signifies that things are somehow or other. But Buridan again emphasizes that while he retains the traditional talk about how a proposition signifies, he regards it only as a summary way of saying that some one of several truth-conditions, based on supposition, is met (Concl. 5; *cf.*, Ch. II, Concl. 14). Propositions signify just what their terms signify, and there is no special sort of "signifying that" done by them.

But truth-conditions may be met, without the corresponding propositions being true, and he summarizes this by saying that it may be as a proposition signifies and yet the proposition not be true (Soph. 1 and its solution). A proposition can be true only if it exists, and since it is a merely physical thing, it can be destroyed. So truth is a property of an inscription or utterance, and such a proposition is true only if it exists *and* if the "case" is as it signifies.

The distinction between what a proposition asserts and its truth is further emphasized by considering other propositional properties. To say that a proposition is possible (or impossible or necessary), for instance, is to say nothing about its truth-value. Some had thought that a state of affairs or a "case" is possible only in the sense that some proposition signifying that state of affairs is possibly true. Buridan rejects this, for the proposition "No proposition is negative" is not possibly true, since whenever it occurs, there exists at least one negative proposition, and since it cannot be true unless it occurs. But what that proposition signifies might be the case, since God might destroy all negative propositions. So he maintains that the proposition "No proposition is negative" is possible, although it is not possibly true. A proposition is possible just because what it asserts could be the case, not because it could be true (Concl. 3). Possibility is a property of propositions, not of "states of affairs," but it is not the property of possible truth. [91]

From this it follows that a man may know that what a proposition asserts is the case, without knowing that proposition to be true. If God eliminates all negative propositions, and if there is a man who knows the proposition "Every proposition is affirmative" and so knows what it asserts to be the case, then he also knows what the proposition "No proposition is negative" asserts to be so. But the latter proposition cannot be true, since it does not exist, so he cannot know it to be true. This distinction between knowledge of a proposition and knowledge of what it asserts and knowledge of its truth is nicely put to use in Sophisms 13–15.

Sophisms 7–12, with the exception of Sophism 8, are all more or less complex forms of self-referential propositions similar to the Liar. [92] So although only one simple form of the Liar will be discussed here, the solution proposed by Buridan can be extended to other forms. The solution brings into play most of the distinctions mentioned above.

[91] So correspondingly, the definition of necessity as eternal truth must be revised to state that a proposition is necessary if it is true whenever it occurs and would be true if it should occur at any other time.

[92] Not all these are strictly forms of the Liar. Sophism 7, for example, is not, although it is the Epimenidean version, for even though the assumption that it is true leads to the conclusion that it is false, the assumption that it is false does not lead to the conclusion that it is true, only to the conclusion that some proposition is true. For some interesting comments on paradoxes of this kind, not all of which may apply to Buridan, see A. N. Prior, "On a Family of Parodoxes," *Notre Dame Journal of Formal Logic*, Vol. II, No. 1 (1961), 16–32. Buridan's claim that Sophism 8 is a paradox may deserve closer examination, but it appears to be due to his supposing that because there is no way of deciding which of the two propositions in question is true and which false, they must have the same truth-value. But of course, it is just because we are sure they have different truth-values that we are unable to decide which is true. The sophism is valuable, however, because it contains his most important discussion of contradiction and equivalence among self-reflexive propositions.

First it is necessary to generate the paradox in an informal way, but in a way that reveals its connection with the traditional definition of truth.[93] According to that definition, a proposition is true if howsoever it signifies the case to be, so it is. And it was further assumed that if the case is as the proposition signifies, then the proposition is true. That is, the following equivalence was assumed: "A proposition 'p' is true if, and only if, p." The proposition "A man is an animal" is true if, and only if, a man is an animal.

Now take the proposition:

(A) The proposition "A" is false,

which involves a self-referential assertion of falsity. Adapting the above formula, we get:

"The proposition 'A' is false" is true if, and only if, the proposition "A" is false.

Or more briefly:

"The proposition 'A' is false" is true if, and only if, "A" is false.

Since the letter "A" in quotation marks names just what is named by "The proposition 'A' is false," namely, the proposition in question, we can replace one by the other. So the equivalence becomes:

"A" is true if, and only if, "A" is false,

which is a contradiction. The paradox thus arises directly from the traditional definition of truth. But before going on to Buridan's solution, it will be instructive to review some others.

The most popular resolution of the Liar in recent years is based on a theory of levels of language.[94] While this may involve either a hierarchy of languages or a hierarchy of semantic levels within a given language, its essential feature is the claim that even if a certain level can contain assertions about the syntax or grammar of propositions of that level, it cannot contain propositions about the semantics of propositions of that level. This means that no proposition can assert its

[93] For a somewhat different account of Buridan's discussion, see Moody, *Truth and Consequence in Mediaeval Logic*, pp. 101–110.

[94] For a classical statement of the position, since developed by others, see A. Tarski, "Der Wahrheitsbegriff in den Formalisierten Sprachen," *Studia Philosophica*, I (1935), 261–405.

own truth or falsity, since a proposition asserting the truth or falsity of any proposition must belong to a different (higher) level from the proposition itself. Buridan does not consider just this sort of solution, but he does mention those who hold that terms that can stand for propositions are never to be placed in one of the propositions for which they stand (Soph. 7). So "true" and "false" cannot stand for the propositions in which they occur, but only for others. He rejects this on the intuitively plausible ground that we often *do* talk about all propositions, including the one we are then using. We can surely think about all propositions, and whatever we can think about, we can talk about. So self-reference is to be allowed.

Other than this, he does not seem to have considered any solution based on the question whether self-referential assertions of falsity are semantically qualified to be called propositions at all. That they are propositions and so either true or false, he takes for granted. And he rejects out of hand the opinion that any proposition can be both true and false at once.

He does consider one position, which he says he had earlier held himself, one also held by his pupil, Albert of Saxony (Soph. 7).[95] On this view, a proposition signifies that it is itself true, in addition to signifying that something "is the case." A proposition which asserts its own falsity is then false, because in signifying both that it is true and that it is false, it must signify *something* that is not the case.[96]

Buridan has two objections to this. The first is based on an acknowledgement of language hierarchies as developed by Ockham in his account of signification.[97] There is a distinction to be made between terms of *first intention*, which signify extra-linguistic objects, and terms of *second intention*, which are signs of signs and not of the objects for which signs stand, *i.e.*, signs *of* first intentions. A proposition such as "A man is an animal" contains only terms of first intention and so signifies only objects, *i.e.*, men and animals. It cannot signify " 'A man is an animal' is true," since the terms of this latter proposition are of second intention, and terms of first intention cannot

[95] *Perutilis Logica Magistri Alberti de Saxonia* (Venice, 1560), VI, Ch. 1.

[96] This solution has been formalized by I. M. Bochenski, "Formalization of a Scholastic Solution of the Paradox of the 'Liar'," *Logico-Philosophical Studies*, ed. A. Menne (Dordrecht, 1962), pp. 64–66.

[97] Ockham, *op. cit.*, I, 12. See also Moody, *The Logic of William of Ockham*, pp. 44–46.

signify second intentions. So even if it is held (as it would be) that in the proposition "This proposition is false," the terms are already of second intention, to say that such a proposition signifies its own truth is to invent arbitrarily a rule that can apply only to propositions that are about their own semantics, syntax or grammar. What is wanted is a general rule that applies to all propositions and which yet provides a solution of paradoxes.

The second objection is more important for an understanding of Buridanian semantics and should be kept in mind when interpreting his solution, since it indicates dissatisfaction with *any* solution that makes use of the notion of signification. In his earlier discussion of the complex signifiable (Ch. II, Concl. 3), he says that a proposition such as "A man is running" can be understood to signify a man to be running (or, that a man is running), but only in two special senses. It can be understood to signify the corresponding mental proposition "A man is running" (and it can be taken in material supposition to stand for both that mental proposition and itself). And it can be understood to signify (and to stand in personal supposition for) something extra-linguistic that may be called a-man-to-be-running. But this latter is not a special sort of entity, it is nothing but a man who is running, a running man. And if no man is running, then it does not signify a running man, since there is no such man. In other words, being is prior to signification, and only what is can be signified.

To say that a proposition "p" signifies itself to be true is to say that it signifies "p" to be true. Now this may mean either that it signifies the proposition " 'p' is true," in which case many propositions of first intention would signify (or claim to signify) second intentions, or that it signifies "p"-to-be-true. But just as a-man-to-be-running is a running man, so "p"-to-be-true is nothing but true "p." But true "p" cannot be signified unless it exists, and it exists only if "p" is true. So to say that every proposition signifies itself to be true is to say that every proposition *is* true, which is absurd.

His own solution of the Liar (in Soph. 7) seems to depend upon a distinction between what is "formally" signified and what is "virtually" implied. A proposition is said to signify formally that something is the case, in the sense discussed above. But it is also said to imply virtually another proposition asserting the truth of the first proposition. This is then qualified, since no proposition can be true unless it exists. So the rule is actually that from any proposition, together with a statement that it exists, there follows a proposition asserting that that first proposition is true. In the case of the Liar, the proposition in question signifies formally that it is itself false. And like every proposition, if it exists, it also implies that it is itself true. But for the truth of a proposition, it is required not only that it is as it formally signifies, but also that it is as that implied consequent signifies. This condition cannot be met by the Liar, since it signifies that it is false, while that consequent signifies that it is true, and it cannot be both true and false. So because it fails to meet this condition of truth, it is false. [98]

This solution can be variously interpreted, but I think that it fails on any likely interpretation. But at the same time, it seems to me that it fails only because of his conclusion that the Liar is false and that he has provided material for a solution that is workable.

Although I do not propose to exhibit the solution formally, some elementary symbolism will simplify the explication. Buridan says that every proposition, together with a statement that the proposition exists, implies another proposition which signifies that the first state-

[98] It is instructive to look at a misunderstanding of Buridan's solution in A. N. Prior, *Proceedings of the British Academy*, XLVIII (1962), 290–291. Prior argues that the distinction between formal signification and virtual implication allows the paradox to recur at the level of formal significations. He takes Buridan to mean that propositions have a special sort of signification which is a "signifying that" something is the case. He then argues that if a proposition "p" signifies that p, we can say that what it formally signifies is not the case. Then consider the proposition "What is formally signified by this sentence is not the case." If we ask of this proposition not whether it is true, but whether what it signifies is the case, the paradox again arises.

Buridan would answer that such an objection takes his talk about formal signification too literally, overlooking all he has said about the signification of propositions. The statement above is no more than an informal way of expressing the proposition "This sentence is false." As he has explained, "not the case" just means "false" and is a way of summarizing many conditions of falsity, none of which is based on signification. Actually, what is formally signified by a proposition is just some concrete things, not a "case" or "state of affairs." In the case of the proposition above, what is signified is just the proposition itself, and "not the case" signifies the attribute of falsity. So this is only the original form of the Liar.

I mention Prior's objection because Buridan in his solution does mention signification of some case or other a great deal. And in my interpretation of his remarks, I do the same. But it must be understood that this is in every case a way of characterizing the supposition of terms and has nothing to do with the doctrine of signification.

ment is true. That is, I take it, if it is as a proposition signifies (*i.e.*, if the relevant suppositional truth-condition is met) and if the proposition exists, then the proposition is true. He says he means by this that every proposition implies another such proposition "as an antecedent implies that which follows from it." And earlier, in Conclusion 5 of Chapter VIII, he explains that an antecedent is said to imply a consequent if it is impossible for it to be as the antecedent signifies unless it is as the consequent signifies. I follow Moody in using the symbol "–|" for this sort of implication.[99] The symbol "=" is used for the equivalence of two propositions that mutually imply each other in this sense. I shall use p (without quotation marks) for any proposition, "p" (with quotation marks) as the name of that proposition, and "T'p'" as an abbreviation for the statement "'p' is true." The requirement that a proposition exist if it is to be true could be met by introducing the expression (Ex) (x="p" · x_sp), to be read "There exists an x, which is the proposition 'p' and signifies that p," where a phrase such as "'p' signifies that p" is to be interpreted not as implying that there exists some "state of affairs" that is signified, but as saying that the proposition "p" is of such form as to assert that some suppositional truth-condition is met, whether or not that condition is indeed met. However, because this is cumbersome and possibly confusing, and because in every one of Buridan's examples, the existence of the proposition is established by the fact that someone is said to utter it, read it on a wall, or something of the sort, the existential condition can be omitted. There are no problems of self-reference with non-existent propositions, and if the proposition does exist and is paradoxical, introduction of the existential condition does not help the solution of the paradox. So it is to be understood that we are here discussing only existing propositions.

Buridan argues that from any proposition, together with the fact of its existence, it follows that that proposition is true. That is, if a proposition exists, it is impossible for it to be as the proposition signifies unless it is as a proposition asserting that proposition to be true signifies. So for any p:

(1) P –| T "p."

If a man is a horse (and if "A man is a horse" exists), then "A man

[99] Moody, *Truth and Consequence in Mediaeval Logic*, pp. 70–79.

is a horse" is true. But he also agrees with the traditional definition that if a proposition is true, then the case is as it signifies. That is, for any p:

$$(2)\ T\text{“p”} \dashv p.$$

Since the antecedent of (1) is identical with the consequent of (2) and the consequent of (1) with the antecedent of (2), this establishes the following equivalence: for any p:

$$(3)\ T\text{“p”} = p.$$

The argument is then that for the truth of any proposition, it is required that both sides of (3) be true. But this condition cannot be satisfied by the Liar (*e.g.*, "This very proposition is false"), since the left side is true only if the Liar is true and the right side is true if the case is as it signifies, which is to say that the right side is true only if the Liar is false, since it signifies that it is false. Therefore, since the Liar fails to meet this condition, it is false.

The conclusion that the Liar is false does not follow from this argument. His error lies in supposing that the equivalence (3) applies only to true propositions, when in fact, it applies to all propositions whatever. So it is not merely the case that if a proposition is true, both sides of (3) must be true, but it is also the case that if a proposition is false, both sides of (3) must be false. And in the case of the Liar, this condition cannot be met either. The left side of (3) is false only if the Liar is false (assuming always that it exists), and if the right side of (3) is false, the case is not as the proposition signifies. But the Liar signifies that it is false, so if the case is not as it signifies, then it is not false and so is true. So for the Liar, if the left side of (3) is false, then the right side is true, and since it is required for falsity that both sides be false, it follows that the Liar is not false. So Buridan's solution will not do as it stands.

But while he has not proved that the Liar is false, he has provided another sort of resolution of the paradox. His contention that the implications of (1) and (2) hold for any propositions whatever seems to me intuitively plausible. And if this is granted, namely, that a proposition has a given truth-value only if another proposition asserting it to be true has the same truth-value, then the equivalence (3) holds for any proposition also. That is, for any true proposition, both sides of (3) are true, and for any false proposition, both sides of (3) are false. But for the Liar, it is impossible for both sides to be either true or false. So the Liar is neither true nor false, and since every proposition is either true or false, it follows that the Liar is not a proposition at all. The equivalence (3) does not provide a truth-condition, but it does provide a means of determining whether a string of words is a genuine proposition, and the Liar fails to meet that test.

If Buridan's solution is understood in this latter way, then it appears to come much nearer the modern solution based on language-levels, for that solution also denies propositional status to the Liar. But it differs from the language-levels solution in that it does not reject *all* propositions that are self-referential or even all that are about their own semantics. In particular, the proposition "This proposition is true" is admissible, which seems desirable on intuitive grounds.

Chapter VIII is rich in all sorts of philosophical material (including a possible contribution to scientific ethics in Sophisms 18–20), but there is space here to mention only one additional problem. That is Sophism 13, which has a logically unsophisticated Socrates read on a wall the proposition "Socrates doubts the proposition written on the wall," which is the only proposition written on the wall. Now while it is true that this is a self-referential proposition, it does not assert its own falsity, nor does it assert anything from which it follows that it is false. So it is not a semantic paradox in the usual sense. If a pragmatic paradox is characterized as one that arises from a relation of a language to its users, then this is a pragmatic paradox, as is the earlier proposition "No proposition is negative." [100] The paradoxical nature of the situation arises from the fact that Socrates sees the proposition, doubts it, and knows that he doubts it. So the proposition is true, since the case is as it signifies, it exists, and it does not assert its own falsity. And Socrates knows both that it exists and that the case is as it signifies. Yet he cannot know that the proposition is true. Furthermore, if Plato should utter an exactly similar proposition in Socrates' presence, he would know Plato's proposition to be true, but would still not know the sophism itself to be true.

[100] Although most pragmatic paradoxes seem to involve situations in which widely accepted and persuasive rules of validity or truth are blocked by the attitudes of language users, it is not possible to give a general characterization of them, since there is no very broad agreement on how to resolve them.

Buridan uses this sophism to reinforce his distinction between what a proposition asserts and the truth of the proposition. But what is most interesting about it is that it stands both as a challenge to a realistic ontology and as a pragmatic argument for an inscriptionist semantics. Given his theory of knowledge and his nominalism, he has no trouble with the sophism. He holds that a proposition is only a sentence token and that knowledge is only of such a token. So he can admit that Socrates can know that some one inscription is true and that the case is as it signifies, without knowing an equiform inscription to be true. On the other hand, the sophism poses a problem for the realist, who holds that every proposition has an intensional "meaning" or significate, which is what it asserts or signifies. On this account, to doubt a proposition is to doubt what it asserts, so Socrates would doubt not only his own proposition, but any proposition asserting what that one asserts. And yet in the case here involved, it seems that Socrates can doubt his own proposition and yet know Plato's to be true. The realist must show either that two equiform tokens of the same language may express different propositions, or he must explain how one may know a sentence to be true, without at the same time knowing the intensional proposition expressed by it to be true.

And finally, even a more moderate position that claims sentence-types as truth-vehicles faces this problem. For just as it is hard to see how two equiform sentences may express different proportions, so it is hard to see how one token of a type may be known to be true, without all tokens of that type being known to be true. So like several of his other sophisms (notably Sophism 15 of Chapter IV), this one attempts a practical refutation of realism, and all such deserve especially careful attention.

SOPHISMS ON MEANING AND TRUTH

CHAPTER I
ON SIGNIFICATION

A. Introduction

In the beginning of my work on the sum of logic, I stated that the ninth and final tract deals with the practice of sophisms, namely, with their solution and formations. And in this tract, sometimes I shall repeat some parts treated in the previous tracts, and sometimes I shall explain them further, as it seems to me to contribute to the solutions of the sophisms.

To this end, I want to divide this tract. First, I shall treat propositions of inherence;[1] second, modal propositions. And although only those that are of present tense are strictly of inherence (since those of past and future tense are not properly of inherence, but of what will be[2] or of what has been[3]), nevertheless, broadly speaking, I want to call "propositions of inherence" all those that are not modal. Now in the first of these parts, I shall first treat propositions with absolute terms; and second, propositions with relative terms. Again, in the first of these parts, I shall first consider simply categorical propsitions; second, simply hypothetical propositions; third, categorical propositions having a hypothetical subject or predicate; fourth, categoricals that require an exposition by hypotheticals, such as exclusive, exceptive, reduplicative, and many others with verbs such as "begins," "ceases," and "differs," and several other syncategorematic expressions. And in the first of these parts, I shall treat first propositions with simple subjects and predicates; second, propositions with compound subjects and predicates, whether they are composed of several terms in the nominative or of terms in both nominative and oblique cases.

[1] *de inesse.*
[2] *de fore.*
[3] *de fuisse.*

And in the first of those parts, I shall treat first the foundation of certain common principles that must be presupposed concerning the said propositions; second, syncategorematic words usually placed in those simple categorematic expressions. And in the first of these parts, I shall treat first the significations of terms and sentences; second, the cause of the truth and falsehood of this kind of proposition; third, supposition and appellation and the ampliations and restrictions of supposition or appellation; fourth, the standards by which a proposition is said to be true or false.

Therefore, dealing with the significations of terms and propositions, there is stated the first sophism.

B. Sophisms

(1) *Every spoken proposition is true.*

This is proved, because howsoever it signifies, so it is correspondingly in the thing signified. Hence, it is true. And the consequence is valid, because this seems to be required and to suffice for the truth of a proposition. [4] The antecedent is clear, since every spoken proposition signifies a mental proposition either similar to itself or proportionally corresponding to it, according to the statement in the first book of the *Perihermenias* that those things that are in the word are marks and signs of concepts [5] that are in the mind. [6]

(2) *A horse is an ass.*

I posit the case that all horses and asses are completely destroyed, so that nothing is a horse and nothing is an ass.

The sophism is proved, because its contradictory is false, namely, that no horse is an ass. This is proved, since in the thing or things signified, the case is not as the proposition signifies. For by hypothesis, the thing signified, namely, a horse and an ass, is nothing. And in a thing that is absolutely nothing, the case is neither so nor otherwise. Therefore, in the things signified, the case was not as it was signified

[4] That is, according to the traditional definition stating that a proposition is true if "howsoever it signifies the case to be, so it is" (*qualitercumque significat esse, ita est*).

[5] *passionum*.

[6] Aristotle, *De Interpretatione* 1. 16a 4–5.

to be by the proposition; so the proposition was not true. Hence, the sophism is true, since its opposite in conceded [to be false].

(3) *God is not.*

This is proved, since howsoever the proposition signifies, so it is. Hence, it is true. The antecedent is proved, because the stated proposition either signifies precisely a mental proposition and its terms—and these are all in the mind corresponding to that proposition, so howsoever it might signify, so it would be. Or it could signify beyond this something outside the mind. And in this case, I ask whether beyond the concepts of the mind, it would signify precisely God; and then since He exists, it would still be the case that to every signification of that proposition there would be a correspondence in things, so that the proposition would be true. Or perhaps it signifies something else besides the concepts of the mind and besides God. And if you say this, you cannot say that that something else is anything except God-not-being.[7] And then I conclude that God-not-being is signified by the proposition "God is not," and furthermore, that God-not-being exists. For the proposition asserting God not to be is affirmative; hence, it is not true unless the subject stands [8] for something.[9] And so God-not-being exists. And this is signified by the proposition "God is not." And nothing else is signified, except God and those concepts that are in the mind; and all these exist. So the proposition follows that howsoever it signifies, so it is. Hence, it is true.

Once again, this is false: "Every God is"; hence, this is true: "God is not." The consequence holds by the argument from contradictories. I prove the antecedent, because the proposition "God is" signifies more than the term "God." Otherwise, it would be true to say "God," just as it is true to say "God is." And similarly, the sentence "A horse is" signifies more than the expression "horse." For it is never false to say "horse," even granting that no horse exists; but it could be false to say "A horse is," which would not be the case unless the latter signified more. I concede, therefore, that the sen-

[7] *Deum non esse*. This sort of expression (an accusative followed by an infinitive) was used by some logicians (but not by Buridan) to designate an intensional entity signified by a proposition. See above p. 16.

[8] *supponit*. The expression "to stand for" and its grammatical forms will be used throughout to translate the technical phrase *supponere pro* and its forms.

[9] Based on a common rule for truth. See the fifth conclusion of this chapter.

tence "Every God is" signifies more than "God." And yet as regards external things, nothing more corresponds to that proposition than to that term. For if there should be nothing besides God, still God would exist. Therefore, as regards external things, there is nothing corresponding to the total signification of the proposition [10] "Every God is"; so it is false. Hence, this is true: "God is not."

The opposite is agreed to by all and must be conceded.

(4) *This name "chimera" signifies nothing.*

It is proved, because it does not signify anything other than a chimera, at least in its principal signification (for we are not here dealing with the grammatical modes of signifying [11]). But a chimera is nothing, so "chimera" signifies nothing. The assumption that this name "chimera" signifies nothing other than a chimera is confirmed. For this name "chimera" signifies nothing other than a chimera in the same way that "man" signifies nothing other than a man or "whiteness" other than whiteness. And the same thing is also confirmed by induction, since it signifies neither ass, nor goat, nor whiteness, and so of all other entities. Moreover, even if it were granted that it could signify something other than a chimera, still it would follow that it signified nothing; for nothing is other than a chimera, since a chimera is nothing. And yet it follows that if B is other than A, both B and A exist, as is clear from Aristotle in the tenth book of the *Metaphysics*.[12] Nothing is either the same as non-being or other than non-being. And again, if this name "chimera" should signify something else, then it would have a corresponding significate outside the mind. And then the proposition "A chimera is a chimera" would be true, which is not admitted. The consequence is proved, since the same thing would correspond to the subject and the predicate of the proposition, and yet an affirmative proposition is true by reason of the identity of the predicate with the subject. And I mean its identity not with the subject of the spoken sentence, but with that which corresponds to it outside the mind. Likewise, if it should signify something, then it ought to stand for it, just as the term "stone"

[10] On the technical expression *significatum totale propositionis,* see above p. 16.

[11] see above p. 27, n. 51.

[12] Aristotle, *Metaphysics* x. 3. 1054b 18–22.

stands for a stone, since it signifies a stone. But "chimera" does not stand for anything; therefore, it signifies nothing. That it does not stand for anything may be proved, since if it did stand for something, the propositions "A chimera exists" and also "A chimera is something" would be true, and these propositions are not admitted. Therefore, "chimera" signifies nothing.

The opposite is argued, since it would then be no more a significant word than "buff" or "baff," which is not admitted. Again, every name is a conventionally significant word, and not only because it can signify, since then "buff" and "baff" would be conventionally significant words, just as are nouns and verbs, which is false. Hence, every name is a conventionally significant word, because it is imposed to signify, and all that is imposed to signify is imposed to signify something. And it signifies that which it is imposed to signify. Hence, every name signifies something, and this word "chimera" is a name; therefore, etc.

One solution is offered as true by some who want to escape difficulties more than to discern truth. They want to maintain that the word "chimera" does indeed signify, but that it does not signify anything, so that it does not follow that if it signifies, then it signifies something. In the same way, many say that this does not follow: A acts, so A acts something. [13] And also some say that it signifies a chimera, but it does not follow that it signifies anything that could appear, since they say that it does not follow that if one builds a house, then one builds something. [14]

Against all these I argue first. Signifying is described as that which establishes the understanding of a thing. So a word is said to signify that the understanding of which it establishes for us. Therefore, if to signify is to establish the understanding of a thing and to signify is always to signify a thing, then to signify is to signify something, since "thing" and "something" are interchangeable. [15] Also to signify is to be a sign. But a sign and its significate are spoken of as correlatives. Hence, "chimera" is not a sign unless it is a sign of something, and consequently, it signifies nothing unless it signifies something or something is a significate—whether present, past, future, or

[13] *A agit, ergo A agit aliquid.*
[14] That is, so long as one is building, what he is building does not yet exist.
[15] *convertibiliter se habent.*

merely possible. For so it is with all relatives—nothing is a father if nothing either is or was or will be or could possibly be a son. And so of a cause and that which is caused, prior and posterior, and so of others. Therefore, if this name "chimera" signifies, it is a sign, and if it is a sign, something either is its significate or at least was, etc. And this we say to be signified by this name "chimera." And so Aristotle, in the first book of the *Metaphysics*, [16] says that all those willing to discuss must presuppose that a name signifies something and that it signifies determinately one or many, thus, either some thing or some things; because "one" and "being" are interchangeable, and similiarly "many" and "beings" are interchangeable, according to the cited passage.

(5) *Chimeras are complex signifiables.*[17]

This is proved, because they are, so they are substances, or accidents, creators or creatures, or chimeras. But they are not substances or accidents or creator or creatures; hence, they are chimeras. The conclusion that they are complex signifiables is proved, because before there was anything besides God there were many complex signifiables. This is proved, since man was not then running, so it was the case that man did not run. But it is certain that then there was neither man nor running nor the combination of man and running nor any proposition, since none of these existed. Nor was it God, since its being so was contingent and God was always necessary. And also that which was the case was signified by the proposition "Man was not running," by which God was not signified. Therefore, God-being-so [18] was then a complex signifiable different from any of the aforesaid statements and not the same as any of them. The same could be said also of the fact that a horse did not then walk, and of the fact that a stone did not then move, and of an infinite number of others; hence, etc. Again, this is true: "Antichrist will be," so it is the case that Antichrist will be. And yet that being the case is neither Antichrist nor any other being, unless it is a complex signifiable, as is clear by induction. And if that is the case, then one must concede

[16] *Cf.*, Aristotle, *Metaphysics* iv. 2. 1003b 23–34.
[17] *complexe significabilia*. See above p. 16.
[18] *Deum ita esse.*

that it was thus before God created anything, since it would have been true to say then just as it is now. Therefore, it was then a complex signifiable. And just as it is argued concerning Antichrist, so it is argued concerning a thousand others that will be and are not yet. Or again, designate something that God can create and call it B, and then this is true: "B can be created," and this is also true: "God can create B." Hence, it is the case that B can be created, and that B-being-created is not God, since God cannot be created; nor is it B nor anything belonging to B itself, since B does not yet exist. Thus, it remains that it is a complex signifiable, and it was so before God created the world, since it is the case that the creation of B was possible then, just as it is now. And so it can be said of this statement "God being able to create B." Likewise, if God creates B, then this is the case, and so God-creating-B exists and is not B itself, nor is it God, since God-creating-B is purely contingent and God is not contingent. Therefore, God-creating-B is a complex signifiable distinct from others. The same thing can be said of others.

Again, some believe, arguing with great difficulty, that Socrates-loving-God is either the same as Socrates himself loving God or it is a complex signifiable. And if it is such a complex signifiable, I have the proposition, for the same will be said of others. But I show that it is not Socrates loving God, for then it would not be anything except Socrates; and then, for the same reason, Socrates-hating-God would be Socrates hating God and nothing else. Therefore, the same thing would be Socrates-hating-God and Socrates-loving-God, and this is impossible, since the latter is extremely good and praiseworthy and the former extremely evil and damnable.

The opposite is conceded by all, since chimeras do not exist. And it is also argued that there were no such complex signifiables before there was anything besides God, since this implies a contradiction, namely, for nothing to be besides God and for the complex signifiables to be and to be other than God. Also they would have to be eternal, and we hold by faith that nothing is simply eternal besides God Himself. And again, all that exists is either God or a creature depending upon God. And yet those complex signifiables were not creatures, since they existed before God created anything. Nor were they God, as those [who support the doctrine of the complex signifiables] admit. And this is true, since such are as many as ten or many more, and God is one. Therefore, these complex signifiables were absolutely nothing. Likewise, they were not accidents, since one could never designate of what they were accidents or to what they belonged. Nor were they substances, as those who posit them concede. Therefore, they were absolutely nothing.

(6) *No man lies.*

This is proved, because to lie is to go against the mind and to assert the contrary of what one has in the mind. But this is impossible, since to every spoken proposition, there must correspond a similar one in the mind, for you cannot assert what you do not understand; therefore, etc.

The opposite is manifest by the common way of speaking.

C. Conclusions

Because of these sophisms, some remarks must be made concerning the significations of terms and propositions.

(1) And the *first conclusion* is that written letters signify sounds spoken or to be spoken, and they do not signify things outside the mind, such as asses or stones, except through the mediate signification of the sounds. This is clear, because masters teaching boys the alphabet teach them on what such letters are imposed and teach them only to pronounce differently the letter "b" and the letter "c," which is just because those letters are imposed to signify the different sounds. But then suppose that someone has Latin as a mother tongue, just as we have French. He would indeed know the signification of this spoken sentence "A man is running." But if the corresponding sentence itself is written, then although he will indeed see the written sentence and the extension or shapes of the letters, he will still be altogether ignorant of what things those letters signify. For he does not know what sounds these letters signify, since those letters do not signify a man running, except mediately, because they signify those sounds.

(2) The *second conclusion* is that significant spoken words signify passions [19] or concepts [20] of the mind, and do not signify other things except through the mediate signification of the concepts. This is clear,

[19] *passiones.*
[20] *conceptus.*

first, because as letters relate to sounds, so analogously do sounds relate to intentions [21] of the mind. But we have said that the letters signify these sounds; therefore, etc. Secondly, this is proved, because there are different significant words and they are not synonymous, but they have diverse significations; and yet, aside from the concepts, they do not signify different things, but rather exactly the same things. And they stand for the same things interchangeably—as for example, "being" and "one" stand for the same; "diverse," "quantity," "essence" stand for the same, etc. Therefore, the significations of these terms are not different because of the different things outside the mind, but only because of the different concepts designated by these terms, through the mediation of which they signify those things. And this is also made clear by authors who commonly posit a difference between an equivocal and an univocal name, because an equivocal name has several significates and a univocal name does not, but rather stands for several things. [22] Thus also, Aristotle says that equivocal names ought to be distinguished and not univocal names. [23] And these things are not true because of the things signified outside the mind, but because of the concepts. Therefore, these concepts are the significates of those names. And it is clear from these two conclusions what Aristotle intended in the beginning of his book *Perihermenias* [24] and also in the fourth book of the *Metaphysics*, [25] where he states that it must be understood that if someone wants to argue with another that a name signifies some one thing determinately—or if many things because it is equivocal, still not an infinite number, but a determinate number—this can only be understood as regards the intentions or concepts. For suppose, as Aristotle believed, that the world has been eternally as it is now; then this term "man"would signify infinitely many men. And this is so even without such an assumption, since this name "continuum" or "magnitude" signifies an infinite number, because it signifies all continua; and continua are infinite, since the parts of a continuum—of which each is continuous—are infinite.

(3) *Third conclusion:* by every concept something is conceived, or perhaps not one thing only, but many things at once. For it would be

[21] *intentiones.*
[22] *habet . . . plura supposita.*
[23] *Cf.*, Aristotle, *Metaphysics* vii. 4. 1030a 32–35.
[24] Aristotle, *De Interpretatione* 1. 16a 4–8.
[25] Aristotle, *Metaphysics* iv. 4. 1006b 12–18.

absurd to say that one understands and yet that he understands nothing, or that he sees and that he sees nothing. For this would be opposed to the condition of an active verb and the signification that an active verb requires after itself, since it signifies in the manner of an act that passes into another. Because of this, these are considered false: "I read and I read nothing," "I see and I see nothing," "I understand and I understand nothing." And I believe all such to be false and impossible by nature. Nor is this opposed by what some say regarding building a house and yet building nothing. For although one could build nothing which was finished, still one could build something subjectively, and from this something subjective comes to be. For one makes wood to be a house, and because of this wood becomes a house. Thus, it appears that if an active verb is truly predicated of some subject, it is necessary that it be properly expressed with an accusative following, in which that active mode of signifying is terminated.

(4) The *fourth conclusion* is that also every significant word and act signifies something. And this ought to be agreed to and proved analogously to the preceding conclusion. And this was also well argued in the second sophism. So this [proof] should be looked up there.

(5) The *fifth conclusion* is that this name "chimera" does not signify a chimera, having conceded that it is impossible for there to be a chimera. And so also this name "vacuum" could not signify a vacuum, if it were impossible for there to be a vacuum, as Aristotle believes. This is now proved, since nothing seems to prevent this consequence from being valid: This name "chimera" signifies a chimera, so a chimera is signified by this name "chimera." But this is false: "A chimera is signified by this name 'chimera,'" for it is an affirmative proposition whose subject, namely, this name "chimera," stands for nothing, since nothing either is or was or will be or can be a chimera. This is a rule which will be further discussed later, namely, that every affirmative proposition whose subject or predicate stands for nothing is false. And so in the same way, one ought to conclude that these are false: "A chimera is knowable" or "A chimera is thinkable" or "A chimera is a chimera" or "A chimera is non-being," and so of others.

There is then some doubt as to what this name "chimera" signifies, since it signifies something, as has been said, and yet does not signify a chimera. Concerning this, I can first say evasively that it signifies some concept which this name "chimera" was imposed to signify. But note that this answer does not suffice, for it is not a question of this spoken name "chimera," but a mental name, *i.e.*, the concept, which that word "chimera" is imposed to signify. I ask, therefore, what is conceived by that concept, since it was said that it is a concept of something and not a chimera. For we said that propositions such as the following are all false: "A chimera is signified," "A chimera is opined," "A chimera is understood," etc. What then is that concept a concept of?

(6) To answer this, I posit the *sixth conclusion*, that a simple concept, if it is a subject or predicate in a mental proposition, stands for that thing of which it is a concept. Nothing prevents this, except perhaps in two cases. The first is that in which a thing is conceived by an accident,[26] as it would be with the concept from which the name "white" comes. For it could be said that it is a concept of whiteness and yet that it does not stand for whiteness, but for the subject to which it belongs, since it is known by way of an accident. But the concept corresponding to this name "whitness" stands for whiteness, since that concept conceives whiteness and not as an accident of something. The other case is that in which a simple concept would not stand for the thing which is designated by it, because that thing was and is destroyed or does not yet exist but will be or can be. In this case, if the copula of the proposition is not suitable[27] but extends to another time, then that concept would not stand for that thing nor for anything. For example, in the mental proposition corresponding to the sentence "Antichrist is running," the concept which is the subject is a concept of Antichrist and yet it does not stand for Antichrist, because the copula in the present tense prevents supposition. Thus, that concept stands for nothing. But if there were this mental proposition "Antichrist will be evil," then the concept of Antichrist would stand for something—indeed, for Antichrist.

There does not appear to me to be any other reason why a simple concept of something, serving as subject or predicate in a mental proposition, ought not to stand for the thing of which it is a concept. And

[26] *per modum adiacentis.*

[27] *consonans.* That is, if the copula is not of the tense which covers the time at which the thing exists.

so I suppose or posit this to be true. But concerning complex concepts, the matter is otherwise. For if there is a determined and determinable complex concept, such as the concept corresponding to the expression "white man," and if there occurs a mental proposition such as "A white man runs," though the concept of man is a concept indifferently of every man, yet that concept does not stand for all men, but only for white ones, since the concept of white combined with it limits it. Nor does the concept of white stand for all white things, but it is limited by the concept of man to stand only for those white things that are men. And so I conclude that although every simple concept stands for all that of which it is a concept (except in the two cases mentioned above), yet this is not so for the complex concept. For the concept corresponding to the expression "white man" stands neither for all men nor for all white things, although every man is conceived by it, on account of the concept of man, and every white thing, on account of the concept of white.

(7) Hence, the *seventh conclusion* is that not every complex concept which is a subject or predicate in a mental proposition stands for all that which it signifies, even without including the two cases mentioned.

(8) The *eighth conclusion* follows, namely, that some complex concepts serving as a subject or predicate in a mental proposition stand for nothing, and yet many beings are conceived by them. This is emphasized, because just as in words one can form the proposition "A risible ass is running," so one can form a corresponding one in the mind. For one can bring together the concept of ass and the concept of risible in a determinate and determinable manner, and from these compose a subject with respect to a concept from which is taken the verb "is running." Then by this complex concept composed of the concept of ass and the concept of risible, I conceive asses by the concept of ass and risible things by the concept of risible. Hence, I conceive through the complex concept many things, namely, men and asses. And yet, that complex concept stands for nothing, since the concept of risible prevents its standing for other than risible things, so it cannot stand for asses. And the concept of ass prevents its standing for other than asses, so it cannot stand for risible things. And so nothing remains for which it can stand, just as in the preceding conclusion, I said that in the proposition "A white man is running," the subject "white man" does not stand for all men nor for all white things, since

this term "white" prevents its standing for other than white things, and this term "man," conversely, prevents its standing for other than men. Hence, finally, it must be noted that although a word immediately signifies a concept, yet through the mediation of the concept, it is imposed to signify that which is conceived by the concept. Thus, the expression "ass" is imposed to signify through the mediation of the concept of ass, for it signifies asses, which are conceived by that concept. So all risible things and all asses are signified by this complex expression "risible ass." Hence also, concerning supposition, it is to be noted that a vocal term, if it is taken in a proposition significatively and not materially, does not stand for itself, nor for the concept that it immediately signifies. Rather, it stands for those same things for which the corresponding concept itself stands, namely, for the things conceived by that concept. And so also a written term, if it is not taken in material supposition, stands neither for itself nor for the spoken term that it immediately signifies nor for the concept that it signifies through the mediation of the spoken term. But it stands for the things for which that concept in the mental proposition stands. So all references in a spoken or written language (if they are taken significatively and not materially) are to be reduced to the suppositions of concepts in mental propositions.

(9) Therefore, as a result, there is a *ninth conclusion*, that a written or spoken term, taken significatively and subordinated to a non-complex concept, stands for the things that it ultimately signifies, namely, for the things that are conceived by that concept, unless it is prevented by the two cases excepted. This is clear from the sixth conclusion. For all men are signified by these words "white man," because of the term "man," and all white things, because of the term "white." And nevertheless, these terms do not stand for all men nor for all white things. Also some spoken and written terms, such as these terms "risible ass," stand for nothing, if they serve as the subject in some proposition. This is clear from the eighth conclusion and from what has been said just now. Thus, this ninth conclusion should be in three parts, as is seen. And it can be added as a corollary that a determination added to a determinate expression neither adds to nor takes away from its signification, but it does either limit or take away its supposition. For example, if I say "A risible ass is running," it is not to be believed that these terms have no signification, and yet they have no supposition.

(10) The *tenth conclusion* will be that to this spoken term "chimera" does not correspond only a simple concept, for then it would stand for the thing or things conceived by that concept, which is false, since nothing is really a chimera.

(11) Then there follows an *eleventh conclusion,* that to this spoken term "chimera" corresponds a complex concept which it primarily signifies and according to which it is imposed to signify. Because, as has been said, a spoken term must correspond to a concept which it signifies in the mind or according to which it is imposed to signify. Therefore, if it does not correspond to a simple concept, it must correspond to a complex concept that stands for nothing. But now it is to be seen how this is true. It should be known that on every non-complex concept there can be imposed a non-complex expression, and on every complex concept a complex expression. But also, because words are imposed to signify by convention, so no matter how complex the concept, we can impose correspondingly a simple word signifying immediately that complex concept, and consequently, all that is conceived by that concept. For example, a certain poet clearly conceives, through a great complex concept, the history of Troy—how Paris abducts Helen and because of this the king of the Greeks invades Troy, etc. And then that poet in accordance with that concept, in a distinct and complex manner, writes a great book signifying that which that extremely complex concept conceived. Finally, he imposed the complex term "Iliad" to signify exactly howsoever that great book signified.[28] Thus, to this name "Iliad" corresponds an extremely complex concept.

However, to turn more specifically to our subject, the expression "place not filled with a body" corresponds to a complex concept, by which we understand place, body, and fullness. And yet this name "vacuum" is imposed to signify all that which this expression "place not filled with a body" together signifies. Hence, this expression "place not filled with a body" is said to be a nominal description of a vacuum, which does not indicate what thing a vacuum is, but what things and how this name "vacuum" signifies. For this reason, this sentence is not true: "A vacuum is a place not filled with a body," unless this be taken in the sense of material supposition, according to which this name "vacuum" signifies the same things and according to the same concept as the expression "place not filled with a body." Thus, this

[28] That is, the term "Iliad" is grammatically simple, but logically complex.

name "vacuum" signifies many things, namely, all that are signified by the terms "place," and "body," and "filled," and there corresponds to it a complex concept that is a concept of many things. And yet neither that concept nor the name "vacuum" nor its nominal definition stands for anything, since the addition of "not filled with a body," or the concept corresponding to it, removes supposition from the term "place," or from the concept corresponding to it, since every place is filled with bodies. In the same way, "non-risible man" stands for nothing, since every man is risible.

Analogously, therefore, this term "chimera" corresponds to a complex concept of many things, and yet it stands for nothing, because the determination is not possibly determinable, as is clear from the nominal description which is posited for such a thing—that a chimera is an animal composed of members of which nothing can be composed. So the same complex concept corresponds in the mind to this vocal expression and to this term "chimera." Thus, this term "chimera" signifies all those things that these terms "animal," "member," and "composed" and also the concept of being signify, and yet it stands for nothing. So neither does the complex concept corresponding to it, because the limitation or addition of "of which nothing can be composed" removes supposition from the other expression "animal composed of members," since it is not compatible with it.

But some have doubts concerning this, because it would follow that the expression "man" would signify all animals, which is false. The consequence is clear, because the definition of "man" is "rational, mortal animal." Therefore, according to what was said before, the same concept corresponds to the term "man" and to the expression "rational, mortal animal" and also that term and that expression signify the same things. And yet the expression "rational animal" signifies, by the term "animal," all animals; and therefore, the term "man" signifies all animals.

It is answered that this is not a nominal definition expressing what or which things and how this term "man" signifies. But it is a definition expressing what the thing is that this term "man" stands for, since it is the same thing for which this expression "rational, mortal animal" stands. But it is not necessary that these terms precisely and adequately stand for the things that they signify. For only a spoken term, to which there corresponds not a non-complex concept, but a complex one, has properly a nominal definition expressing precisely the significates which that term signifies. Thus, the signification of such a spoken term is explained by the spoken terms corresponding to the simple concepts from which the corresponding complex concept of this term is composed. But when any spoken term corresponds to a simple concept, as the term "ass" to the specific concept of an ass (assuming that it is simple), then it is not possible for another spoken term precisely and adequately to signify that and those things which that term signifies, unless it is a pure synonym of it. Nor is it possible to give a spoken expression composed of terms of different concepts or significations, without other concepts corresponding to them that did not correspond to that term. But of such a simple term corresponding to a simple concept, one can give a causal definition or a definition expressing what are the causes or the properties of the thing or things for which that term stands; or a quidditative definition from genus and difference to which a complex concept corresponds, yet which adequately stands for the same things for which that non-complex concept, corresponding to the spoken term, stands. And more should be emphasized about this in the tract on definitions, divisions and demonstration, which I have published. [29] And I am happy to have this understood.

Other things will have to be said about suppositions and the cause of the truth of propositions, but first I want to respond to the sophisms that were stated long ago.

D. Solutions of Sophisms

(1) Concerning the first, I say that it is false. And I say that for the truth of a spoken proposition, it is not sufficient that there be a similar mental proposition corresponding to it, for this is common to every proposition, that howsoever it signifies concerning the concept, so it is in the mind. But what else is sufficient or required will be said later. [30]

(2) Concerning the second sophism, I answer that it is false and its contradictory is true, namely, the proposition "No horse is an ass." And when it is argued that that is not true, since it is not so in things

[29] *Summula de Dialectica*, Tract VIII.
[30] See Conclusions 8-14 of Chapter II.

signified—namely, in horses and asses—I concede that it is neither so nor otherwise. But they are not. And it is not required for the truth of a negative proposition that it is somehow in things ultimately signified, that is, outside the corresponding concepts. And what is required and suffices will be said later. [31]

(3) Concerning the third, I say that it is false, and I also say that this sentence "God is not" signifies nothing which is not or could not be. That is, it does not correspond to a concept in the mind, which in turn corresponds to what is not or could not be outside the mind. But neither does this suffice for the truth of a proposition, as will be said below.[32] And also, I concede that the sentence "God is not" does not signify God-not-being, for God-not-being neither is nor will be nor can be. Thus it is false that God-not-being is signified, since this proposition is affirmative and its subject stands for nothing. Concerning the other argument, I say that this proposition "Every God is" is not false, but rather most true. And when it is said that this proposition "God is" signifies more than this term "God," I agree that more is signified within the mind, for it signifies a mental proposition, and this term signifies only a simple concept. But it is a good question whether it signifies more outside the mind, namely, in the things conceived by the concepts corresponding to that term "God" and to that sentence "God is." And concerning this, it is to be noted that far different things are designated outside the mind by the propositions "God is" and "God is God." For this proposition "God is" also has within the mind a subject, predicate, and copula, namely, this: "God is being." And this signifies much more than "God is God," since it signifies also all that is signified by this term "being." But "God is God" signifies nothing outside the mind except God, since "is," being precisely the copula, signifies nothing outside the mind, beyond the signification of the categorematic terms. It signifies only that complex concept by which the intellect forms propositions from the terms "God" and "God."

But then there is a difficult doubt, since it has been said before that every concept is a concept of something. What then is conceived by the complex concept corresponding to this copula when it is said "God is God" or "A man is a stone"? I say that concerning this some-

[31] See Conclusion 11 of Chapter II.
[32] See Conclusion 8 of Chapter II.

thing has been said in the third chapter of the first tract of the *Summula de dialectica*, but I say further that since the intellect could not form that complex concept without the categorematic concepts that compose it, that concept conceives no one thing. But we conceive the same things with simple concepts in a complex manner which were conceived by those simple concepts without that composition, in a non-complex way. So there are not different things conceived by the concept corresponding to the sentences "God is God" and "God is not God" and "Every God is God" and "No God is God" and by the simple term "God." But that thing is conceived differently in the different cases, namely, in a complex or non-complex manner, affirmatively and negatively.

I return, therefore, to the solution of the sophism, and I say that although more is signified within the mind by the sentence "God is God" than by the name "God," still outside the mind nothing more is signified, but the same thing in different ways.

(4) Concerning the fourth sophism, I say that it is false and I agree that it does not signify a chimera nor anything other than a chimera. For nothing is other than a chimera, since a chimera is nothing, and nothing is other than non-being. But still it signifies many things that are not chimeras nor is any of them a chimera. Nor is it similar to these terms "man" and "whiteness," since these correspond to simple concepts and stand for some things. And briefly, all the arguments given seem to be resolved by these remarks.

(5) Concerning the fifth sophism, I say that it is false. Rather, all entities in the world are complex signifiables. Also every being, no matter how simple, is a complex signifiable. For example, God, who is simple to the highest degree, is signified in a complex manner by the sentence "God is God," as was said in the solution of the third sophism. I say also that before God created the first creature, there was nothing except God. Thus, no complex signifiable existed except God. But then when it is argued that man did not then run, I agree, and when one infers that it was, therefore, the case that man was not running, I answer that this is so in the sense that there was something which was not a running man, namely, God. But then it was neither so nor otherwise in things signified by the proposition "Man was not running." Nor is this required for the truth of a negative, as commonly could be said. Similarly, when you say that this is true: "Antichrist

will be," I agree. But when you conclude that it is the case that Antichrist will be, I deny this, except in the sense that something exists which will not be Antichrist. But Antichrist-to-be-going-to-be or Antichrist-will-be does not exist. Thus, whence this proposition is said to be true will be discussed later.[33] Concerning the other, I concede in the case posited that God can create B and that B can be created by God and that these propositions are true. But you conclude, therefore, that it is the case that B can be created. I deny this, since B-being-able-to-be-created is nothing, but it can indeed be, for B can be. But then you ask whether there is not God-creating-B. I say that this is so, and similarly, if God creates B, then God-creating-B is God. But you argue against this, since God-creating-B is contingent. I deny this. Rather, God-creating-B is necessary, taking the subject "God-creating-B" significatively. But if it is taken according to material supposition, then it is true that God-creating-B is contingent, since in this case that subject stands for the proposition "God creates B," which is contingent.[34] Concerning the other argument, I say that Socrates-loving-God is Socrates, if Socrates loves God. But if Socrates does not love God, then I say that Socrates-loving-God is nothing. And similarly, Socrates-hating-God is Socrates, if Socrates hates God. But if Socrates does not hate God, it is nothing. You argue then as follows: Socrates-loving-God is Socrates, and I agree, positing the case that Socrates loves God. But you say similarly that Socrates-hating-God is Socrates, and I deny this. For Socrates-hating-God is nothing when Socrates loves God. But I agree that Socrates-hating-God was Socrates, if perhaps Socrates previously hated God. Then when it is further said that Socrates-loving-God is good and praiseworthy, I agree, for he is a good man loving God. And when it is said that Socrates-hating-God is evil and damnable, I deny this, for Socrates-hating-God is nothing. But Socrates-hating-God was evil, since there was an evil man hating God. And this is not inconsistent. Since a good man was an evil man, so neither is it impossible that [someone]-loving-God was [someone]-hating-God.

(6) Concerning the sixth *sophism*, I say that it is a contingent proposition and such a proposition is often false, since men often lie. And when it is said that every man pronouncing a proposition has a

[33] See Conclusion 10 of Chapter II.
[34] See above p. 16.

similar one in the mind, I say that this is true. Nor is it the case that because of this man does not lie or is excused for a lie. But a man lies because of this, that he states a verbal proposition assertively and does not assent to the corresponding mental proposition, but dissents. And this is possible. Or in other words, it is to be said, and amounts to the same thing, that a man lies because he verbally asserts a proposition that he believes to be false.

These remarks that have been made about the sophisms concerning the significations of terms and propositions should be placed as the first chapter of this work.

CHAPTER II

TRUTH-CONDITIONS FOR CATEGORICAL PROPOSITIONS

The second chapter will be about the cause of the truth and falsehood of simply categorical propositions. Already in the preceding sophisms, difficulties concerning this have been touched upon. But they will be repeated by stating some brief sophisms.

A. Sophisms

(1) *Aristotle's horse does not exist.*

I posit the case that Aristotle did indeed have a horse, and indeed it was walking. But it is dead, or rather, it was destroyed by divine power. Therefore, the sophism is manifest by the case.

But the opposite is also proved, namely, that this proposition "Aristotle's horse does not exist" is false. For a proposition is true when howsoever it signifies, so it is in things signified, and a proposition is false when it is not the case that howsoever it signifies, so it is. [1] This condition is commonly agreed to, and it is confirmed by ordinary speech, since if it appears to us that somebody has truly spoken, we say that it is as he said. But if it appears to us that he speaks falsely, then we say that it is not as he asserts. And therefore Aristotle says in the fifth and sixth books of the *Metaphysics* that in a signification of being and non-being, being signifies what is true and non-being signifies what is false. [2] Nor does it appear that another cause of the

[1] See note 7 Chapter I. Some philosophers apparently interpreted the definition as asserting that a proposition is true only if what it signifies exists at the time the proposition is written or uttered. Buridan will want to maintain that the definition is not concerned with existence in any way.

[2] Aristotle, *Metaphysics* v. 7. 1017a 31–32, and *Metaphysics* vi. 2. 1026a 33–35.

truth and falsehood of propositions could be assigned. Thus, supposing this to be true or proved, it appears that the proposition "Aristotle's horse does not exist" is false, since in things signified, it is not as the proposition signifies. For the thing signified, namely, Aristotle's horse, is nothing, and nothing is neither so nor otherwise.

(2) *Aristotle's horse walked.*

This is proved by the case posited at the beginning of the preceding sophism.

But it is also disproved in the same way as the preceding one, since it is not in the thing signified as is signified by the proposition. The same argument could be used concerning the propositions "Aristotle's horse is dead" and "No horse is an ass," positing that there is no horse or ass, but that all were destroyed. For concerning any such propositions, it is true that in things signified, it is not as those propositions signify.

(3) *A chimera is a chimera.*

This is proved by Boethius' saying that no predication is more true than that in which the same thing is predicated of itself.[3] Likewise, if it were not true, it would be because the term "chimera" stands for nothing. But that does not prevent the truth of the proposition "Aristotle's horse walked," and yet its subject stands for nothing. I prove this because it does not stand for anything other than Aristotle's horse and that is nothing, according to the case previously posited. Therefore, it stands for nothing.

The opposite position is held because of the fact that it is an affirmative proposition whose subject and predicate stand for nothing And such affirmative propositions are false.

(4) *A vacuum is a place not filled with a body.*

This is proved since it predicates a definiens of its definiendum or a description of that which it describes, and such a proposition is true, because Aristotle states that it is. Therefore, etc.

[3] Boethius, *In librum Aristotelis de interpretatione Commentaria majora*, in *Patrologiae cursus completus, seu bibliotheca universalis omnium SS, patrum, doctorum scriptorumque ecclesiasticorum ab aevo apostolico ad tempora Innocenti III* (*anno* 1216). *Series Latina*, ed. J. Migne (221 vols; Paris, 1844–1880), vol. 64, col. 577.

The opposite is argued, since it follows that if a vacuum is an empty space, then a vacuum is. But the consequent is supposed to be false, according to Aristotle,[4] and, I think, according to the truth. Therefore, the antecedent is also false. Also, the proposition is an affirmative one whose subject stands for nothing; therefore, etc.

(5) *A man is an ass.*

This is proved, since absolutely howsoever the case is signified to be by the proposition, so it is. Therefore, it is true. The antecedent is proved, for if it signifies a mental proposition, then there is in the mind a similar and corresponding proposition. And if it signifies something outside the mind, that is nothing except a man or an ass, and they exist; thus, still, so it is. If you say that it signifies not only a man or an ass, but that it signifies man-being-ass, I prove this to be false, since man-being-ass is nothing, nor was it nor can it be anything. And so in this proposition "Man-being-ass is signified by the proposition," the subject stands for nothing, namely, man-being-ass. Therefore, the proposition is false, since it is an affirmative proposition whose subject stands for nothing. And if you say that the proposition is affirmative signifying some situation,[5] I ask whether that situation exists or does not exist. If you say that it does not exist, then that which you say, namely, that some situation is signified by the proposition, is false. For just as I said, the proposition is affirmative and its subject stands for nothing. If you say that it does exist, then we have our purpose, since howsoever it signifies the case to be, so it is.

The opposite [is agreed to] by all.

(6) *I am speaking falsely.*

I posit the case that I utter this proposition "I am speaking falsely" and no other.

The sophism is proved, since in so speaking, I speak either falsely or truly. If I speak truly, then it is true that I speak falsely. Thus, the sophism is true. But if I speak falsely, then the case is as I say. Therefore, I speak truly, and so the sophism is again true. Again, if the sophism is false, then the subject and predicate, namely, "I" and "speaking falsely," stand for the same, because they stand for me,

[4] Aristotle, *Physics* iv. 7. 214a 16–19.
[5] *aliqualiter esse.*

since I am speaking falsely. And such an affirmative proposition is true, so the sophism is true.

The opposite is argued, since if the sophism were true, it would also follow that it was false, and so it would be both true and false, which is impossible. This consequence is proved, since if the proposition is true, then it is true that I speak falsely, and so what I say is false. And yet it is posited that I say nothing other than that sophism. Therefore, it is false.

It is noted that this sophism has been called one of the insolubles, and it cannot be solved until after a consideration of the reasons for which a proposition is said to be true or false. Therefore, it seems to me that a tract on the insolubles ought to follow this present chapter, or shortly after. Hence, I plan to treat of these immediately after I have spoken of supposition and appellations and the standard by which a proposition is said to be true or false. [6]

B. Conclusions

Now, therefore, toward the solution of the above and similar sophisms, I shall state some conclusions concerning the reasons for which propositions are said to be true or false. And in order to speak intelligibly, I suppose, according to previous statements, [7] that expressions have two significations—one within the mind, since in the mind they signify concepts corresponding to them, or something similar, which they were imposed to signify. And they have another signification, since by mediation of these concepts, they signify things conceived by the concepts. And because many times those things conceived are outside the mind, such as stones and asses, so customarily I shall call the first "signification within the mind" and the second "signification outside the mind."

(1) I state then the *first conclusion:* it is not necessary that a spoken proposition be true if howsoever it signifies within the mind, so it is within the mind. For it would follow that every spoken proposition was true, since every spoken proposition, whether true or false, corresponds to a similar one in the mind.

(2) *Second conclusion:* it is not required for the truth of a spoken

[6] Chapter VIII.

[7] See Conclusions 2 and 3 of Chapter I.

proposition that howsoever it signifies outside the mind, so it is according to things signified outside the mind. Or the conclusion can be stated in the following way: some proposition is true, and yet it is not the case that howsoever it signifies outside the mind, so it is in the things which are signified outside the mind. This conclusion can be proved: I posit that Antichrist does not yet exist, but will exist and will walk. Then this proposition "Antichrist will walk" is true; and Antichrist and his walking are signified outside the mind by this proposition. Yet they are nothing. And in that which is nothing, it is neither so nor otherwise. Therefore, in things signified by that proposition outside the mind, it is not as it is signified to be by the proposition. So similarly, it could be argued concerning the proposition "Aristotle disputed," having posited that Aristotle is destroyed; and likewise, concerning the proposition "Antichrist can walk." And so also, the same could be argued concerning this negative proposition "A horse is not an ass," positing that God should destroy all horses and all asses, from which it would follow again that the things signified did not exist and that it was neither so nor otherwise in them.

(3) The *third conclusion* is that this proposition "Man is an ass" does not signify man-being-ass. Nor is man-being-and-ass-being signified by this proposition "Man is an ass." For man-being-ass neither is nor will be nor can be. For just as if there is man-running, then there is a running man, and if there is man-being-white, then there is a white man, so if there is man-being-ass, then there is an ass man existing. And this is impossible. Therefore, the proposition "Man-being-ass is signified" is affirmative, and yet its subject stands for nothing. From this it follows that man-being-ass can be nothing else; therefore, the proposition is false. And from this it follows that this is true: "Man-being-ass is not signified by such a proposition." In the same way, it is proved than man-being-ass cannot be imagined or understood or opined, and so of others. But you might ask whether "Man-being-ass" is not false. I answer that it is neither true nor false, properly speaking, that is, taking the total signification and not according to material supposition. But nevertheless, it is to be conceded that such propositions of the infinitive mode [8] are often taken materially and

[8] I have translated these phrases as gerundive, even though this leaves them awkward at times, because it is less inelegant than an infinitive translation. It is important that the translation be uniform, since they are technical expressions.

stand for some proposition. For example, "man running" stands for a proposition such as "Man runs" and "man being ass" stands for a proposition such as "Man is an ass." In this case, it is to be agreed that "man being ass" is false, which is to say that a proposition such as "Man is an ass" is false. So it is to be granted that man-being-ass is nothing, but ["man being ass"] is a false proposition.

In this regard, it is to be noted that some, in order to avoid the difficulty, wanted to say that such sentences of the infinitive mode stand only for propositions—for example, "man running" for a proposition such as "Man runs," and "Man being ass" for a proposition such as "Man is an ass," and so of others. But this is not true, since according to Aristotle in the *Categories*, cutting is acting and being cut is being acted upon. [9] So also a man cutting is a man acting, and wood being cut is wood being acted upon. And a man being white is a man being colored. Therefore, such propositions are to be conceded, and yet all these would be false if they should stand for propositions. For this proposition "Man cuts or man is white" is not this proposition "Man acts or man is colored." Again, all agree that loving God is indeed good and hating God indeed evil, and this would not be true referring to propositions. For I can without malice form in my mind a proposition such as "A man hates God."

But it is still doubtful whether man-being and also Aristotle-being are signified by the proposition "A man is an ass," or by this term "man." And it is also doubtful concerning man-having-been or Aristotle-having-been. And concerning these doubts, some conclusions are stated.

(4) One of these is the *fourth conclusion* of this chapter, namely, that man-being is signified by this term "man," since every man is signified by this term "man." But every man is man-being, as is seen in the fourth book of the *Metaphysics*.[10] And also this is stated elsewhere in the first book of the *Physics*, that man-generating is a generating man, and man-being-white is a white man. [11] Thus, it follows by DARAPTI in the third figure that man-being is signified by this term "man"; and ass-being is signified by this term "ass," and sim-

[9] *Cf.*, Aristotle, *Categories* 9. 11b 1–4, where action and passion are discussed. A better reference would have been to *Metaphysics* v. 15. 1020b 28–30.

[10] Aristotle, *Metaphysics* iv. 1. 1003b 26–29.

[11] Aristotle, *Physics* i. 7. 190a 10–12.

ilarly, man-being-animal or ass-being-animal. Indeed, also, if a man runs, then man-running is signified by this term "man," since every man is signified by this term "man," and yet some man is man-running. Therefore, it follows in the third figure by DATISI.

(5) The *fifth conclusion:* man-being is signified by this proposition "A man is an ass" since all that is signified by the terms or by some term of a proposition is signified by that proposition. Indeed the proposition is not itself imposed as a whole alongside of the signification of its [categorematic] terms, which we understand it composes affirmatively or negatively as one will. Thus, from the signification of the terms the proposition has, its signifies outside the mind that which it signifies. Therefore, if man-being is signified by this term "man" and ass-being is signified by this term "ass," it follows that this is also signified by this proposition "A man is an ass."

(6) A *sixth conclusion* must be posited, that man-having-been is signified by this term "man," and consequently, by this proposition "A man is an ass." For indifferently, every man—present, past, and future—is signified by this term "man," because its signification is independent of time. Therefore, Aristotle is signified by this term "man"; for terms such as "to signify," "to understand," "to know," etc., ampliate the terms to stand for past and future, as will be said later.[12] Moreover, just as this predicate "dead" ampliates supposition to the past, so for the same reason does this predicate "having been." Therefore, just as it is conceded that Aristotle is a dead man, so Aristotle-having-been-a-man is to be conceded. Then the argument runs as follows: Aristotle is signified by this term "man," and Aristotle is something which was a man; therefore, man-having-been is signified by this term "man."

(7) *Seventh conclusion:* Aristotle-being is signified by this term "man," and consequently, by this proposition "A man is an ass," or by "A man is an animal." For it is to be noted that a participle in present tense or future tense is carried by a verb of past tense to stand for the past. For example, it is true that Aristotle was running and that a running thing was Aristotle, and it is true that Aristotle was to be generated and that a thing to be generated was Aristotle. And similarly, a sentence of the infinitive mode[13] is carried to supposition

[12] *Cf.*, the seventh sophism of Chapter V.
[13] Again translated as gerundive.

for the past; for example, "Aristotle saw Alexander riding." Thus, with this verb "to signify" or "to be signified," one ampliates suppositions to past or future. Similarly, if Aristotle is signified by this term "man," and Aristotle was Aristotle-being, it follows that Aristotle-being is signified by this term "man."

(8) From this, then, I infer the *eighth conclusion*, namely, that a true affirmative proposition of inherence and of the present tense is not true because whatever or howsoever the case is signified to be by it, so it is. For this proposition "A man is an animal" is true, by which, however, Aristotle-being is signified, which is not so in fact. Also, whatever or howsoever the case is signified to be by these two propositions "A man is a man" and "An ass is an ass," that is also signified to be by this proposition "A man is an ass," as is evident from what has been said. And yet the latter is false, while the first two were true. And so it seems to me that in assigning the cause of truth and falsehood, it is not sufficient to go to the significations of terms, but one must also go to suppositions.

(9) And concerning suppositions, I state the *ninth conclusion*, namely, that it does not follow that if the terms of an affirmative proposition stand for the same thing, then the proposition is true. Take first the case of universal propositions. For if only one man is running, then the subject and predicate of this proposition "Every man is running" stand for the same, and yet the proposition is false. But even if the predicate should stand for all that for which the subject stands, there would still remain the instances of the so-called insolubles. For example, if Socrates states only the proposition "Socrates is speaking falsely," this proposition would be false, as will be shown later;[14] and yet the subject and predicate—"Socrates" and "speaking falsely"—would stand for the same thing, namely, for Socrates. And so it is often with other insolubles, but concerning these, I shall speak more especially later.

(10) The *tenth conclusion* is that for the truth of an affirmative categorical proposition it is required that the terms, namely, the subject and predicate, stand for the same thing or things. Hence, it is also sufficient for its falsity that they do not stand for the same thing or things. And this is not a conclusion but an indemonstrable principle—or if it is a conclusion, it is almost an indemonstrable principle.

[14] See the eleventh sophism of Chapter VIII.

Yet in the *Posterior Analytics*, it appears that sometimes indemonstrable principles are well in need of some clarification or examples or remarks or something of this sort.[15] Thus I will so clarify the statement of the tenth conclusion. It is certain that in the proposition "A is B," this term "A" stands for nothing or its stands for A, and so with "B." And similarly if I say "Aristotle argued" or "Antichrist will walk," this term "Aristotle" stands for nothing or it stands for Aristotle, and so with "Antichrist" and others. Moreover, it is manifest that in saying that A is B (assuming that the terms are not ampliated to past or future), to say that A is B is the same as to say that A is the same as B, just as to say that it is not B is the same as to say that A is not the same as B. And yet if this is true—that A is the same as B—then it is necessary that these terms "A" and "B" stand for the same thing, because "A" stands for A and "B" for B, and because A is posited to be the same as B. The case is similar with propositions of past or future. Thus, it is the same to say that Aristotle was disputing as to say that Aristotle was that which was disputing. Therefore, in that proposition, the terms "Aristotle" and "disputing" stand for the same thing, since "Aristotle" stands for Aristotle and "disputing" for a disputant. It is not stated that Aristotle and disputing are now the same, but that they were the same. And the case is similar with propositions of the future and the possible.

(11) The *eleventh conclusion* is that for the truth of a negative categorical, it suffices that the subject and predicate do not stand for the same thing or things—although some such proposition may be true in which the subject and predicate do stand for the same thing or things, as in "An animal is not a man." And for the falsity of a negative, it is required that the subject and predicate stand for the same—although it does not follow that if the subject and predicate stand for the same thing, then the negative is false. This conclusion is clear from the preceding, since an affirmative and a negative are always contradictory, and it is necessary for one to be true and the other to be false (if they are formulated together), and never can they be true at the same time or false at the same time. And this is so only because how many and whatever are the causes of the truth of one, so many and the same are the causes of the falsity of the other, and conversely. Thus, whatever is required for the truth of an affirmative,

[15] Aristotle *Posterior Analytics* i. 3. *passim*. *Cf*., also ii. 19.

that is required for the falsity of the contradictory negative. And also whatever suffices for the falsity of an affirmative, that suffices for the truth of the contradictory negative.

(12) The *twelfth conclusion* is that for the truth of an indefinite or particular categorical affirmative, it is required and it suffices that the subject and predicate stand for the same thing, unless because of the reflection of that proposition on itself, it follows from it, together with the circumstances of its assertion, that it is false. I say that a proposition reflects on itself if it asserts itself to be false or asserts something from which it follows that it is false, either simply or with accompanying circumstances—or also if it denies its own truth or denies something from which it follows that it is not true, as in the example above. [16] This condition is involved in the so-called insolubles, as will be seen later. [17]

This conclusion is clear, first, because its truth is required for that which was stated in the tenth conclusion. But in order to make it sufficiently clear, it is proved by induction, since no instance of such a proposition is found, because such a proposition is always true. And this is also clear from the terms. For "A being B" signifies the same as "A being the same as B," and "A having been B" signifies the same as "A having been the same as B," and "A being able to be B" signifies the same as "A being able to be the same as B."

But it may well be asked why there is an exception to this rule in the case of the so-called insolubles. Concerning this, it is briefly answered for now that this is because such a proposition, either simply or with accompanying circumstances, implies a contradiction. It affirmatively asserts itself to be false, from which it follows that it is affirmative and that the term standing for it and this term "false" stand for the same thing—since this is required for the truth of an affirmative proposition. And again, from the fact that it asserts itself to be false, it follows that its terms do not stand for anything or do not stand for the same thing. Thus, it is false, because it implies a contradiction. So from the proposition, it not only follows that it is false, but also that it is true (assuming that it exists), [18] and then it implies this copulative: "It is false and it is true." And this copulative

[16] *Cf.*, the ninth conclusion.
[17] Chapter VIII.
[18] Concerning the existence of propositions, see above pp. 35 and 51.

is false because of the falsity of the second categorical, which is affirmative but whose terms do not stand for the same thing. This will be discussed in greater detail later.[19]

(13) The *thirteenth conclusion* is that for the truth of an affirmative universal, it is required and sufficient that whatever thing or things the subject stands for, the predicate also stands for, unless the proposition reflects on itself, as was discussed in the previous conclusion. This is proved by induction, and also in a way analogous to the preceding conclusion.

From these conclusions, it is seen whence any true proposition is said to be true and any false proposition false, except in the case of the so-called insolubles, concerning which there will be a special discussion later. Thus, it seems that the conditions are not the same for all propositions, but are different for universal and particular affirmatives, and still otherwise for negatives.

(14) By way of summary, a *fourteenth conclusion* is stated. It is that every true particular affirmative is true because the subject and predicate stand for the same thing or things. And every universal affirmative is true if whatever thing or things the subject stands for, the predicate stands for that thing or those things. And every particular affirmative is false if the subject and predicate do not stand for the same thing or any of the same things. And a universal affirmative is false if the predicate does not stand for every thing or all things for which the subject stands. And every particular negative is true if the universal affirmative which is its contradictory is false, and it has been said whence this is. And this is the fourteenth conclusion which contains eight partial conclusions.[20] It results from previously established propositions, on account of the principle that whatever is the cause of the truth of one contradictory or is required for its truth, that is the cause of the falsity of the other or is required for its falsity.

Finally, it is to be noted that since we can employ names conventionally, if many people commonly use this mode of speaking, we can say concerning all true propositions "it is so," and concerning false propositions "it is not so." I do not intend to eliminate this way of speaking, for in speaking briefly, I shall often use it, not meaning by

[19] *Cf.*, the seventh sophism of Chapter VIII.

[20] He omits the conditions for the falsity of a particular negative, as well as those for the truth and falsity of a universal negative.

it what it signifies according to any primary imposition. But I shall regard the causes of truth and falsity previously assigned as different for different propositions, as has been said.

C. Solutions of Sophisms

Now I shall respond to the sophisms in proper form.

(1) Concerning the first, I agree that Aristotle's horse does not exist. And when it is argued that it is false since that which the proposition signifies is not, I agree. But I say that this is not necessary, especially in negatives. But it is true because the subject stands for nothing, so the subject and predicate do not stand for the same thing, which suffices for the truth of a negative.

But it is objected that I am contradicting Aristotle in the fifth book of the *Metaphysics*, where he says that "it is so" and "is" signifies that it is true, but "it is not" that it is not true, but simply false, both in affirmatives and in negatives.[21] These are the words of Aristotle, and he clearly seems to say that every true proposition, whether affirmative or negative, is said to be true because so it is in things. Whence also, it is said in the *Categories* that from the fact that a thing is or is not, a proposition is said to be true or false.[22]

I answer that Aristotle notes here that this is not the principal signification of "being," according to which being is said of the ten categories. According to this principal signification, not only true propositions, but also false ones are being or beings. But because names are imposed to signify by convention, there has been another imposition, according to which this name "being" or "to be" could signify the same as this name "true." And so also concerning "non-being" and "non-true." And this caused men to err, because if it is said that a proposition is true, we say that it is as he says. And here men understand badly and believe that it is said that in things signified, it is as the proposition signifies. But they do not understand. Rather, this phrase "it is so" ought to be understood to say only that the proposition is true. Aristotle expresses this better in the sixth book of the *Metaphysics*, where he talks about being as true and non-being as false—and so they are according to composition and division, and

[21] Aristotle, *Metaphysics* v. 7. 1017a 31–34.
[22] Aristotle, *Categories* 10. 13b 26–35.

speaking altogether in terms of participation in contradiction.[23] And later he says that this composition or division is in the mind and not in things. [24] Thus, it is absurd to believe that by "so it is" ought to be understood "so it is in things."

(2) Concerning the second sophism, it is answered that these are to be conceded: "Aristotle's horse walked" and "Aristotle's horse is dead," not because so it is in things signified, but because the subject and predicate stand for the same thing, not asserting that it is, but that it was. For the same thing is dead and was walking and was Aristotle's horse. And it is not required that it is the same, but that it was the same, because this verb "was" and this participle "dead" are of past tense. Similarly I say that this is true: "A horse is not an ass," although there may be no horse or ass, not because it is so outside the mind, but because the subject and predicate stand for nothing, and so they do not stand for the same thing.

(3) Concerning the third sophism, I say that this proposition "A chimera is a chimera" is false. Nor is the authority of Boethius to be understood to apply except where the terms stand for the same thing. But when it is said that this is true: "Aristotle's horse walked," that is conceded. And when it is said that the subject "Aristotle's horse" stands for nothing, that is denied. But I agree that it does not stand for anything which is, but for something which was. Yet you argue that it does not stand for anything other than Aristotle's horse, and that is nothing; hence, it stands for nothing. I grant the premisses but deny the conclusion. For the verb "stands" ampliates the supposition of the subject to past and future; and in the minor premiss there was no such ampliation, but restriction to the present—indeed, a removal of supposition. Hence, in this proposition "Aristotle's horse is," or "Aristotle's horse is not," the subject stands for nothing. Thus, you argue as if it were argued that A is nothing, so A was nothing. But concerning this sort of supposition, or the restriction of supposition, more will be said later. [25]

(4) Concerning the fourth sophism, it is said that this is false: "A vacuum is a place not filled with a body," because the terms stand for nothing. And neither does a definition, speaking essentially, affirm

[23] Aristotle, *Metaphysics* vi. 4. 1027b 17–27.
[24] Aristotle, *Metaphysics* vi. 4. 1027b 24–27.
[25] Chapter V.

truly concerning what is defined, unless what is defined stands for something. But if the proposition is taken materially, it is necessary to explain it as follows: a vacuum is a place not filled with a body—that is, this name "vacuum" signifies precisely that thing or those things which are signified by the expression "place not filled with a body," so that the same concept in the mind must correspond to that name and to that expression, according to the signification.

(5) Concerning the fifth sophism, I say that this is false: "A man is an ass," because the terms do not stand for the same. Nor does it follow that it is true if howsoever it is signified to be by the proposition, so it is—as has been said in the preceding.

(6) Concerning the sixth sophism, it is said that it pertains to the insolubles. Thus I reserve its solution to the chapter on insolubles, which ought to be treated immediately, except that because of their difficulty, I want to treat first of suppositions.

So this is the end of the second chapter of this book.

CHAPTER III
ON SUPPOSITION

The third chapter will be about suppositions,[1] for there have often been deceptions in arguments due to variations in supposition. And it will now be seen in what way this is so.

A. Sophisms

(1) *God being unjust*[2] *is to be denied by all the faithful.*

This is proved, since that is to be denied which it is heretical to affirm. But to affirm God to be unjust is heretical; therefore, etc. Likewise, every false statement is to be denied. But "God being unjust" is a false statement; therefore, it is to be denied.

In the same way, it would be argued concerning this sophism: "God not being is to be denied." It is proved because that is to be denied whose opposite is to be affirmed. But the opposite of this, namely, "God being," is to be asserted; therefore, this is to be denied.

The opposite is argued, because that which is nothing is neither to be asserted nor to be denied. But God-being-unjust or God-not-being is nothing; therefore, etc. Again, the proposition "God-being-unjust is to be denied" is affirmative, and its subject stands for nothing because nothing is God-being-unjust. Therefore, it is false.

(2) *You are an ass.*

It is proved, because you being an ass is denied by you, so you-being-an-ass is.[3] The conclusion is clear, since the argument moves from a verb occurring as a third member[4] to the same verb occurring

[1] On the doctrine of supposition see above pp. 29–42.
[2] *Deum esse iniustum.*
[3] There is a shift from a linguistic expression to a non-linguistic entity.
[4] *Tertio adiacente.*

as a second member.[5] And since that which is nothing ought to be neither affirmed nor denied, and since you-being-an-ass is nothing unless you are an ass, therefore, you are an ass. Likewise, you are something. Therefore, in saying that you are an ass, one says that something is an ass. And in saying that something is an ass, one speaks the truth. Hence, in saying that you are an ass, one speaks the truth. And consequently, you are an ass. Again, whoever says that you are an animal speaks truly; and whoever says you are an ass says you are an animal, since every ass is an animal; therefore whoever says that you are an ass speaks truly. And again, if I say that you are an ass, it is either as I say or it is other than I say. If it is as I say, then I have my purpose. If it is other than I say, and I speak falsely, and it is the true that is other than the false, then I speak the truth. So you are an ass.

The opposite is conceded by all.

(3) *Man is a species.*

This is proved by the authority of Porphyry, who often says that man is a species and animal is a genus.[6] And it is proved by the definition of a species, since "man" is predicated of many things, namely, of Socrates and Plato, who differ numerically. Thus, man is a species.

The opposite is argued, since its contradictory is true, namely, "No man is a species." This is clear by induction. For Socrates is not a species, Plato is not a species, and so of others; therefore, no man is a species. But some answer that "No man is a species" is not the contradictory of "Man is a species," but rather that "Man is not a species" is its contradictory. But this is wrong, since particular and indefinite propositions are judged alike. And the proposition "No man is a species" contradicts the particular proposition "Some man is a species," so it also contradicts the indefinite proposition "Man is a species."

(4) *A genus is in more than a most general genus.*[7]

This is proved, since that which is predicated of another truly, universally, and not convertibly is in more or is more common. For example, animal is in more than man, or is more common, for it is true to say that every man is an animal and the converse is not true, namely,

[5] *secundo adiacente.* On the distinction, see above p. 34, n. 64.
[6] Porphyry, *Isagoge* 3. 5–14.
[7] *genus generalissimum.*

that every animal is a man. But a genus is predicated universally of a most general genus, and the converse is not true. For instance, every most general genus is a genus, but not every genus is a most general genus. Therefore, a genus is more common or is in more than a most general genus.

The opposite is argued, since every genus is either a most general genus or a subaltern genus, and neither of those is in more or is more common than a most general genus. Thus, no genus is in more than a most general genus.

(5) *A name is trisyllabic.*[8]

It is proved. From the preceding, it could be said that there is an error due to a change from material to personal supposition, or conversely. I assume that one should not make this change, but the entire sentence should proceed according to material supposition. And from this it appears at once that the sophism is false, for "name"—or this term "name"—is not trisyllabic.

But it is argued that the sophism is true, since *asinus* [*i.e.*, "ass"] is trisyllabic, and *asinus* is a name; therefore, etc. And it is manifest that the propositions are true, taking the subject materially, and it is a good expository syllogism. For many say that such propositions, in which the subject is taken materially, are singular, and if they are not singular, yet they are made singular by prefixing a demonstrative pronoun and saying "This term *asinus* is trisyllabic, and it is a name; therefore, etc."

B. Remarks

These sophisms are simple, but in discussing their solutions, a few remarks must be made about the suppositions of terms, about which more has been said in the *Summula de dialectica.*[9]

(1) [*First remark*]: I say, therefore, that I do not mean to use "supposition" as it is spoken of by the grammarian, namely, where a nominative noun is said to be a subject with respect to a verb, because it gives to it the same person. So this term "chimera" stands for this verb "runs" in this proposition "A chimera runs." But in logic suppo-

[8] *Nomen est trisyllabum.*
[9] Tract IV.

sition is properly attributed to the subject and the predicate of a proposition; and at times, less properly, some terms which are parts of the subject and predicate are agreed to have supposition. But supposition as it is here used is the taking of a term in a proposition for some thing or things, in such a way that if that thing or those things are indicated by the pronoun "this" or "these," or the equivalent, then that term is truly affirmed of this pronoun, by the mediation of the copula of the proposition. For example, in the proposition "A horse is running," the term "horse" stands for every horse which exists, since whatever one should be indicated, it would be true to say "This is a horse." And in this proposition "A horse was running," "horse" stands for every horse which is or was, since of every such, if it should be indicated, it would be true to say "This is or was a horse." And something similar would be said, if a copula of future tense should be used. I say, disjunctively, "is or was," because although a verb of past or future tense ampliates supposition to the past or to the future, it does not remove supposition for the present. Something analogous is to be said concerning "to be able." For if it is said "A horse can walk," this term "horse" stands for every horse which is or can be, since, pointing to one of these, it would be true to say "This is or can be a horse." And again, if a term does not stand for one only, but for many things simultaneously—as when it is said "The populace is large"—this term stands for those of which, if indicated simultaneously, it would be true to say "These are the people." And if there should not be any such, then this term would stand for nothing, just as this term "chimera" stands for nothing in logic, since nothing is or was or can be a chimera. And similarly, there are not some things which are or were or can be chimeras. But in what way God or Aristotle or Antichrist can be referred to has been sufficiently discussed in the *Summula de dialectica.* [10]

(2) [*Second remark*]: It is to be noted that a term is said to have supposition in two senses, namely, personally or materially. And I am not concerned with whether this division has applied also to verbs, properly speaking; for names signify conventionally. Hence, I am only concerned to show what should be understood there by these terms "personally" and "materially." I say, therefore (as has been said in greater detail in the *Summula*), that any term or word which can be placed in a proposition stands materially if, in that proposition, it is

[10] *Ibid.*

not taken for its ultimate significates or its ultimate significate, but for itself or for something like itself. For example, "to love" is a verb and a word such as "to love" is a verb. Similarly, "man" is a species and a term such as "man" is a species. Again, "Man runs" is a sentence, and such an expression, or even such a concept as "Man runs" is a sentence. And again, "ba" is a non-significative expression. Similarly, "if" is a conjunction, "I" is a pronoun, etc.

This kind of supposition is also often possessed by expressions of the infinitive mood,[11] such as " 'man reading' is true." And such a sentence does not stand for itself, nor for anything similar, but for a similar proposition having a subject, predicate, and copula, but with the subject and predicate changing to nominative from accusative and with the verb changing from infinitive to indicative mood.[12] For example, " 'Socrates running' is true," " 'Socrates running' is an affirmative proposition," and a proposition such as "Socrates is running" is true and affirmative. Sometimes, however, such a sentence stands personally and is taken significatively, whether it should so stand or not, as when I say "Man being white is man being colored," "Cutting is acting," "Being cut is being acted upon." And then they signify the same for me, as has been said elsewhere. This sentence "Cutting is acting" signifies the same as "[Someone] cutting is [someone] acting." And this sentence "Man being white" signifies the same as "Man being colored." And generally, just as it is true to say that generating is [someone] generating, so being-generated is that which is generated, being-white is a white thing, and so of others. So also "chimera" and "being-chimera" signify the same thing or things, but since the term stands for nothing, it is not true to say "Chimera being chimera," just as it is not true to say "A chimera is a chimera."

C. Solutions of Sophisms

Now, therefore, the sophisms are solved by the fact that it is not a valid process or argumentation if the supposition changes from material to personal or significative.

(1) Hence, concerning the first sophism, I make the distinction that this sentence "God being unjust," in the said syllogism, can be

[11] Again translated gerundively.

[12] For example, *Hominem esse asinum* becomes *Homo est asinus*.

taken materially, and then it stands for a proposition such as "God is unjust." And in this case, it is agreed that "God being unjust" is a false and impossible proposition, to be denied and heretical (*i.e.*, rendering a man heretical who asserts it tenaciously). In another sense, it is taken significatively, and then in this second case, this expression "God-being-unjust," although it has supposition in grammar, nevertheless, as intended by the logician, it does not have supposition, since nothing is God-being-unjust, since an unjust God is nothing. Thus, it is false that "God being unjust" is to be denied, as has been well argued.

(2) Response to the second sophism. Concerning the second, I deny that you are an ass. And when it is said that you being an ass is to be denied by you, I agree, if this subject "you-being-an-ass" stands materially, since it is a false proposition. But if it is taken significatively, then you-being-an-ass is nothing, so it is neither to be denied nor to be confirmed.

Concerning the other objection. I say again that no one can say you-being-an-ass, if this expression "you being an ass" is taken significatively. But if it is taken materially, then someone can indeed say "you being an ass," and he says this proposition "You are an ass," which is false. But then when it is said that whoever says you to be an ass says you to be something, I deny this. For the sense of this is that whoever, speaking materially, says "you to be an ass" says "you to be something," and this is false. And if someone says both of these, he speaks the truth insofar as he says the second and not insofar as he says the first.

In the same way, concerning the third objection, I say that no one can say you-being-an-animal, speaking significatively, since you-being-an-animal is you, and no one can say you or me or a horse or a cow. For we cannot say anything except expressions.[13] But if one speaks materially, then it is false that whoever says "you being an ass" says "you being an animal," since I can say one without saying the other.

To the last argument, I concede that I say "you to be an ass," speaking materially, if I say this proposition "You are an ass." And when it is said further that it is either as I say or other than I say, I answer that that which you say is, but how you say it is otherwise. And where and when you say it, there and then it is, and it is a false proposition. But perhaps you meant to ask whether the case in the

[13] *voces*.

thing signified is as your proposition signifes. But then, concerning this we have spoken in the preceding chapter.[14]

(3) Response to the third sophism. Concerning the third sophism, it can be answered that the sophism is false, since propositions, using language properly, ought to be understood as taking the terms or sentences significatively. Nevertheless, a distinction can be made in order to see the difficulty, by saying that the sophism is true, taking this term "man" materially, and false, taking it personally or significatively. But suppose you ask what is the contradictory of the proposition " 'Man' is a species," taking this term "man" materially. I say that its contradictory is " 'Man' is not a species," also taking the term "man" materially. But you ask whether this is not the same as "No man is a species." I say, rather, that always taking "man" materially, it is "No term 'man' is a species," and then it is false. Nor is your induction valid, for you ought to argue that this term "man" is not a species, nor is that other term "man," and so of others. And in this way, the whole would be false.

(4) Response to the fourth sophism. Concerning the fourth sophism, it is to be said that it is false, according to personal supposition, that a genus is in more or is more common than a most general genus. But according to material supposition, it is true that this term "genus" is in more or is more common than this term "most general."[15] And so the arguments proceed.

(5) Response to the fifth sophism. Concerning the last sophism, I deny that "name" is trisyllabic, taking that term "name" materially. And when you prove that the term *asinus* is trisyllabic and is a name, I concede these premisses, taking the terms "trisyllabic" and "name" personally. Hence, it would be conceded indeed that a name would be trisyllabic, taking "name" as above, namely, personally. But the consequence is not valid, taking "name" materially. For it was not so taken in the premisses, if they were true.

D. Sophisms

There follows a division of personal supposition, or the way in which terms and sentences are taken.

After the division of supposition, or the taking of terms or sentences significatively or materially, there remains another division of

[14] See Conclusion 8 of Chapter II.

[15] *generalissimum.*

personal or significative supposition into discrete and common, and of common into confused and determinate, and of confused into distributive and non-distributive. From this, there also arise some sophisms, whose solution involves some difficulties. Thus, concerning these types of supposition, some sophisms are stated.

(6) *There has always been some man.*

This is proved, since today there has been some man and yesterday there has been some man, and so of every other time; hence, there has always been some man. The conclusion is clear by induction or by the approach from the parts of the whole—sufficiently enumerated in quantity or in time—to the whole.

The opposite is argued, because nothing which is or has been generated or created has always been. But every man has been generated or created; hence, no man has always been.

(7) *Some ass every man sees.*[16]

It is posited that there are only three men—namely, Socrates, Plato, and John—and that each has one ass, which he sees, and that none of these men sees the ass of another.

Then the sophism is clear, since some ass Socrates sees, some ass Plato sees, and also some ass John sees, and there are no more men. Therefore, some ass every man sees.

The opposite is argued, since neither this ass does every man see, nor this nor this; and there are no more asses. Therefore, no ass does every man see. And this contradicts the sophism, so the sophism is false.

(8) *Every man is an animal.*

It is proved, because "animal" belongs to the definition of every man, since every man is an animated, sensible substance.

But it is disproved, since from "Every man is an animal" there follows a false proposition. Therefore, it is false. The consequence holds. The antecedent is proved, because by conversion, it follows that if every man is an animal, then every animal is a man. And yet the consequent is false. I prove that the proposition "Every man is an animal" ought to be converted into the proposition "Every animal is a man," because just as an affirmative proposition is related to an

[16] *Aliquem asinum omnis homo videt.*

affirmative, so a negative to a negative and conversely. And just as a particular is related to a particular, so a universal to a universal, by the same analogy. But the universal negative is converted into a universal negative, so a universal affirmative is converted into a universal affirmative. And also a particular affirmative is converted into a particular affirmative, so similarly, a universal converts into a universal.

This is also confirmed by the fact that an affirmative is stronger and of greater force than a negative. On account of this, Aristotle concludes in the first book of the *Posterior Analytics* that affirmative demonstration is more powerful than negative demonstration.[17] Thus, if a particular negative can be inferred from a universal negative, then a particular affirmative can be inferred from a universal affirmative. Hence, I conclude that from the proposition "Man is an animal" something false follows. Because from this proposition there follows the proposition "That man is an animal," by the argument from the whole in quantity to its part. And then, there is a possible case in which the proposition "That man is an animal" is false, if it is posited that a stone is indicated by the pronoun "that."

(9) *Every man is not an animal.*

It is proved, since Socrates is not the animal which is Plato. Thus, Socrates is not an animal. And similarly, Plato is not the animal which is Socrates, so Plato is not an animal. And the same is true of others. Therefore, every man is not an animal. The consequence is valid.

The opposite is argued, because the propositions "Every man is an animal" and "Every man is not an animal" are contraries, since they are universal affirmative and universal negative. And yet this proposition "Every man is an animal" is true, so by the law of contraries, the proposition "Every man is not an animal" is false. Thus, its equivalent is false. Hence, it is false. The antecedent is proved, because this proposition "No man is an animal" is its equivalent, since "every" and "no" are equipollent.

E. Remarks

(3) [*Third remark*]: Because of these sophisms, that which was said in the *Summula* is to be remembered, that of terms taken per-

[17] Aristotle, *Posterior Analytics* i. 25. *passim.*

sonally or significatively, the supposition is twofold, namely, discrete and common.[18] And next, common supposition is twofold, namely, distributive and non-distributive. Also, non-distributive or indefinite supposition is twofold, that which is determinate and that which is merely confused.[19] And I presuppose this as determined elsewhere.

(4) [*Fourth remark*]: Then you should note, as was said in my treatise on consequences,[20] that from every proposition containing a distributed term, there follows a proposition in which that term occurs not distributed, other things remaining the same. But from a non-distributive, a distributive does not follow. For example, "some" follows from "every," but "every" does not follow from "some." Similarly, it follows negatively that if none runs, then some does not run, but it does not follow that if some does not run, then none runs. Moreover, as I explained in the same place, from a proposition containing a term with merely confused supposition, according to the distribution of the preceding term, there never follows a proposition containing the same term with determinate supposition, unless the distribution is removed. But if the distribution is removed, then the consequence is good. Thus, it does not follow that if every man is an animal, then an animal is every man, but it follows that an animal is a man. But from determinate supposition, confused supposition does follow, as in this consequence: A is every B, so every B is A. And the causes of these are assigned in that treatise. It is clear, therefore, that a change of supposition from non-distributive to distributive, prevents a consequence, and so does a change from merely confused supposition to determinate, unless the distribution, which was the cause of the confusion is removed. And from this, we can easily reply to the sophisms.

F. Solutions of Sophisms

(6) Concerning the first sophism (which was the sixth sophism of this chapter), it should be agreed that if the world were eternal, as seems to have been asserted by Aristotle, then the sophism would be true—that is, that there has always been some man—as the argument

[18] *Summula de Dialectica,* Tract IV. See also above pp. 35–38.
[19] *confusa tantum.*
[20] *Consequentiae,* I, 6, Conclusion 10.

well shows. And with this, it is also conceded that no man has always been, as the reasoning proves. But these two propositions are not contradictory. Indeed, the propositions "No man has always been" and "Some man has always been" are contradictory. But that does not follow from the proposition "There has always been some man," because this changes merely confused supposition to determinate supposition.

(7) Concerning the second [*i.e.*, seventh] sophism, I say that in the case posited, this is false: "Some ass every man sees." But this is true: "Every man sees some ass." They differ, for in the first, this term "ass" stands determinately, and in the second, it has merely confused supposition. So the induction was not a valid proof, since from singulars, one ought not to move to a common distributed term, unless by that distribution, some other common terms should be confused (if there are other terms). And according to this, the following is also not a valid induction on the part of the predicate: a man is Socrates, a man is Plato, and so of singulars; hence, a man is every man. But it ought to be concluded thus: every man is a man.

(8) Concerning the third [*i.e.*, eighth] sophism, I say that this is true: "Every man is an animal." Nor from this does a false proposition follow. Nor is the conversion valid—every man is an animal, so every animal is a man—for it proceeds from the non-distributed term "animal" to the same term distributed. Nor does the analogy [with negative propositions] hold, for in other respects, they are not comparable. In the conversion of a universal negative, one does not alter the supposition of any term, while in the conversion of a universal affirmative into a universal affirmative, one changes the supposition of one term from non-distributive to distributive. Similarly, the other argument is not valid, for the affirmative is stronger than the negative in the sense that a syllogism can be constructed from pure affirmatives, but not from pure negatives. But this does not hold for a consequence in which some term is changed from non-distributive to distributive supposition. Concerning the last argument, I say that it is not a formal consequence to descend from a common distributive term to a singular term, unless on the assumption that the singular term stands for something for which that common term stands.

(9) Concerning the fourth [*i.e.*, ninth] sophism, I agree that every man is not an animal. And I say that "Every man is an animal" is not

its contrary, for it does not have a distributed predicate. Rather, these two sentences are both true. For it is actually required that both the subject and the predicate of the contrary negative be distributed. Indeed, these are contraries: "Every man is an animal" and "Every man is no animal." But you say that since this proposition "Every man is not an animal" is a universal negative, there must be a universal affirmative which is its contrary. I reply that nothing is its contrary, unless perhaps this: "Every man is every animal." For it is necessary that the predicate in one of the contraries be distributed. But neither do I say that this is really the contrary, since it does not have the same predicate. For the sign applied to the predicate is the sign of the whole predicate. Similarly, I say that these are not equivalent: "Every man is not an animal" and "No man is an animal," because "animal" was distributed in one and not in the other.

So the third chapter is finished.

CHAPTER IV
ON CONNOTATION

The fourth chapter will be about connotations.[1] And there will be some sophisms.

A. Sophisms

(1) *Socrates and the white are the same.*

I posit the case that Socrates is white today, and tomorrow he will not be white, but black.

Then it is proved as follows: pointing to Socrates, it is true to say "This is Socrates, and this same thing is white." Therefore, the same thing is Socrates and the white; and converting, it thus follows that Socrates and the white are the same. And this was the sophism.

The opposite is argued, since those are not the same of which one will remain tomorrow, while the other does not remain. But Socrates will remain tomorrow and he will not remain white. Therefore, the white, etc. Or in another way, as long as Socrates will be, so long will be all that which is the same as Socrates. But tomorrow, Socrates will be and he will not be white. Hence, Socrates and the white are not the same thing. Again, Socrates and the white are no more the same than action and passion or motion and time; but in the third book of the *Physics*, it is said that learning is not the same as teaching, nor is action the same as passion, properly speaking, but they belong to the same motion.[2] And in the fourth book, he concludes also that it is manifest that time is neither motion nor in motion.[3] Likewise, Socrates and the white do not differ less than Socrates differs

[1] *Appellationibus*. On the doctrine, see above pp. 42–49.
[2] Aristotle, *Physics* iii. 3. 202b 1–20.
[3] Aristotle, *Physics* iv. 2. 219a 1–2.

from himself when he is doing something and when he is at rest. But Porphyry says that Socrates doing something differs from Socrates at rest.[4] Therefore, etc. Again, Socrates is accidentally white, but Socrates is not accidentally himself. Therefore, etc.

(2) *You ate raw meat today.*

I posit the case that you bought a piece of raw meat yesterday, and today you ate it well-cooked. Then it is argued thus: whatever you bought yesterday, you ate today. But yesterday you bought raw meat; hence, today you ate raw meat.

On the contrary, whatever you ate today you ate well-cooked, by the case; hence, it was not raw.

(3) *The white will be black.*

I posit the case that this wood is now white, and tomorrow it will be black. Then it is argued as follows: this wood will be black and this wood is white; therefore, the white will be black.

The opposite is argued. A proposition of the future is not true if the corresponding proposition of the present will never be true. For example, if this is true: "Antichrist will preach," it follows that at some time this will be true: "Antichrist is preaching." Similarly, the proposition "Aristotle argued" is not true, unless at some time it was true to say that Aristotle is arguing. And so of others. But it has never been true to say that the white is black, nor will it ever be true to say this. Therefore it is the case neither that the white is black nor that the white was black.

And it is similar concerning the sophism "The white can be black." It is argued that it is true, because this wood can be black, since tomorrow it will be black. But this wood is white. Hence, the white can be black.

The opposite is stated, because from the positing of the existence of a possibility, there follows no impossibility. But there follows an impossibility from positing that white is black. Therefore, it is not true that the white can be black. Likewise, a proposition of impossibility contradicts a proposition of possibility; and yet it is true that it is impossible for the white to be black. Therefore, this is false: "It is possible for the white to be black," which is equivalent to "The white can be black."

[4] Porphyry, *Isagoge* 3. 2–3.

(4) *An old man will be a boy.*

This is proved since it is the equivalent of the statement that he who is or will be an old man will be a boy. This is true for Antichrist.

The opposite, however, is clear by induction, since this old man will not be a boy, nor this one nor this one, and so of singulars, because whatever old man is indicated, it is false to say that he will be a boy.

Likewise, it can be argued as in the preceding sophism, concerning what is going to be and what can be.

(5) *Socrates will be running tomorrow.*

The sophism is clear, positing that he will run tomorrow, because "will run" is resovled into "will be running," if one wishes to explain the copula apart from the predicate.

The opposite is argued, because if a proposition of the future is true, it is necessary, as has been said, that in the future it should correspond to a true proposition of the present tense, keeping the predicate in proper form, although not the subject, because the predicate always connotes [5] its form. But it will never be true to say "Socrates is running tomorrow" or "This is running tomorrow," pointing to anything whatever. It is similar concerning the sophism "Socrates argued last year," because it was never true to say "Socrates is arguing last year."

(6) *I saw Peter and Robert.*

Posit that I saw Peter yesterday and Robert the day before yesterday. And then the sophism is manifest by the case.

The opposite is argued, since assuming that I have never seen them at the same time, it was never true to say, in the present tense, "I see Peter and Robert." The same is true of this sophism "I shall see [6] every star," positing that I shall remain under the equinox. The sophism is proved by induction for every star whatever, because a star which I do not see in the summer, I shall see in the winter, and conversely. Therefore, etc.

[5] *appellat.*
[6] Reading *vibebo* for *vidi.*

The opposite is argued as before, because it will never be true to say "I see every star."

B. Remarks

In order to solve these sophisms, a few remarks are required concerning connotations and a fuller discussion should be sought in the *Summula de dialectica.*[7]

(1) [*First remark*]: First, it is to be known that a term which is of a nature to stand for something is said to connote all that which it signifies or consignifies besides that for which it stands, unless it is restricted, as was said elsewhere. For example, "white" standing for men connotes whiteness, and "great" greatness, and "father" past generation and someone else whom the father generated. And "the distant" connotes that from which it is distant and the mediate space by which it is made distant, and "being somewhere" standing for Socrates connotes a place, and so of others.

(2) [*Second remark*]: Secondly, it is to be noted that a term connotes that which it connotes as being somehow determinant or not determinant of that for which it stands or is of a nature to stand.[8] I say it is determinant if it connotes that thing positively, and I say that it is not determinant if it connotes the thing privatively. Thus "white" connotes whiteness positively, as belonging to that which is white, and "father" connotes past generation, as that by which he generated and another as one whom he generated, and "wealthy" connotes exterior goods, as those which the wealthy possess. But "blind" standing for the eye connotes vision privatively and as not belonging to that eye. And "poor" connotes exterior goods not as determinant of them, but as not possessing them.

(3) [*Third remark*]: Thirdly, it is to be noted that according to the different kinds of positive determination by the things connoted of the things for which the terms stand, there are correspondingly different kinds of predication, such as how, how many, when, where, in what way this is related to that, etc. From these different kinds of prediction, the different categories are taken, as should be seen above

[7] Tract IV.

[8] *terminus appellat illud quod appellat per modum adiacentis aliquo modo vel per modum non adiacentis ad illud pro quo supponat vel est natus supponere.*

in the book on the categories.[9] For example, the terms "white" and "black" connote [10] qualities of the substances for which they stand, by which they are called such and such. And the terms "bicubit" and "tricubit" connote quantities by which things are measurable. And in another way of determining or conditioning,[11] the terms of the category "when"—for example, "today" or "tomorrow"—connote the motion of the heavens concerning those which we say to be today or to be going to be tomorrow. And so of others.

(4) [*Fourth remark:*] Fourthly, it is to be noted that connotative terms connote differently in respect of a verb of inherence and of the present tense and in respect of a verb of the past or future tense, and in respect of this verb "can" or "possible." For in respect of a verb of the present tense (if there is not an ampliative term), a connotative term, whether it is the subject or predicate, connotes its thing as something related in the present to that for which the term is of a nature to stand, and as related to it in some determinate way, according to which it connotes it. And then to whatever things such a connoted thing belongs, that term stands for all those things and for no others. And such a term, standing for some things, not only would cease to have supposition because of the destruction or annihilation of those things, but because of the removal of the connoted things or of the manner in which they are related to those things. For example, the term "shod" stands for you, and it would cease to stand for you if your shoes were removed from you. But in respect of other verbs, the subject and predicate connote differently. For the predicate connotes its things only for the time covered by the verb—for whatever time the verb has been restricted to. And if for this time, the mode of relation of the thing connoted does not correspond to that for which the term is of a nature to stand, then it does not stand for that thing, regardless how well the mode of relation corresponds for the [whole] time of the verb. For example, if I say "Socrates was white yesterday," the term "white" in this proposition does not stand for Socrates unless whiteness was related to him yesterday, whether or not it is still so related or was previously so related to him; and so the proposition would be false. But the subject connotes its thing indifferently and in a dis-

[9] *Summula de Dialectica,* Tract III.
[10] *connotant.*
[11] *habitudinis.*

junctive manner for the present time and for the time of the verb, as is also the case with supposition. Hence, the proposition "The white was black yesterday" is exponible as "That which is white or was white yesterday was black yesterday." And just as this is so of past time, so it must be said analogously of the future.

And from this, there follows one noteworthy thing, that if in a proposition of past or future, the subject should be connotative—as for example, when I say "The white will be black"—it is not required, in order for such a proposition to be true, that at some time in the future a proposition of the present corresponding to it will be true. Still, I suppose that in every future time, there is such a proposition corresponding to it in such a way that it has the same subject and predicate. For although this is true: "The white will be black," because it is equivalent to the true statement "That which is or will be white will be black," nevertheless this will never be true: "The white is black," although it could always be formed. But in the reduction of a proposition of future tense to one of present tense, one must remove connotation from the subject of the proposition and change the connotative subject to a non-connotative one, standing for that for which the connotative subject stood and for which the proposition was true. For example, if in the given case, we make the subject of that proposition the pronoun "this" and say "This is white," then it is necessary that if the proposition of the future were true, then at some time the proposition of the present will be true. However, this is not so concerning a connotative predicate, for in such a reduction, a predicate ought to retain the same form with regard to connotations.

And there is a reason for this kind of diversity between the subject and the predicate. For as has been said, the predicate connotes its thing for the time of the verb determinately and precisely. Thus, the connoted thing must be related in the time for which a proposition of future was true. Thus, it is necessary for the proposition of the present to be true with that connotation, and so the connotative term ought to remain. But the subject did not connote its thing precisely for the time of the verb, but in disjunction with the present. And so it suffices that in the time in which the proposition of the future is stated, the connoted thing is related to that for which the subject stands. And it is not required that it be related in that time in which the proposition of the present was true. And so in that present proposition, the connotation must not remain. And therefrom also proceed the causes of the truth of the propositions stating that the white will be when it will not be white and that Robert's horse will be when it will not be Robert's horse. This term "Robert's horse" stands for a horse and connotes Robert as the possessor of that horse. And this is what we should understand by that common saying that the predicate connotes its form and the subject does not. For this is not literally true. Rather, the subject, if it is a connotative term, always connotes its form. But the dictum is true in the sense that it is not necessary for the subject to connote its proper form determinately and precisely for the time of the verb, if the verb is of past or future tense, or also if it is the verb "can" or "possible to be." Hence, to put it properly, it is necessary for the predicate to remain in proper form with its connotation, but not the subject. It is also to be noted that if the subject should not be connotative, then it is not necessary to change it in reducing a proposition of past or future or of possibility to a proposition of inherence and of the present, unless it should be a universal proposition. Then it is not required that one make the reduction to a universal proposition of the present or of inherence. But it suffices that the reduction be made by singulars taken in conjunction. As for instance, this is true: "Every horse will die," but it is not necessary that this be true at the same time: "Every horse is dead." But it is true, because whatever horse, present or future, should be indicated, the following either is or will be true: "This dies" or "This horse dies."

But now concerning these remarks, there are some doubts. For this is true: "Socrates will run tomorrow," and yet this will never be true: "Socrates runs tomorrow." And this also was true: "Socrates was in Paris last year," and yet this was never true: "Socrates is in Paris last year." Similarly, it is true that I saw John and Robert, positing the case that I saw John yesterday and Robert the day before yesterday, and at no other times. And yet in this case, it would never be true to say "I see John and Robert." Similarly, I can see every star, and yet this can in no way be true: "I see every star," and so of many others from which many sophisms can be formed.

To these objections, it seems to me I have to reply. First, concerning the first two. In reducing a proposition of the past or the future to a proposition of the present, signification of the past or the future is to be removed. So there is to be removed every determination of this past or future, in whatever part of the proposition it should be found. Of this kind are the terms "tomorrow," "yesterday," "last year," "at that time," "long ago," etc. And thereby, all the other previously stated sophisms are solved. Likewise, concerning the other doubts, it seems to me that I should say that the term "every" is not properly connotative, since it is not categorematic. Also, it does not signify or connote anything outside the mind, beyond the significations and connotations of the categorematic terms. Rather it only signifies within the mind a manner of conceiving things, according to which the concept of those things stands for them distributively. And so reducing those propositions of past or future or of possibility to those of present or of inherence, it is not necessary to leave such signs distributive, whether in the subject or in the predicate. But it suffices to reduce from each of the copulatives separately, since the copula neither signifies nor connotes anything outside the mind. And thus, certain sophisms are solved.

Yet many say, and indeed commonly, that in reducing to a proposition of the present and of inherence, it is necessary that whatever is after the verb remain absolutely in the same form. Thus, they say that this is to be posited: "John and Robert I saw," but not this: "I saw John and Robert." And similarly, "Yesterday I walked" and "Tomorrow I shall walk," but not "I walked yesterday" or "I shall walk tomorrow." Nor do they allow this: "Tomorrow will be tomorrow's day"; [12] but they allow this: "Tomorrow tomorrow's day will be." And so of others. And either of these ways of speaking is probable and difficult to attack, since the controversy is perhaps due to different uses of conventional words. But I rather accept the first way. Thus, the first sophisms previously posited must now be solved in proper form.

C. Solutions of Sophisms

(1) Concerning the first sophism, I say that the sophism is true; for Socrates and the white are the same. But in the first argument for the opposite, there are implied some difficulties. The first is whether

[12] *Cras erit dies crastina.*

different things are the same. And I say that it is so, because the parts which are diverse from each other are a whole which is one and the same with itself. But no diverse things are the same with themselves, so that this is the same thing as that.

The second doubt is whether this is to be admitted: "Socrates and the white are the same," positing that Socrates is the same as what is white. And for the sake of the subject, I grant that they are something, rather that they are beings, for Socrates is beings, since he is his parts. But in things not having parts, it is doubted. For example, are God and the First Cause the same? I say that this is so and that they are and they govern the world. But they are neither some things nor are they beings nor governors of the world, but they are some thing, a being, a governor of the world. For the plural number consignified by the verb is used to correspond to the plurality of the nouns which convey the person to the verb, and not because those nouns stand for several things.

The third doubt is whether some things are mutually the same. And it seems to be so, for Socrates and the white are mutually the same, since Socrates is the same as the white, and the white is the same as Socrates.

I answer that things are never mutually the same. Nor is the argument valid, since Socrates and the white are something and not some things, unless perhaps something is some things, namely, the whole is its parts. But it will be discussed elsewhere that insofar as they are mutually relative, it is indeed true that some things are truly said to be mutually the same—such as these terms "Socrates" and "white" or the terms "God" and "First Cause." I do not say that they are mutually the same, but that they are called the same. That is, it is truly said of them, taking the predicate "same" significatively and joining them with the verb "are." For it is true to say "Socrates and white are the same" or "God and the First Cause are the same."

Thus, I answer directly the argument where it is said that those are not mutually the same of which one will remain tomorrow and the other will not remain tomorrow. I agree. And when it is said that Socrates will remain tomorrow and that he will not remain the white, I agree. But the white will remain. Similarly, I agree that as long as Socrates will be, so long will be all that which is the same as Socrates. And I agree that it will be. And I agree that tomorrow Socrates will be and also that that which is white will be tomorrow. But he will not be the white.

To the other argument, I say that action and passion are the same and also motion and time are the same. And I say that Aristotle, when he said these not to be the same, meant only that these names are not called the same. That is, one is not affirmed of the other according to essential predication, but according to denomination, and this is even more clear in the third of the *Physics*.[13]

To the other, it is said that this is false, properly speaking: "Socrates doing something differs from Socrates being at rest." Rather, Socrates being at rest is not other than Socrates running or doing something. But this saying of Porphyry ought to be understood in the sense that Socrates' situation is different when he is at rest than when he moves, or at least it is not the same kind of situation.

To the last, it is said that taking the whole significatively, this is false: "Socrates is accidentally white," since the same thing is Socrates and being white. But this proposition is conceded in the sense of material supposition, namely, in the sense that the proposition "Socrates is white" is true accidentally—or in the sense that the predicate "white" is said of the subject "Socrates" accidentally—that is, denominatively and not essentially.

(2) Concerning the second sophism, I say that it is false. And when it is said that whatever you bought yesterday you ate today, perhaps this could be denied, since I bought not only the substances of the meat, but also its accidents and properties.[14] And so I bought raw things which I do not eat, and it is certain that in cooking, something of the substance of the meat disappears and evaporates. Thus, in the aforesaid case, I do not eat whatever I bought. But if the major premiss is conceded, then the minor is also to be conceded, since I bought something raw. But it does not follow that I eat something raw, nor does it follow that something raw is eaten by me. And the reason for your position is that you proceed from a wider supposition or connotation to narrower, without distribution. And it will be said elsewhere that this is not a valid process. I say that this is so, for in the minor proposition "Something raw you bought," the term "raw" connotes rawness indifferently and disjunctively for present or past time,

[13] Aristotle, *Physics* iii. 3. 202b 18–23.
[14] *inherentia.*

while in the conclusion "I eat something raw," the term "raw" connotes rawness only for the present. Hence, it does not stand for that to which rawness was related before, unless it is still so related at present.

This is answered in another way by some. They say that this distributive term "whatever" is a substantial distributive and cannot apply to "raw," since it belongs to the category of quality. But this solution is not sufficient, because "whatever" is distributive for every being. Thus, its distribution applies to all terms which stand for something. And this is a valid syllogism: whatever is something is being, a raw [thing] is something; hence, a raw [thing] is being. The defect in the conclusion is thus due to the aforesaid cause.

But perhaps the argument will be stated that I bought a round loaf of bread, and afterward I altered its shape, adding nothing and removing nothing. For this is possible, assuming that a shape does not differ from what has the shape. And so I eat the whole of that bread. Then I form a syllogism: Whatever I bought I ate. This is true by the case. Nor is there the exception which was made in the case of raw [things]. Then the minor should be assumed, that I bought [something] round; and it is concluded that, therefore, I ate [something] round; which is false by the case, since I ate something having another shape, and since that proposition of the present was never true, namely, "I am eating [something] round." Thus, there is a legitimate doubt whether in this case the following is to be conceded: "I ate [something] round." It seems that it is so, since this is true. "[Something] round I ate," because what was round I ate. Therefore, analogously, in this case, this is true: "I ate [something] round." The consequence is proved, because the connotation was related correctly to the tense of the verb, since in the case posited, that was round. Thus, the connotative verb can be placed as the predicate as well as the subject.

I believe that the proposition should not be conceded, because although the connotation was related for past time, yet it was not in that time that I ate. For it is necessary that all the connotations of the predicate be related to the same time at once. For example, if I say that I have been eating raw fruit in Paris, it is necessary at one and the same time that I should be eating, and eating fruit, and that the fruit should be raw, and that I should be eating it in Paris. Therefore,

I say that this argument is not valid: whatever I bought I ate, and I bought [something] round; hence, I ate [something] round. But it could be concluded that [something] round I ate, or I ate that which was round.

(3) Concerning the third sophism it is said that it is true. For as has been said, in reducing a proposition of the past or the future, or of the possible, it is not required that the subject, if it is connotative, remain in proper form. Concerning the further argument that it is impossible for white to be black, I agree, according to material supposition. That is, this proposition "white is black" is impossible. But from this it does not follow that this is false or impossible: "It is possible for white to be black," since those propositions are very different. For one is in the divided sense [15] and the other is in the composite sense.[16]

(4) Concerning the fourth sophism, it is said that it is true. Nor is the induction valid, for it takes account of supposition for present things only, and it ought to account for the future, because of the ampliation to the future. But from this induction, it does indeed follow that nobody who is an old man will be a boy.

(5) Concerning the fifth sophism, I say that it seems to me that a distinction must be made in order to more clearly determine the truth. For the expression "tomorrow" can be undestood determinately as belonging with the verb "will be" with respect to time known, or as belonging with the predicate "running." Thus, if it is understood determinately as belonging with the time of the verb, then the proposition is true, and in reducing to a proposition of present tense, the expression "tomorrow" is to be removed. But if the expression "tomorrow" is construed with the predicate "running," then the sophism is false, because then it would be required that that predicate be retained in proper form in the reduction. So therefore, concerning the proper way of speaking, this would have to be conceded: "Socrates will be tomorrow running." And this would have to be denied: "Socrates will be running tomorrow." And it is to be said that the proposition "Socrates will run tomorrow" ought to be resolved into "Socrates will be tomorrow running." And also, I believe that in this case, the whole expression "will be tomorrow" is the copula and this term "running"

[15] *in sensu diviso.*

[16] *in sensu composito.* On the distinction, see above p. 33, n. 60.

alone is the predicate. Similarly, I say that this proposition "Socrates argued last year" ought to be resolved into "Socrates was last year arguing," and this whole expression "was last year" is the copula of the proposition.

(6) Concerning the sixth sophism, I say that it implies two sophisms, and it seems to me that the sophisms are to be conceded. And it has been seen in the remarks in what way one should respond to the arguments for the opposite.

D. Sophisms

Still, for this chapter on connotations, other sophisms can be stated.

(7) *This dog is your father.*

This is proved, because this is a father and this is yours; hence, it is your father. Similarly, pointing at a black monk it is argued that there is a white monk, because this is white and it is a monk; hence, it is a white monk. And similarly, it is argued that it is not a black monk, since he is not black but white. Hence, he is not a black monk, by the argument from the whole in quantity to its parts. So also it could be argued concerning your father that he could not be your father, because he is not yours, but rather, conversely, you are his; hence, he is not your father.

(8) *The whiteness of Socrates is his similarity to Plato.*

I posit the case that Socrates and Plato are white and possess equal degrees of whitness, and that they are not similar in any other qualities except whiteness. Then I posit that Socrates continues to become whiter, while Plato does not change.

Then the sophism is proved, because Socrates is similar to Plato, because of his similarity to Plato, and he is not similar to him except in whiteness; hence, his whiteness is his similarity to Plato.

The opposite is argued, because the whiteness of Socrates continues to grow in intensity, since he continues to become whiter. And yet his similarity to Plato does not become more intense, but rather less so, because Socrates continues to become less similar to Plato, or more dissimilar. Therefore, the similarity is not that whiteness.

Likewise, no quality is related to anything, because these are distinct categories, since whiteness is a quality and similarity is a relation. Therefore, etc. Or it is argued as follows: no absolute is relative, but whiteness is an absolute thing and similarity is a relative thing; hence, etc.

E. Remarks

(5) [*Fifth remark*]: Because of these sophisms, it is to be noted concerning connotations, that connotative terms connote their things in one way, when the connotative term alone is the subject or predicate of a proposition, and otherwise when it is conjoined with another connotative term. For if it is taken alone, it connotes its thing as relative to the thing for which it stands, and not to another. But often when it is conjoined to another connotative term, it connotes its thing as somehow determinant of what that other term connotes. For example, if I say "Socrates is good," the term "good" connotes the goodness of Socrates. But if I say "Socrates is a good cleric or poet," then the term "good" connotes the goodness of knowledge or art, and not the goodness of Socrates.

(6) [*Sixth remark*]: Sometimes a connotative term, by primary or principal imposition, is imposed to connote its thing by some mode of connotation which it retains if it is in itself the subject or predicate. But by addition, it is carried to another mode of connotation by the requirements of the terms to which it is adjoined. For example, the pronoun "your," by principal signification or imposition, connotes you as the thing which possesses that for which it stands. But when I say "your father," then it connotes you as that of which that for which it stands is the father. And in the same way, if I say "your lord," "your husband," and so of others. And so, because of such changes in the mode of connotation, it is not valid to conclude from conjoined terms to the same terms divided or from these terms divided to them conjoined, since thus is committed the fallacy from that which is by virtue of something [17] to that which is simply,[18] which would be valid if the modes of connotation did not change.

[17] *secundum quid.*
[18] *simpliciter.*

F. Solutions of Sophisms

By this, the aforesaid sophisms are solved.

(7) Concerning the seventh sophism, I say that this is not a valid consequence: this dog is a father, and it is yours; hence, it is your father. For the connotation of this term "your" changes, as has been said. Nor is this valid: this is white, and it is a monk; hence, it is a white monk. For in the first premiss, "white" connotes the whiteness of his body, and afterward it connotes the whiteness of his monastic garb. And for the same reason, this conclusion is not valid: the monk is not black, so he is not a black monk. Nor for the same reason is this valid, concerning your father: he is not yours, so he is not your father. Nor is this valid, for the same reason: you are white with reference to your teeth; therefore, you are white. Similarly, you are a good thief, so you are good. And so of others.

(8) Concerning the eighth sophism, I say that it is true. The argument that it is false can be answered by the preceding. I concede that the whiteness becomes continuously more intense. But when it is said that the similarity of Socrates becomes not more intense but less so, I deny this. But the similarity does not become more intense, because the connotation of the term "more intense" changes. For when I say "The similarity becomes more intense," the predicate "more intense" connotes only intensity or augmentation of that for which "similarity" stands, namely, whiteness. But when I say "The more intense becomes the similarity," then "more intense" connotes that the relation they [*i.e.*, Socrates and Plato] bear to each other becomes the one of those qualities that is more.

But others, not so attending to logic, say that neither does the whiteness become more intense nor is the similarity diminished. But it is true that the white becomes more intense, that is, that it becomes a more intense white and less similar, that is, it becomes less similar. And then if one should argue as follows: Socrates becomes a more intense white and not more intensely similar, then one can conclude only that something which is more intensely white is not more intensely similar, which is not against the sophism.

To the other objection, I say that substances and qualities are indeed similar or dissimilar to something, because Socrates is similar or dissimilar to something, or rather, to many things; and the white is also white and similar to something [white] and dissimilar to something black. And similarly, whiteness is the same as itself and different from another. But I say that the terms of one predicate are not of another predicate. Yet in the material sense it is understood that no quality is a substance or a quantity or a relation. And so also, I concede that an absolute term is not relative. Thus, the terms "whiteness" and "similarity" differ. But they still stand for the same thing.

G. Sophisms

There are still other difficulties concerning some kinds of connotations, because of which they posit other sophisms. And this will be the ninth sophism of this chapter.

(9) *You know the one approaching.*

I posit the case that you see your father coming from a distance, in such a way that you do not discern whether it is your father or another.

Then it is proved, because you do indeed know your father, and he is the one approaching; hence, you know the one approaching. Likewise, you know him who is known by you, but the one approaching is known by you; hence, you know the one approaching. I prove the minor, because your father is known by you and your father is the one approaching; hence, the one approaching is known by you.

The opposite is argued, because you do not know him of whom, if you are asked who he is, you will answer truly "I do not know." But concerning the one approaching, you say this; hence, etc.

(10) *You know the coins in my purse to be even in number.*

It is proved, because you know every pair to be even in number, so you know every two to be even. But the coins in my purse are two; hence, you know them to be even.

The opposite is argued. I posit that you believe that in my purse, there is only one coin, and so you believe there not to be an even number of coins in my purse. Then it is argued thus: You do not know that whose opposite you believe, since opinions or beliefs about opposites—*i.e.*, contradictories or contraries—cannot be in the same intellect simultaneously, because they are contrary, as is said in the fourth of the *Metaphysics*.[19] But these are opposites; "The coins in my purse are not even in number" and "They are even in number," and you believe that they are not even. Therefore, you do not know them to be even. And so the sophism is false.

(11) *You believe yourself to be an ass.*

This is proved, because whoever believes his father to be an ass believes himself to be the son of an ass, and consequently, an ass. But you believe your father to be an ass. I prove this, positing the case that your father is covered with the hide of an ass, and from afar you see him walking on his feet and hands, so that you believe that this thing is an ass. Then it is argued by an expository syllogism: this you believe to be an ass, and this is your father; hence, your father you believe to be an ass.

The opposite is argued, because you do not believe this, but rather, you know the opposite, namely, that you are not an ass.

(12) *Socrates appears to be other than he is.*

This is proved by the aforesaid case, namely, that that father who is thus covered with the hide of an ass is Socrates. Then Socrates appears to be an ass, and he is not that, but other than that, because he is a man; hence, he appears to be other than he is. Or it can be argued thus: every ass is other than Socrates, but Socrates appears to be an ass; hence, he appears to be other than he is. Or again: Socrates appears to be an ass, which he is not, but something other; hence, etc. The consequence seems to be known. The antecedent is clear, because he appears to be an ass, and this he is not. And this is again confirmed, because I posit that he appears to be an ass, and you have no other appearance; thus, he appears to you to be other, since he appears to be an ass, and he does not appear to you to be other than an ass, by the case. However, he is not. Whereby, he appears to be another, which he is not; so consequently, he appears to be other than he is.

The opposite is argued, because whatever thing in the world is shown to me, I judge that it is that which it is, thus, not that it is other than it is, because such would be contrary judgments, which cannot simultaneously be in the same intellect. Likewise, this verb

[19] Aristotle, *Metaphysics* iv. 3. 1005b 28–32.

"is," occurring without a predicate following it [20] can be resolved into "is" and "being," just as "runs" is resolved into "is running." Otherwise, one could not convert propositions such as "A man runs" and "A man is." Therefore, if something appears to be other than it is, it follows that it appears to be being other than it is being, and thus it appears to be other than being, which is impossible. Again, it follows that it is possible for Socrates to run. Therefore, this is possible: "Socrates runs." Hence, by the same argument, it follows that Socrates appears to be other than he is, so this is appearing: Socrates is other than he is, which is impossible.

H. Remarks

(7) [*Seventh remark*]: Because of these sophisms, it is to be known that these verbs "understand," "be acquainted with," "know," and others of this kind (of which more will be said later), and participles and names descended from them—such as "understanding," "being acquainted with," "acquaintance," "knowledge," etc.—effect some special kinds of connotation in the terms with which they occur. For since I can understand the same thing in many different ways, and, corresponding to these diverse ways, impose different names on it to signify it, therefore, such verbs cause the terms with which they occur to connote the reasons [21] for which their names are imposed to signify them, and not only the external things known, as happens with other verbs.

(8) [*Eighth remark*]: However, the case is different when the term occurs before the verb than when the term occurs after the verb. For when it occurs after the verb, the term connotes the reasons for its imposition determinately and precisely. But when terms occur before the verbs, they connote the reasons for their imposition indifferently, and they connote disjunctively other ways in which the things signified can be signified and understood. Because of this, this proposition "I know the one approaching" is not true, properly speaking, unless I know him according to the reason for which he is called the one approaching, although I may indeed know him according to some other reason. And so it does not follow: I know Socrates, and he is the one approaching; hence I know the one approaching. For although

[20] *secundo adiacens.*
[21] *rationes.*

I may know him according to the reason for which he is called Socrates, yet I do not know him according to the reason for which he is called the one approaching. But taking the term as subject, it does indeed follow: Socrates is known by me, and Socrates is the one approaching; hence, the one approaching is known by me. So also, we say that the sense of sight knows and judges the white but not the sweet, although the same thing is both white and sweet. However, we may say that the sweet is judged by him and known by him, as is clear by an expository syllogism. For this white [thing] is judged by him, and it is sweet; hence, the sweet is judged by him. Therefore, it does not follow: the one approaching is known by me, so I know the one approaching. Rather, it is possible that I do not know the one approaching. But it does follow: I know the one approaching, so the one approaching is known by me. In the same way, in other connotations it did not follow that the white will be, so it will be white; but conversely, it did follow that it will be white, so the white will be.

(9) [*Ninth remark*]: Furthermore, it is to be noted that we impose names to signify things by means of the ways in which we understand things. Thus, also, this verb "to signify" effects such connotations, just as "to understand" or "to be acquainted with," and so also this verb "appears" and these verbs "to know," "to opine," "to consider," "to believe," etc. Furthermore, since our desires are effected in us by means of cognition, it follows that similar connotations are effected by the verbs "to want," "to desire," and "to long for." And also, since it is under concepts that we make our promises and obligations, it follows that the verbs "to owe," "to promise," "to obligate," etc., and other terms derived from these, effect these kinds of connotations.

(10) [*Tenth remark*]: But also it is to be noted that there are differences between these verbs "to understand," "to be acquainted with," on the one hand, and the verbs "to know," "to believe," etc., on the other hand. For we can be acquainted with a thing or understand it or apprehend it by simple and non-complex concepts. But it does not happen that we know a thing or believe it or opine it, except by complex concepts. Thus, the verbs "to know," "to opine," etc., cause terms to connote not only according to simple reasons, but also complex ones. Thus, it is not proper or perfect to say that I know or opine a man or a stone, but one must say that I know a man to be an animal and I opine a stone to be hard—or conversely, that a man to

be an animal is known by me and a stone to be hard is opined by me. Or, by way of division, that a man is known by me to be an animal and a stone is opined by me to be hard. However, we admit this way of speaking, that of men or of stones we have knowledge, which is not true, unless because we have knowledge that one is an animal or risible or hard, and so of other predicates.

In this way, therefore, if the whole dictum should follow such a verb (as in saying that I know an isosceles to have three angles equal to two right angles) it is necessary, if the proposition is true, that this knowledge be according to this proposition "An isosceles has three angles, etc." Whence, it does not follow: I know every triangle to have three angles, and an isosceles is a triangle; hence, I know an isosceles to have three angles. Nor does it follow: it is necessary for every ass to be an animal, and Brunellus is an ass; hence it is necessary for Brunellus to be an animal.

And Aristotle somewhat superficially speaks of this in the first of the *Posterior Analytics*,[22] saying that in knowing every triangle to have three angles, one knows, in a certain manner, an isosceles, or the figure inscribed in a semicircle, to have three angles, but he does not know absolutely. He does not actually know this unless by introducing a minor under a major, he should know that an isosceles is a triangle. But he knows it potentially, since there is lacking only the introduction of that minor under that major.

However, that statement of Aristotle is not sufficient for the argument involved. For I raise a difficult question, by not placing the subject of the expression before the verb and the predicate after the verb. For example, I ask whether it follows: I know every B to be A; so every B is known by me to be A. Or, I know every triangle to have three angles, so every triangle is known by me to have three angles. And from this question, one can add a sophism to the prior sophisms, namely, the thirteenth of this chapter.

I. Sophisms

(13) *Anyone knowing the conclusion that every triangle has three angles equal to two right angles, every isosceles is known by him to have three angles equal to two right angles.*

[22] Aristotle, *Posterior Analytics* i. 1. 71a 19–30.

I posit that everyone who knows this conclusion has knowledge of every triangle, and yet of every triangle he has knowledge only that it has three angles, etc. For I posit that concerning triangles, he knows no other conclusion. Therefore, concerning every triangle he knows that it has three angles; therefore, etc. And then that conclusion should form the major of the other syllogism, and adding the minor that every isosceles is a triangle, it will be concluded in the first mood of the first figure that concerning every isosceles, he knows that it has three angles; hence, etc. And this signifies the same as to say that every isosceles is known by him to have three angles. And I return to declare what I assumed, namely, that whoever knows this conclusion "Every triangle has three angles," he has knowledge of every triangle. Whoever would deny this must for the same reason say that the doctor has no knowledge of health or illness, or that the natural philosopher, having all natural knowledge, has no knowledge of heaven and earth or of generation and corruption or of animals and plants; or that the astronomer has no knowledge of the heaven and the stars, and so of others, which is patently absolutely absurd. Therefore, this sophism is to be conceded.

The opposite is argued. It is posited that at a distance you see a figure which is an isosceles. But you believe that it is a circle. Therefore, that isosceles is not known by you to have three angles. Rather, you believe that it does not have angles. Hence, not every isosceles is known by you to have three angles. Likewise, knowing that all pairs are even in number, you would know that the coins in my purse are even, and it was argued before that this is false. For if you are asked whether they are even, you will answer "I do not know." Again, from this known proposition "Every triangle has three angles," to conclude that every isosceles has three angles, there is required the minor proposition that every isosceles is a triangle. But it is not necessary that from the knowledge of the major without the minor, the conclusion is known. Therefore, it is not necessary that knowing, concerning every triangle, that it has three angles, one knows this about every isosceles.

The whole difficulty seems to lie in this, whether it follows: I know every triangle to have three angles, so concerning every triangle, I have this knowledge, namely, that it has three angles. Hence, because of this difficulty, some people have said that we have knowledge only of the conclusions of demonstrations and not of other things, neither of stones or animals or others. Others say that it is not the case that of every triangle I have knowledge, but I have knowledge of every triangle, from which it does not follow that I have knowledge of an isosceles, because the mode of connotation is changed to that which the term has after the verb.

But this answer seems very hard to accept. For it would follow that concerning no triangle do we have knowledge, for what is the case with some is the case with all. So we have knowledge either of all or of none. And then for the same reason, it would follow that although we have knowledge of God, of heaven, of animals, of health or illness, yet of heaven we have no knowledge, nor of God nor of animals. Nor would doctors have knowledge of health or illness. And this seems hard to concede.

And yet this opinion had cogency, because from a composite modal, a divided one does not seem to follow. For example, it does not follow: it is necessary for every ass to be an animal, so every ass is necessarily an animal. For Aristotle would allow the first and deny the second, because every ass can not be, and consequently not be an animal. Likewise, it does not follow: it is possible for every being to be God, so every being is possibly God, since the first is true. For it was so before the creation of the world, and it would be so if God should destroy every creature. And yet the second would be false, since it is not possible for a creature to be God. Thus similarly, it is seen that it ought not to follow: I know every B to be A, so every B is known by me to be A. Or also: I know every triangle to have three angles, so every triangle is known by me to have three angles.

But it can be said that it is not the same for all modals, for although it does not follow in all, still nothing prevents its following in some. For example, it follows: it is true that every B is A, so every B is truly A. Thus, it is seen to be still probable that it follows: I know every triangle to have three angles, so concerning every triangular figure, I know that it has three angles, or also, every triangle is known by me to have three angles.

Now the arguments for the opposite are answered. Concerning the first, I say that concerning the same thing, I could doubt about one proposition and have true knowledge about another conclusion. For example, concerning the first elements, I know truly that they are corruptible, and I doubt whether they remain in a mixture. So also, if I see a mule, which I think to be a pregnant horse, then concerning this beast I have true knowledge that he is sterile by the proposition known to me: "Every mule is sterile." And in spite of this, I have a false belief about him, by the proposition "This beast is pregnant." And so also concerning the isosceles, I have true knowledge that it has three angles by the proposition "Every triangle has three angles." Yet also, I have a false opinion about it by the proposition "This figure is a circle."

Concerning the other argument, I say similarly that the coins in the purse are known by you to be even in number, but not by the proposition "The coins in my purse are even," but by the proposition "All pairs are even."

Similarly, to the other argument, I say that it follows, if I know every triangle to have three angles, that by this name "isosceles," I know it to have three angles. But it does not follow that I know every isosceles to have three angles.

(14) *Socrates the astronomer knows some stars to be above our hemisphere.*

This is proved, because a good astronomer, of which kind I want Socrates to be, knows that every hemisphere is a half of the sky containing a multitude of stars. Thus, he easily concludes that many stars are above our hemisphere.

The opposite is argued, positing the case that this Socrates is in a dark dungeon, so that he does not know whether it is day or night. Thus, he does not know what part of the sky is above our hemisphere; it follows that he has knowledge of some stars that they are above our hemisphere. The conclusion is false, so the antecedent is false. The falsity of the conclusion is proved, for he does not know the sun to be above our hemisphere. Rather, he doubts whether it is above or below, as is posited by the case. The same is true of the moon. He does not know that it is above our hemisphere, nor the stars of Aries nor the stars of Libra, and so of others. Therefore, he does not know about anything that it is above our hemisphere; and this contradicts that conclusion, so that conclusion will be false.

But then the consequence is proved by the fact that in a preceding sophism, it was said that it follows: I know every B to be A, so every B is known by me to be A. So it follows: I know some B to be A, so some B is known by me to be A. Thus, similarly, if I know some stars to be above our hemisphere, it follows that of some stars I know that they are above our hemisphere.

Likewise, [one might argue that] he either knows concerning all stars that they are above our hemisphere or he knows it concerning none, since he knows no more of some than of others, since all are equally in doubt. But it cannot be said that of all he knows that they are above, for he would know a false, impossible proposition. Therefore, he knows concerning none that they are above.

But from this, it seems to follow that he does not know this conclusion, namely, that some stars are above our hemisphere. In other words, one must say that by knowledge of natural or medical conclusions, we have no knowledge of natural or medical things outside the mind. And this we have already said to be hard to admit.

Concerning this sophism, just as the preceding, it seems to me one must say that the whole of the difficulty consists in whether this follows: I know some stars to be above our hemisphere, so some stars are known by me to be above our hemisphere. And it is similar to a contradiction posited of which I do not know what part is true. Does it follow: I know one or the other part of this contradiction to be true, so of this contradiction one or the other part is known by me to be true, or also, concerning one or the other part of this contradiction, I have knowledge that it is true?

And it seems to be a good consequence and so the sophism would be conceded, namely, that Socrates knows some stars to be above our hemisphere and that, also, some stars are known by him to be above our hemisphere. And similarly concerning that contradiction, he knows one or the other part to be true, and one or the other part of the contradiction is known by him to be true.

And then I answer the argument in opposition, by which it was argued that Socrates knows no stars to be above our hemisphere, just as neither part of that contradiction does he know to be true. For he knows neither the sun nor the moon to be above the earth; and so of others. I deny the induction. Rather, those stars which are above the earth, he knows to be above the earth. For example, when the stars of Aries are above the earth, he knows concerning them that they are above the earth. But he does not know this by the proposition "The stars of Aries are above the earth." Similarly, one or the other part of that contradiction I know to be true, and the other I know to be false. And if the affirmative is true and the negative false, then the affirmative is known by me to be true and the negative false, but not by the proposition "The affirmative is true and the negative is false"—rather I doubt concerning this—but by the proposition "One part of the contradiction is true and the other false."

Concerning the other argument, I say that neither of all nor of none does he know that they are above, but of those which are above, he knows that they are above, and of the others he knows that they are not above. However, he does not know this by the proposition "Those are above and those are below," but by the proposition "Some are above and some are below." And if it is asked whether, concerning the sun, he knows that it is above, it is answered that he does if the sun is above, but if it is not, he does not know. Thus, I agree that although he knows of the sun that it is above, yet he does not know whether it is above.

J. Solutions of Sophisms

Furthermore, the other sophisms are also solved, which were stated long ago and not solved.

(9) Concerning the sophism which was the ninth of this chapter, I say that in the case posited, the sophism is true, namely, "You know the one approaching." For you know from the reason by which he is said to be approaching, since you see him approach. And when it is argued that it is not so, since if you are asked "Who is that?" you answer that you do not know, I say that I know to respond that he is something, for he is a substance—or perhaps that he is also an animal or a man. But I do not know, indeed, to answer whether it is Socrates or Plato, since I do not know him by that proposition "This is Socrates" or "This is my father." But I know to say that this is approaching, for I know it by the proposition "This is approaching."

But still there may be posited the case that he approaches and you do not see him approach nor consider anything about his coming. In this case, do you know the one approaching? I say that you do not, although I know the one approaching. Nor is the following argument valid: you know your father, etc. Because the term is altered to have connotation after the verb.

But then another more difficult argument could be stated as follows: You know one who is known by you, but the one approaching is known by you; hence, you know the one approaching. I grant the major and the minor, but I deny the consequence. For the inference ought to be: hence, the one approaching is known by you; or it ought to be inferred; hence, you know the one who is approaching. So please note that the last proposition, namely, "You know the one who is approaching" is hypothetical.[23] Thus, the verb "I know" which is in the first categorical does not have connotation for the term "approaching," which is in the second categorical, so that it does not force it to connote precisely its concept. In the same way, I could say that this is true: "Antichrist will preach"; and yet this is false: "Antichrist is one who will preach." For in the first proposition, which was categorical, the verb "will preach" affects "Antichrist," making it stand for the future. But in the second proposition, which is hypothetical, it does not affect it, because it is in another categorical.

(10) Concerning the second [*i.e.*, tenth] sophism, I answer that the sophism is false, for you do not know the coins in my purse to be even in number. Yet I agree that the coins in my purse are known by you to be even, by the proposition known by you that every pair is even. Nor is that argument that you know the coins to be even valid for the conclusion, because the connotation of the term is changed to that which it has after the verb. And I say that these propositions are not repugnant, but are simultaneously true: "These coins are known by you to be even" and "These coins are believed by you to be uneven." For this knowledge and this belief are due to different propositions. But these would be repugnant: "You know these coins to be even" and "You believe these coins not to be even." More will be said of this hereafter.

(11) Concerning the eleventh sophism, I can deny it. And I could deny the major premiss "Whoever believes his father, etc." But in this case, it does no harm to concede it and to deny the minor proposition "You believe your father to be an ass." For proof, I concede the case and I concede the whole expository syllogism. Thus, I concede that my father is believed by me to be an ass. But this does not follow: hence, I believe my father to be an ass. For my father was

[23] Terminist logicians called any proposition composed of two or more categoricals as main clauses a hypothetical proposition. The class thus included disjunctives and conjunctives, as well as conditionals.

believed by me to be an ass, not by the proposition "My father is an ass," but by the proposition "This is an ass."

(12) Concerning the twelfth sophism, I say that it is false. And please note that this is false: "Socrates appears to be another, which he is not." For if he appears to be another, then he is also something. But I would indeed concede this: "Socrates appears to be something, which he is not," and similarly, "Socrates appears to be other than he is." And likewise, I concede that Socrates appears to me to be an ass, which he is not, but something else. Thus, when it is argued: Socrates appears to be an ass, and he is not that, but something other; hence he appears to be something other than he is; I concede the antecedent, but I deny the consequent. For the cause of the term's connotation is changed to that which it has after the verb. But with this the relation is changed just as before. For if I say "He appears to be an ass and he is not that, but something other," this has the sense that he is not an ass, but other than an ass. But if I say "He appears to be something, and is not that, but something other," this has the sense that he is not something, but other than something, which is false. And in the same way, concerning the second argument, I concede the premisses and deny the conclusion.

But concerning the third argument, I deny this: "Socrates appears to be something, which he is not, but he is other." For proof, I say that the consequence—that he appears to be an ass, which he is not, so he appears to be something which he is not—is not valid. But furthermore, when it is said "I posit that he appears to you to be an ass, and that you have no other appearance," I say that the case is impossible. For that appearance is complex, so it includes non-complex appearances, every one of which is other than that one. But I concede that you have no other appearance which is not required for that one to be. But when it is said also "This appears to you to be something," I say that this must be denied by the case posited; because this is another appearance and requires another proposition. For the proposition that this is an ass and that this is something are different, and there can be the appearance of one without the appearance of the other. Hence, there is no doubt that this thing can appear to be something without its appearing to be an ass. And perhaps this can be so conversely, if the inferior concept can be freed from the higher one, which is not now to be discounted.[24] Rather, I assume that Socrates appears to you to be an ass and to be something. Yet when beyond this it is said that he does not appear to you to be something other than an ass, I agree that it does not follow from the aforesaid appearances that the same thing appears to me again by the proposition "Clearly, this is something other than an ass." But from this it does not follow that he appears to you to be something which he is not. But all such conclusions are false, since they change the predicates and the reasons connoted after the verb.

But notwithstanding all the preceding, there is still another argument, whether it is possible that something appears to you to be something which it is not. For although according to the preceding, this is not possible concerning those that are as they were posited to be, yet it is probable that this is possible concerning those that are not. I posit the case that my horse Brunellus is dead. Still, by his appearance preserved in my imagination, he can appear to me in memory or in dreams, as though he were present. And I posit that Brunellus appears to be something, and yet that he is not, since he is nothing. And from this, there follows a proposition, namely, that he appears to me to be something which he is not.

And it seems to me that the proposition "Brunellus appears to me to be something which he is not" ought to be distinguished. For it can be a hypothetical, and is equivalent to the proposition "Brunellus appears to me to be something, and he is not that"; and this is a true proposition. In another way, it can be understood that it is a categorical proposition, so that the whole expression "something which he is not" is placed as a hypothetical predicate. And then it would have the sense that Brunellus appears, by this proposition and complex expression "Brunellus is something which he is not"; and this is false and impossible. And if you ask which of those senses is the more proper, I say that this depends on how the vocal proposition is spoken and how the written proposition is written. For if it is spoken with a pause and if it is written with a comma between the proposition "Brunellus appears to you to be something" and the remainder "which he is not," then the proposition is clearly hypothetical, since it is then signified that this whole expression "which he is not" is not a predi-

[24] That is, the concept of something is broader or more general than the concept of ass.

cate. But if it is spoken or written continuously, without pause or comma, it seems more properly that it is a categorical proposition. Hence, often in propositions there is such a difference, because of which, if the inflection is not perceived, there is committed the fallacy of composition or division.

K. A Final Sophism

Finally, concerning this matter, there is posited a fifteenth sophism, which seems to be very difficult.

(15) *I owe you a horse. (Or similarly: I owe you a denarius).*

I posit the case that for a good service which you performed for me, I promised you a good horse. And I have obligated myself before a competent judge to make suitable payment to you of a good horse. Thus, the sophism appears manifest, for it is commonly said that every promise is included in one's debt. And since I owe this, until I have paid that concerning the payment of which I have obligated myself by legal obligation before a judge, you could rightly take action against me to bring about payment to you of a horse, which you could not do if I did not owe you. And similarly, I posit that I bought some mustard from you for one denarius, and I have not paid you. It follows that I owe you a denarius.

But the opposite is argued in a difficult way, conceding the aforesaid case. For I owe you nothing, so I owe you neither a horse nor a denarius. The consequent seems clear of itself. Hence, if before a judge, you should declare that I owe you nothing, the judge would rule that I was free from debt. But I assert the antecedent, because I do not owe you this horse, namely, Morellus, nor this one; hence, I owe you no horse. And consequently, I owe you nothing, since I promised nothing other than a horse. But it remains to prove the two consequences.

First, I shall prove this consequence: this horse, namely, Morellus, I do not owe you; hence, no horse I owe you. And secondly, I must prove the antecedent of this consequence. Thus, I prove first the consequence, since I no more owe you Morellus than Favellus, since I no more promised you one than the other, and I could fulfill my obligation equally with one horse as well as another. Therefore, it follows that if I do not owe you Morellus, neither do I owe you Favellus, for the same reason. And the same is true of other horses. Therefore, I owe you no horse. And so that consequence is clear.

But then I prove the antecedent, because just as was said at first, I owe you no more Morellus than Favellus. Hence, I owe you either both or neither. If neither, then the proposition is proved, namely, that I do not owe you Morellus. But it cannot be said that I owe you both, since I promised only one. Hence, I owe you only one. And it does not follow that if I owe you one, then I owe you two. Likewise, I could obligate myself to you for one horse or for one florin, if I do not actually have a horse or a florin, just as if I did have. For I am capable of having them before the assigned payment. Thus, I posit the case that I, having no horse, promise to pay you a horse before Easter, and to this I obligate myself. Then in this case, I argue as before, because I owe you nothing, or because I do not owe you the king's horse, since I neither promised that nor have I obligated myself to pay that. And so also I do not owe you the pope's horse nor Peter's horse, and so of others. For the same reason, therefore, I owe you no horse. And yet I owe you nothing else, nor have I promised [anything else]; hence, I owe you nothing.

This sophism appears difficult. Yet to the first argument, I say that in the case posited, I should owe you a horse. But then it is doubted whether I owe you Morellus. And it is to be said that I do not and that also in promising you a horse, I did not promise you Morellus. Because as was said before, these verbs "promise," "owe"—just as these verbs "know" or "understand"—make the terms following them connote the reasons for their imposition. Thus, a consequence is not valid which changes the reason for the predicate after the verb. Indeed, neither does it appear to be a valid consequence to descend from a species to an individual without distribution.

However, it is to be said that it makes a difference whether "horse" is placed before the verb or after the verb. Because the mentioned verbs, since they connote their reasons, confuse whatever terms are following them, so that one cannot make a descent to singulars by a disjunctive proposition. For example, it does not follow: I owe you a horse, so I owe you Morellus, or I owe you Favellus, and so of others, since each of these is false. But a term occurring before the verb is not thus confused. So one can descend by disjunction.

Whence, if this is true: "A horse is owed by me to you," it follows that Morellus is owed by me to you, or Favellus, and so of others.

But then, I concede, according to the aforesaid case, that this is true: "I owe you a horse," because I promised you a horse, and I obligated myself precisely with words such as "I promise you a good horse, and I acknowledge that I owe you a good horse." Then there is great doubt whether this is true: "A horse is owed by me to you" or "Some horse is owed by me to you" or also "One horse is owed by me to you." And there is doubt whether it follows: I owe you a horse, so a horse is owed by me to you.

And for the solution of these doubts, I suppose that in the proposition "A horse is owed by me to you," the expression "horse" is not confused, but stands determinately, for no cause of confusion precedes it.[25] Similarly, I suppose that it does not connote determinately and precisely the reasons for which this name "horse" is imposed. And it is not placed after the verb "owe," but before it, so that verb does not effect such connotation in it. Thus, also I posit that there neither are nor could be any horses other than Brunellus, Morellus, and Favellus, so that if one must argue inductively, it is sufficient to take account of these three. For in a proposition, it is the same as if there were or could be an infinite number. Although there should be an infinite number, still an induction taking account of three or two would be sufficient, with the clause "and so of singulars." And then supposing these, I posit this conclusion, that if this is true: "A horse is owed by me to you," this disjunctive is also true: "Morellus is owed by me to you, or Favellus is owed by me to you, or Brunellus is owed by me to you." For one is permitted to descend disjunctively under a common term standing determinately and not connoting precisely any reason.

A second conclusion is that if this is true: "A horse is owed by me to you," it is necessary for one of these three to be true: "Brunellus is owed by me to you," "Favellus is owed by me to you" or "Morellus is owed by me to you." For the disjunctive followed from these, which cannot be true unless some part of it is true.

A third conclusion is that if some one of these is true, any one is true, and if some one of these is false, any one of them is false, since

[25] Concerning these types of supposition, see above pp. 35–40.

there is no more reason for one of them than for another, by the case. Thus, none is true or any one is true.

Thus also, it is fourthly concluded that in the aforesaid case, it follows that if a horse is owed by me, then every horse is owed by me, and if a horse is not owed by me, then no horse is owed by me.

Hence, fifthly, I conclude that in the given case, it is necessary that one of these universals be true, namely, that every horse is owed by me to you or that no horse is owed by me to you. This is proved, because these are subcontraries or have the laws of subcontraries: "A horse is owed by me" and "A horse is not owed by me." Thus, both cannot be false, so one of them is true. And in the fourth conclusion immediately preceding this, it is said that from each of these, there follows its universal. Thus, it is necessary that one of those universals be true. And then there remains the doubt as to which of these is true —namely, "Every horse is owed by me to you" or "No horse is owed by me to you."

And concerning this, there is to be drawn a conclusion. The sixth conclusion is that in the given case, it follows that if no horse is owed by me to you, then nothing is owed by me to you, since nothing was promised by me to you except a horse. And it seems that I owe you a horse more than anything else. And if nothing else is owed by me, then it follows that nothing is owed by me. Hence, one must concede that nothing is owed by me to you, or that every horse is owed by me to you. Now it is to be seen which of these is true.

And it is argued that this is true: "Every horse is owed by me to you," since all that is owed by me which I pay to give satisfaction and to be freed from debt. But if I hand this horse over to you, I would be free from debt. Therefore, the first one was owed by me, and so of the others for the same reason. Hence, every horse was owed by me to you.

Likewise, whoever owes and says that nothing is owed by him clearly denies the debt, since the negation precedes this verb "to owe." But inconsistent and unfaithful is it for the debtor that he denies the debt. Therefore, it is not to be said that nothing is owed by him. And if this is not to be said, one must concede the other part, namely, that every horse is owed by him. Hence, every horse is owed by him.

Likewise, in the earlier sophisms, it was said to be inconsistent to say that someone knows a triangle to have three angles and that no triangle is known by him to have three angles. Hence, it is inconsistent to say that someone owes a horse and that no horse is owed by him. Likewise, if the creditor confessed before a judge that I owed him nothing, the judge would free me. Hence it would be very hard for the creditor, and the debtor would be absolved, without paying anything. Thus, it is not to be said that nothing is owed by me.

The opposite is argued, because the debtor is not freed from the debt if he does not pay all that which he owes, even if he should pay the major part. Therefore, if every horse should be owned by me, I could not be absolved unless every horse was paid by me, which is not true. So not every horse is owed by me to you.

Again, if every horse were owed by me to you, then the king's horse would be owed by me, which is false, since I have not obligated myself to pay that, and the judge would call you foolish if, because of such a promise, you should demand from me the king's horse.

Again, in the proposition "I owe you a horse," this term "horse" is confused without distribution, and in "A horse is owed by me," "horse" stands determinately. In no way is it a valid consequence from a term standing confusedly to the same standing determinately, unless the confusion is removed, as has been said elsewhere.[26]

Likewise, whether there were confusion or not, still it was said that from a non-distributive a distributive does not follow. But in this: "I owe you a horse," there is not anything distributive, and in this: "Every horse is owed by me to you," there is something distributive. Therefore, it does not follow: a horse is owed by me, so every horse is owed by me.

Likewise, if every horse were owed by me to you, then Morellus would be owed by me, and Favellus. Therefore, two would be owed by me, which is false, since in fact the obligation was made for one only.

It is to be known that some, wanting to escape, say that it is not properly said "I owe you a horse" or "A horse is owed by me to you," but this expression is taken in this sense: "I owe or am bound to pay to you, so that from me you would have one horse." And so this proposition "I owe you a horse" or "A horse is owed by me to you" is neither true nor false, except in this sense.

But this solution seems to me superfluous, since there can be many ways to pay. For one way to pay would be to give you Morellus,

[26] See the fourth remark of Chapter III.

another would be to give you Favellus. Thus, there is a genuine doubt as to whether I am bound to pay all or none. Likewise, although a chimera cannot be seen nor an eclipse destroyed, yet these are acceptable grammatically: "A chimera is seen by me" or "An eclipse is destroyed by me," so it is necessary for any one of them to be true or false, as is stated; therefore, it is similar concerning this: "I owe a horse," even though it would not be possible to owe a horse.

And so others concede this: "I owe a horse" or "I owe something"; but they deny this: "A horse is owed by me" or "Something is owed by me," because of the reasons given.

But it seems that it must be said that every horse is owed by me to you. For it appears to me that I could satisfy the debt only by paying that which I owe. And yet I could satisfy the debt by paying Morellus; hence, Morellus was owed by me; and so of Favellus. But I do not believe that this is to be conceded: "I owed Morellus or also every horse," since I was not obligated for this. And yet these propositions signify this because of the reasons for the connotation of the term after the verb.

Concerning the arguments in opposition. To the first, I deny that I must pay all that which I owe, but it suffices that I pay something or some things which are suitable to the terms according to which the debt was contracted. For example, if I owe five solids, it is not sufficient to pay only four solids, for they are not five solids, although they are parts of five solids.

To the other, I say that the king's horse is owed by me and to pay the king's horse I have obligated myself. Thus, if I should buy that horse or if it should be given to me and I should pay, I would be freed. But neither do I owe the king's horse, nor am I obligated to pay the king's horse, nor can you demand the king's horse, except in disjunction with others; for I have not promised that to you according to the reason for which it is called the king's horse, but according to the indeterminate and confused concept of this term "horse."

To the other, I say that there is not here such confusion as there would be for the distribution of a term preceding the verb, but the confusion is such that it is not allowed to descend from a term occurring after the verb. Nor is it permissible to change the term, due to the fact that it connotes its reason. Yet it is permissible to change it when it occurs before the verb. Thus, from a confused term after the verb, there can follow a non-confused before the verb, although it is not so concerning confusion by distribution.

To the other, I say that sometimes from a non-distributive, there follows the same with distributive [supposition], due to its matter, because there is no more reason for one than for the other. For example, it follows: some man is, so every man is. And if I say "B runs," it follows that if "B" stands for something, then every B is stood for by "B." Yet it does not follows that it stands for all B, for this would signify that it stands distributively, since this verb "stands" makes terms connote their reasons.

To the other, I say that I do not owe two, but two are owed by me, not taking "two" collectively, but distributively, *i.e.*, either of these two.

CHAPTER V
ON AMPLIATION

The fifth chapter will be about ampliations and restrictions of supposition,[1] about which must be presupposed what was said in the *Summula*, in the chapter on suppositions.[2] And now concerning this some easy sophisms are formed.

Sophisms

(1) *Some horse does not exist.*

It is proved, since nothing which is corrupted exists, but some horse is corrupted; hence, some horse does not exist. The manner of arguing is valid and formal in the fourth mood of the first figure. The major is true, because corruption is a change from being to non-being, and what is corrupted does not return as numerically the same, as is clear in the second of *De Generatione*.[3] Also it is clear because every horse that dies is corrupted by dying, since its form is withdrawn from material potency. But many horses have died and are dead. Therefore, not only is some horse corrupted, but many. Similarly, concerning generation, since nothing which is going to be generated exists and some horse is going to be generated, namely, that which will be generated tomorrow; therefore.

The opposite is argued, because the opposite of the sophism is true, since every horse exists, as is clear by induction. Thus, the sophism is false.

I answer that the sophism is false. And I say that the form of arguing is not valid. For from the ampliated supposition of a term

[1] On the doctrine of ampliation, see above pp. 32–34.
[2] *Summula de Dialectica*, Tract IV.
[3] Aristotle, *De Generatione et Corruptione* ii. 11. 338b 6–20.

without distribution, there does not follow that term with a less ampliated supposition. But in the second premiss "Some horse is corrupted," the term "horse" is ampliated to stand for the past, because the predicate "corrupted" is of past tense, and in the conclusion, it is not thus ampliated. And so similarly, in the second premiss—"Some horse is going to be generated" or "will be generated"—the term "horse" is ampliated to stand for the future, and it is not so ampliated in the conclusion.

But one must be careful about the proposition "Nothing dead is," [4] since it can be distinguished. For this whole phrase "dead is" could be one expression, namely, a verb of past perfect tense. And then only the expression "nothing," as a neuter substantive, would be the subject, and the proposition would be false, since it would be the equivalent of the proposition "Nothing is dead." [5] In another way, the whole phrase "dead is" can be two expressions, namely, "is," a verb of present tense, and "dead," a participle. And then "dead" would be the subject of the proposition, and the proposition would have to be conceded.

(2) *No man is dead.*

This is proved by induction for all men. Likewise, by a syllogism in the first mood of the second figure: no [dead thing] is an animal, and every man is an animal, so no man is dead. Similarly, in the third figure by a syllogism concluding the impossible: every man is an animal, a certain man is dead, so a certain dead [thing] is an animal. The conclusion is false, so one premiss is false; but not the major; so the minor.

The opposite is argued, because the contradictory of the sophism is true, namely, "Some man is dead." Indeed, many are dead; hence, etc.

I answer that the sophism is false, and your induction is insufficient if it takes into account only men who are. Rather, all who have been ought to be taken into account, because the subject of the sophism is ampliated to the past by the predicate "dead."

Similarly, the syllogism in the second figure is not valid, for "man" in the minor premiss was not ampliated, and in the conclusion

[4] *Nullum mortuum est.*
[5] *Nihil est mortuum.*

it is ampliated and distributed. But from a less ampliated there does not follow a more ampliated with a distribution of the more ampliated. For example, it does not follow: every man runs, so every animal runs. Similarly, the syllogism in the third figure is not valid, since the middle term "man" in the major premiss is distributed under a lesser ampliation, since it is only of the present; and in the minor, it had a greater ampliation, since it was ampliated to the past. Thus, the minor could have been true for some past time and not for the present, since it did not fall under the distribution of the major. And so the connection of the extremes by the middle was for none of the same things.

And from the solutions of those two sophisms, it is to be concluded correlatively, that the aforesaid ways of syllogizing in the first, second, and third figures are not formal. For they do not hold for any propositional content, although they would hold always where there is no ampliation. Even this conclusion about the Holy Trinity, which is also in the first mood of the first figure, would not be valid under this form of syllogizing: every God is the Son, every Father of God is God, so every Father of God is the Son. But for the construction of those formal syllogisms, it is necessary to form propositions with the addition "which is." For example, all which is B is A, and all which is C is B, so all which is C is A. But if this syllogism were valid about divine things, then, for example, this syllogism would be valid: all which is God is the Son, all which is the Father of God is God, so all which is the Father of God is the Son. But some denied the conclusion, since they deny the major, and others concede the major, the conclusion, and the whole, since the expression "which is" is a substantive in neuter gender and is a substantial and not a personal term. But I offer no opinion about this and leave the whole thing to our doctors of sacred theology.

(3) *Antichrist is.*

It is proved, because Antichrist is intelligible, so Antichrist is. The antecedent is clear, because "intelligible" and "can be understood" signify the same. And this is true: "Antichrist can be understood," since he could be signified by this name "Antichrist." Thus, this is true: "Antichrist is intelligible." But the consequent is also clear by the argument from a part of a whole, in a way, to its whole. Nor could anyone deny that argument in the proposed case on the ground that there is a limiting determination. Since nothing is limited by reason of its being intelligible.[6] For God Himself is most intelligible. And the argument from the part to the whole would not seem to be hindered except by a limiting determination, since it is limited by reason of that which is attached to it, as is commonly said. For example, I argue: Socrates is a dead man, so Socrates is a man, or: Antichrist is in potency, so Antichrist is. The antecedent is commonly conceded. The consequent is clear, because if I say "Antichrist is in potency," then I ask concerning that potency whether it is something or nothing. If it is something, then Antichrist is in something, so he is. And if that potency is nothing, then it is the same to say "Antichrist is in potency" as to say "Aristotle is in a chimera" or "Antichrist is in nothing"; and to say this is absurd. Again, Antichrist is generable, so by conversion, the generable is Antichrist, from which it follows that Antichrist is, since the predicate connoted its reason as applicable for the time of the verb.

I answer that the sophism is false. And then concerning the first proof, I concede that Antichrist is intelligible. But it does not follow that Antichrist is, since this predicate "intelligible" is a name of a potency and so stands for that which can be but is not. And so the subject and predicate do indeed stand for the same, so the proposition is true. But in the proposition "Antichrist is," the subject stands for nothing, since the predicate does not permit it to stand for things which are not. So the proposition is false.

But there is an objection, because there is not a limiting determination which could hinder the argument from the whole. Likewise, if the consequence should be hindered, it would be because of the ampliation. But there is no ampliation, since the subject is a singular term, whose supposition cannot be ampliated, since it can stand for one only.

To the first objection, it is to be said that not only a limiting determination, but also the ampliation of the conclusion hinders the consequence, as a process from an ampliated term without distribution to a less ampliated term. But to the second objection I concede that there is not here properly an ampliation of the term "Antichrist," nor is the process from greater to lesser ampliation. Rather, what is worse, it is a process from a term standing for something to a term standing for nothing.

[6] That is, intelligibility is not a predicate.

Concerning the other, I agree that Antichrist is in potency, only in the sense that Antichrist can be, and not because he is in something which is called potency. Thus, this is not a proper expression.

Concerning the last, I say that it is not valid to convert "Antichrist is generable" to "The generable is Antichrist," since in the antecedent the term "Antichrist" is permitted to stand for things which can be and are not, but in the consequent it is not so permitted. Rather, it must be converted thus: "Therefore, the generable is or can be Antichrist." And the proposition "Antichrist will be generated" ought to be converted to "What will be generated is or will be Antichrist." So also: a horse is dead, so a dead thing is or was a horse.

(4) *Every old horse is going to die.*

I posit that there neither are nor will be other than two horses, that are or will be Favellus and Morellus, and that both of them are young, but will grow old and then are going to die. And it is posited with this that God miraculously will conserve all other things eternally, and that also nothing else will grow old or die.

And then the sophism is proved, since all which is or will be an old horse is going to die, as is clear by the case. Therefore, every old horse is going to die. And the conclusion is apparent from the relation of an equivalent to an equivalent.

The opposite is argued, because every horse that is going to die is young, as is clear by the case, and every old horse is a horse that is going to die, as is posited in the case. Therefore, every old horse is young. This is a syllogism in the first mood of the first figure. And yet the conclusion is false and impossible. Therefore, one of the premisses is false, and not the major, since it agrees with the case. Therefore, the minor, which is the sophism, is false.

It is answered that the sophism, in the case posited, is true. Nor is your argument valid, since it removes the reason of the connotation. For this term "old horse" in the minor proposition connotes oldness disjunctively for present and future times, and in the conclusion, only for the present. Thus, it proceeds from a disjunction to a part of it, which is not a valid consequence. So a corollary is inferred, just as previously it was inferred, that those kinds of syllogizing are not formal, unless the propositions are formed with the addition "which is."

(5) *The corrupt is to be generated, and that which is to be generated is the corrupt.*

It is proved, since the predicate which is "to be generated," since it is of future tense, ampliated its subject to stand for the future. Thus, the proposition "The corrupt is to be generated" is equivalent to this one: "What is or will be corrupt is to be generated." And this is true by the second part of the disjunctive. For something will be corrupt which is to be generated, such as a horse which will be generated tomorrow. Therefore, the sophism is true. And similarly, it is argued that this is true: "That which is to be generated is the corrupt," since because of ampliation, it is equivalent to this: "That which is or was to be generated is corrupt," which is true of Aristotle's horse. For it was to be generated and yet it is corrupt.

But the opposite seems to have been determined by Aristotle at the end of the second of *De Generatione*, for it is impossible, as he says, for the corrupt to be restored as the same numerically.[7] And yet it would be restored if it were generated. So the sophism is false. Again, nothing which is corrupt is to be generated, but every corrupt thing is corrupt; hence, no corrupt thing is to be generated. And again, this term "to be generated" stands only for what is to be generated, and this term "corrupt" only for the corrupt. And no one thing is both to be generated and corrupt. Therefore, in the given sophism, the terms do not stand for the same. Thus, it is false, since the proposition is affirmative. Also, in the given proposition "The corrupt is to be generated," this term "to be generated" stands only for future things, which neither are yet nor have been. And this term "corrupt" does stand only for those which have been, since it is a participle of past tense. Thus, the terms do not stand for the same. So it is concluded as before.

I answer that the sophism is true and well-proved. Concerning the first argument for the opposite, I say that this proposition "The corrupt can be generated" is true, since what is or can be corrupt can be generated. And so also it is true that the corrupt will be generated, because what is or will be corrupt will be generated. But these are false: "The corrupt will be regenerated" or "The corrupt can be regenerated" or "The corrupt is to be regenerated," because they sig-

[7] Aristotle, *De Generatione et Corruptione* ii. 11. 338b 12–20.

nify that after something has been generated, the same thing could be regenerated, which is impossible in nature. And this is what Aristotle said about recurrences.[8]

Concerning the second [argument for the opposite], I agree that this is true: "Nothing which is corrupt is to be generated," since that first "is" prohibits the ampliation of this term "corrupt" to the future. And I concede also the minor, since every corrupt thing is corrupt. But the conclusion is badly inferred, for it ought to be inferred, by the requirement of the major, with the addition "which is"—namely, "Nothing which is corrupt is to be generated."

Concerning the other [argument for the opposite], I say that in the given sophism, it is true that the term "corrupt" stands only for the corrupt, but this is with ampliation to the future, that is, for those which are or will be corrupt. Hence, it is to be noted that this does not follow: it stands only for the corrupt, so it stands only for those that are corrupt. In the same way, it also does not follow that it stands only for men, so it stands only for those who are men. For just as these terms "to understand" and "to signify" ampliate to past, possible and future, so also this term "to stand."

Concerning the other [argument for the opposite], I say in the same way that this term "corrupt," because of ampliation, not only stands for those who are and have been but also for those who will be and have not been yet, because of the fact that they will be corrupt. But you say "How then will the mode of signifying of the term "corrupt," which is of past tense, be saved?" I say that it will indeed be saved, since the future things for which it stands will then be past, when they will be corrupt. Thus, if I say "Aristotle was to be generated," the term "to be generated," which is of future tense, retains its signification, since in the time signified by this verb "was," Aristotle was still in the future.

(6) *Young Socrates was going to argue.*

The case is posited that Socrates who was young is now old and that he has never argued nor does he now argue, but tomorrow he will argue.

Then it is proved, since due to the ampliation of the subject, the sophism is equivalent to this proposition "Whoever is or was young Socrates was going to argue"; and this is true.

[8] *reiteratione.*

The opposite is argued, since whoever has been going to argue either argues or will argue or has argued. Young Socrates has been going to argue. Hence, young Socrates argues or will argue. The process is valid and the conclusion is false, so one premiss is false, and not the major; so the minor, which is the sophism, is false. I now prove that the conclusion is false, since it is false by the case, that he argues. But it is also false that young Socrates will argue, since it is equivalent to the proposition "Whoever is or will be young Socrates will argue," which is wholly false, as is clear by the case.

I answer that the sophism is true. But in order to disprove it, some say that that syllogism is not valid, since under this distributive "whoever," which is a substantive distributive, the term is taken with another predicate, which is inconsistent where there is ampliation. Yet subject to better judgment, I believe that that process as it concerns a syllogism is valid, because under substantive distribution, it is permissible to take any term whatever subjectively, whether it is ampliated or not, so long as there is not a different ampliation in the premisses and in the conclusion. For example, it does not follow: whatever I saw I see, and I saw white, so I see white. For in the conclusion, the ampliation is removed. But this does indeed follow: whatever I saw I ate, and I saw a white [thing], so I ate a white [thing]. For in the conclusion, the ampliation is not changed.

Because of this, it is to be known that in the proposition "Young Socrates was going to argue," the subject is ampliated to past and future. I say "to past" because of the verb "was," and I say "to future" because of the participle "going to argue." Thus, this proposition is equivalent to this: "Whoever is or was or will be young Socrates was going to argue." And so also in the major the term "whoever" is ampliated to past and to future; and in the conclusion "Young Socrates has argued or will argue," the subject is ampliated to past and future, because of the verbs "has argued" and "will argue." Thus, this conclusion is equivalent to this: "Whoever is or was or will be young Socrates argues, will argue or has argued." And this is true and the whole syllogism is valid. It is to be noted that the conclusion is a categorical with a disjunctive predicate. But this disjunctive is false: "Young Socrates argues or young Socrates has argued or young Socrates will argue." For none of the categoricals of that disjunctive retains the ampliation which was in the premisses. For one excludes ampliation from the future and another excludes ampliation from the past and the third from both. But if in that categorical of the future, you should place the ampliation which was in the premisses, it would be true, namely, this: "Whoever is or has been or will be young Socrates will argue."

(7) *Non-being is known.*

I posit that the proposition is an affirmative with an infinite subject.

Then the sophism is proved, because such infinite terms are resolved in this way. For it is the same to say "non-man runs" as to say "what is not a man runs." [9] And one states an equivalence in saying "non-being is known" and in saying "what is not being is known." But the second of these is true, since Antichrist, who is not a being, is known.

The opposite is argued, because the term "non-being" stands for nothing, and yet an affirmative proposition is false if the subject stands for nothing; therefore.

I answer that the sophism is false, since this term "non-being" stands for nothing. This is clear, since the verb "to know" or "I know" is ampliative of supposition to past and future, indeed, also to every possible thing. Thus, if I say "non-being is known," this name "being" stands indifferently for every being, present, past or future or possible. But the rule is that a negating infinite added to some term prevents its standing for all that for which it stood and makes it stand for all that for which it did not stand, if there is any such. So in the proposition "Non-being is known," this term "non-being" stands for nothing present, past, or future or possible. So it stands for nothing, and the proposition is false. And I say that those two sentences are not equivalent: "Non-being is known" and "What is not being is known," because by the verb "is," you restrict the infinite term to the present. Thus, there remains supposition for past and future, and so this is to be conceded: "What is not being is known." Therefore, if by resolution we want to give an equivalent to "Non-being is known," it is "What is not nor has been nor can be being is known"; and this is false, as was the sophism. The same sort of thing would be said about the proposition "Non-being will be." For it is false and yet this is true: "What is not being will be."

[9] *quod non est homo currit.*

But against this conclusion, there is a strong objection, because in this proposition "What is not being is known" or also "What is not being will be," this verb "is" restricts the term "what,"[10] so that it stands only for those that are. Furthermore, concerning all such, it is false to say that it is not being. Thus, this whole subject "what is not being" implies a contradiction. So it stands for nothing, just as this whole expression "man who is not man," stands for nothing. Likewise, also, "something which is not being" stands for nothing. And since it is the same to say "What is not being" and "Something which is not being," so this is false: "What is not being is known" or "What is not being will be." For the subject stands for nothing.

Then I say to this, as before, that these are true. Because of this, it is to be known that such propositions or such a proposition is not completed except through that which is known, namely, "What is not will be" or "What will not be is known." There are two reasons for this. The first is because this relative "what" is here placed without an antecedent. The second is because there are here two verbs, on account of which the single nominative cannot determine that for which the subject stands. Thus, it is necessary to add "What is not will be," that is, "Something which[11] is not will be." For in this proposition, the term "something" is not construed with the verb "is" but with the verb "will be." So it is not restricted to the present but is ampliated to the future. Moreover, although this relative "which"[12] is construed with the verb "is," yet it is not thereby restricted to the present, for the condition of a relative is that it stands just as its antecedent does. So this whole subject "something which is not being" does indeed stand for something not present, but future. Thus, the proposition will be true. And so also it should be said that this is true: "A man who is not a man will be," or "A man who is not a man is known," since that term "man" stands for future men who are not.

(8) *Everything which will be is (Or: Everything which will be being is being).*

It is proved from the preceding, for this expression "everything" is not construed with "will be" but with "is." Therefore, it is restricted

[10] *quod.*
[11] *Aliquid quod.*
[12] *quod.*

to the present and not ampliated to the future. And so also this relative "which" stands in the same way. So this whole subject "everything which will be" stands only for those who will be and are. For concerning every such it is true to say that it is. So this is true: "Everything which will be is." And it could be similarly argued that this is true: "Everything which can be is."

The opposite is argued, since something will be, such as Antichrist, which, however, is not yet. Therefore, not everything which will be is. Likewise, if everything which will be is, and Antichrist will be, then Antichrist is. The conclusion is false, so one premiss must be false, and not the minor, so the major, which is the sophism. Likewise, these are seen to be equivalent: "Whatever will be is" and "Everything which will be is." But the first cannot be conceded as true, so neither can the second.

I answer that the sophism is true, and yet this is false: "Whatever will be is." For they differ very much, since the expression "whatever" is construed with this verb "will be"; and it is necessary to understand a relative which is construed with "is"—namely, saying "whatever will be, it is." And so this term "whatever" is ampliated to the future, and consequently, so is the relative, namely, the expression "it." And so the objection concerning all future things that are not yet is against the proposition "Whatever will be is." But the converse is [asserted] in this proposition "Everything which will be is," for "everything" is construed with this verb "is" and it is restricted to those which are, and every such thing is. Thus, everything which will be is. And so it is concluded that all such as the following are true: "Everything which has been is" and "Everything which can be is." But these are false: "Whatever has been is" or "Whatever can be is." And since by not considering carefully the diversity of expression, the latter seem to be equivalent to the former, so at first glance, the former appear to be false, just as the latter. And similarly, in particular propositions, I say that this is true: "Something will be which is not," and this is false: "Something which will be is not."

Concerning the arguments for the opposite. To the first, it is said that I concede the antecedent, namely, "Something will be which is not yet"; and I deny the consequent. Rather, it ought to be concluded: "Hence, not whatever will be is." [13]

[13] *non quicquid erit ipsum est.*

To the other [argument], I say that the syllogism is not valid, since you do not take the minor under the distribution of the major. For in the minor you take distribution for the future, because of the ampliation. And in the major, there was distribution only for the present. But if in the minor, you were to say "I am restricting to the present the [statement] that Antichrist is what will be," then the syllogism is concluded of necessity. But in fact the minor is false.

Concerning the last argument, it is said that those propositions are not equipollent.

(9) *"Man" and "risible" are convertible.*

It is proved, because "risible" is imposed on a quality [14] proper to man, and a proper quality is convertible with the subject of which it is a proper quality.

The opposite is argued, because it is true to call certain things risible which it is not true to call men. Hence, they are not convertible. The consequence is clearly valid. And the antecedent is clear, for "risible" is the name of a potency, since it signifies the same as "possible to laugh"; so it ampliates supposition to those that can be and are not. Thus, Antichrist is risible, because he can laugh. Indeed, many times he will in fact laugh, which could not be if he were not able to laugh. And so this term "risible" can be predicated of Antichrist and of all men who will be generated, since every man who will be generated is risible. But of none can this term "man" be predicated, since no man who will be generated is presently a man.

I respond by conclusions: The first is that terms are not said to be convertible on the ground that each can be universally affirmed of the other, by means of this verb "is," without any further addition. For although every man is risible, yet not every risible thing is a man, since it could be argued thus: Antichrist is risible and yet he is not a man.

But some object, because it seems that this is true: "Every risible [thing] is a man," because "risible" is restricted by the verb "is" to stand only for those things which are. Hence, to say "Every risible [thing] is a man" is equivalent to saying "Every risible [thing] which is is a man." But this second is true, so the first is true.

It is answered that a past participle which is the subject in a proposition cannot be restricted by the copula or the predicate of the

[14] *passio.*

proposition so as not to stand for the past. For it does not lose its mode of signifying because of the copula or predicate. So also neither is the name of a potency thus restricted, so that it does not stand for things which can be but are not. Nevertheless, any term can be restricted by a determination attached to it. For example, if I say "A white man runs," "man" does not stand for all men, but only for those who are white. Similarly, if I say "The man who ran yesterday is eating," "man," with the addition, does not stand for all men, but only for those who ran yesterday. Also, it is to be said that in the proposition "The risible which is is man," "risible" is restricted by this determination "which is" adjoined to it, and it is not so restricted in this proposition "The risible is man."

The second conclusion is that these terms are convertible (each can be universally predicated of the other), with this addition "which is"; because by that addition the supposition of "risible" is removed, in so far as it exceeded the supposition of "man." For example, every risible [thing] which is is man, and every man who is is risible.

The third conclusion is that these terms also would be convertible with this addition "which has been," with respect to the verb "has been," and with the addition "which will be," with respect to the verb "will be," and with "which can be," with respect to the verb "can be." For example, every risible [thing] which has been has been a man, and conversely, every risible [thing] which will be will be a man, and every risible [thing] which can be can be a man, and conversely.

The fourth conclusion is that just as something is risible which is not a man, so there has been something risible which has not been a man, and something will be risible which will not be a man. But whatever can be risible can be a man. And this fourth conclusion is clear, since however much "risible" is ampliated, so much is "man" ampliated, by this verb "can." But the first and second are clear because Antichrist is risible, and he has been risible, and yet neither is he a man nor has he been a man. The third clause is also clear by this, that many men can be created, who will never be created, and just as those can be, so they can laugh. Thus, they are risible and they also will be risible, since it is not necessary that tomorrow the possibility of their creation cease. Therefore, those will be risible and they will never be men.

The fifth conclusion is that these are true: "Everything which is risible is a man," "Everything which has been risible has been a man" and "Everything which will be risible will be a man." But this is not so of "whatever." And these appear to be clear from the preceding sophism.

(10) *Socrates will die today.*

I posit that for this whole day, or rather, for a whole year after this, he will continue to live in good health.

Then, by the case, it appears that the sophism is false, since by the case, he will die neither today nor tomorrow.

But it is argued that the sophism is true, because the proposition "Socrates will die today" is a proposition of the future. Hence, it is true, if sometime in the future a proposition of the present corresponding to it will be true. And yet it will be so, because I posit that he will die on the first day of next year. And then on that day it will be true to say in the present "Socrates will die today." Therefore, the sophism is true.

I answer that the sophism is false by the case posited, since this term "today" is a term with discrete supposition, standing only for this indicated day, just as "this man" stands only for this man. Hence, it is the same to say "today" and "on this day." Hence, pointing at Socrates, this term "this man" stands for Socrates and it cannot stand for anyone else, by this act of pointing. Thus, it cannot be ampliated by some verb or predicate to stand for another. And so also, indicating this day, the term "today" cannot be ampliated by any verb or predicate, so it could not be taken for another day. But if tomorrow, you should indicate another day by that term "today," then it could stand for another day, just as this vocal term "this man," not indicating Socrates, would stand for someone other than Socrates, whether with respect to a verb of past or future or any other time. But indicating Plato, this term or one like it would then stand for Plato and not for Socrates. And so the argument which held that the sophism is true was not valid, since the supposition of this term is changed according to different indications. Nor is it thus ampliated, because it is a singular term.

CHAPTER VI

ON CONVENTIONAL SIGNIFICATION

The sixth chapter will be about that which words conventionally signify. And concerning this, some sophisms are formed.

A. Sophism

(1) *You will be an ass.*

I prove this, since tomorrow this will be true: "You are an ass." Therefore, today this is true: "You will be an ass." The consequence is held because of the order of present, past, and future times to one another. For what is now present will later be past and was previously future. And also it is thus with propositions. For if it is true that you will run, at some time it will be true that you run.

The antecedent of the first consequence is proved, positing the case that you and others voluntarily change your name, and impose on you the name "ass." Then it appears that tomorrow this will be true and to be agreed to by you: "You are an ass." But that it is permissible to change names in this way appears in many cases. First, of St. Paul, who was first called Saul and later Paul. Second, of the Pope, because when someone becomes Pope, his name is changed voluntarily. Third, because in confirmation the name is sometimes changed. Fourth, because sometimes names signify conventionally and it does not appear that they ought to signify according to the convention of those who are more than of those who were, especially concerning things which are now. Fifth, because every day some impose new names on things in their disputations, as when an acute angle is called A and a straight line is called B.

The opposite is argued, because I believe that you will not concede this, namely, "You will be an ass." For then by the same reasoning, it is valid that every man will be an ass or that God will be unjust. At least, you would have to concede these heretical propositions as possible: "God can be unjust" and "An ass can be God." And you must concede that this is possible: "God will not be God," and even "A chimera will be God." Indeed, in this way, every proposition would be possible or contingent and none would be impossible or necessary.

B. Conclusions

I posit concerning this matter some conclusions.

(1) The *first conclusion* is that according to some language a proposition such as "A man is an ass" can be true, namely, positing that by flood or divine will, the whole Latin language is lost, because all those knowing it are destroyed. And then the new ones following impose by convention this word "man" to signify the same as it now signifies and this word "ass" to signify the same as our word "animal" now signifies. This case is possible. And positing it to be so, nothing impossible should follow. And yet it follows that according to such a language, this spoken proposition "A man is an ass" would be true, since it would signify a mental proposition of the sort that is now signified by us by the proposition "A man is an animal." Thus, it would signify a true mental proposition, and it would indeed be subordinated to that mental proposition. And yet a spoken proposition is said to be true when it is subordinated to a true mental proposition, and false when it is subordinated to a false mental proposition. Therefore, it is not impossible that such a proposition is false.[1]

(2) The *second conclusion* is that it is impossible for the proposition "A man is an ass" or any such to be true, retaining, that is, just those significations which it now has. For it would always signify a false mental proposition just as it now signifies, so it would always be false.

(3) The *third conclusion* is that this proposition "Man is an ass" is an impossible proposition. For if it should be stated now, it would be stated according to the signification which it now has, and according to this, it signifies to us an impossible mental proposition. And yet a vocal or written proposition is said to be impossible if it

[1] *Vera* would have seemed more natural than *falsa*.

designates an impossible mental proposition, or possible if it designates a possible mental proposition, or necessary if it designates a necessary mental proposition. Therefore, that one is absolutely impossible.

(4) The *fourth conclusion* is inferred, that the same written proposition numerically, which is now an impossible proposition, could be a necessary proposition, when this proposition "A man is an ass" is written in stone. This written proposition is now impossible, and yet if that written proposition and that stone endure, the language could change in the way indicated, namely, this term "ass" could signify the same as "animal" now signifies to us. Then that written proposition would be necessary, since it would signify a necessary mental proposition.

(5) The *fifth conclusion* seems to me to follow, that the same or a similar spoken or written expression could be at the same time a true proposition for me and a false one for you. It is proved concerning this proposition "A man is a species." For if you do not take the subject according to material supposition, but according to personal, then it signifies for you a false mental proposition, and so it is false for you. But if I take it according to material supposition, in the way stated by Porphyry,[2] then it signifies for me a true mental proposition, and is thus true for me. Hence, it is not required that propositions be taken always in that sense which would be the more proper way of speaking. But it is often acceptable to take them in some other sense, as has commonly been done by the doctors.

But also in another case more to the point, if it should be written on a wall that a man is an ass, that proposition is false for me, who am of this language, and it is true for you, assuming that you are of some other language, in which this term "ass" signifies exactly the same as that which the term "animal" signifies for us. Still, another case commonly occurs in required disputations in the schools. The master states that for the time of those disputations, this term "ass" signifies for them exactly the same as what the term "animal" signifies for us, according to its common significations. And if the respondent and others agree, then the proposition "A man is an ass" is for them true and to be conceded. And yet without such an obligation, a similar one in wording would normally be false and impossible, even if it should be stated in church by the Blessed Mary.

[2] Porphyry, *Isagoge* 4. 26–27.

(6) The *sixth conclusion* is that a vocal proposition, stated without such an assumption or obligation, ought to be considered true, if according to the signification which it commonly has in the language of those hearing and speaking it, it is true, and false [if under the same conditions], it is false.

C. Solution of First Sophism

And so I reply, concerning the sophism, that it is false. And when it is said that the proposition "You are an ass" will be true tomorrow, I agree, concerning either this proposition or a similar one in wording. But this will not be according to the signification which this term "ass" now has, according to which the sophism is now stated. Thus, it does not follow: hence, you are an ass.

D. Sophisms

(2) *Baf will be baptised.*[3]

I posit the case that this word "baf" is not significant, so that it is not yet imposed to signify anything. But tomorrow this boy will be baptised and the name "baf" will be imposed on him as his proper name.

Then the sophism is proved, since this boy will be baptised tomorrow, and then he will be Baf, so Baf will be baptised. This is apparent by syllogistic demonstration. Likewise, what is or will be Baf will be baptised, so Baf will be baptised. The consequent is clear, because it proceeds from expounding terms to the [expounded] proposition.[4] The antecedent is clear, because, by the case, this boy who tomorrow will be Baf will be baptised.

The opposite is argued, since the proposition, if it is true, ought to be true according to the signification which it actually has when it is stated, and not according to that which it will perhaps have and does not yet have, as was said in the preceding sophism. But "baf" does not now signify this boy, as is clear by the case. Therefore, it is not true for him. But also, it is not true for another. So it is not true.

I answer that no proposition, if its terms are not taken materially,

[3] Reading *baptisabitur* instead of *baptisatur*.

[4] That is, the proposition "Baf will be baptised" is exponible as "What is or will be Baf will be baptised." See above p. 33.

ought to be called true or false, except according to the signification which it and its terms have when it is stated, and not according to a signification which it can have or perhaps will have, but does not yet have. For otherwise, it would be necessary to say that these propositions "God can be unjust" and "A man can be an ass" are true, since the significations of the names can be changed. And to concede this is absurd and heretical. And then I say that if that written expression "baf" stands materially for itself or for its concept, then a spoken or written expression such as "Baf will be baptised" is a manifestly false proposition. But if it is not taken for itself or for something similar, I deny, in the case posited, that this spoken or written expression "Baf will be baptised" is either true or false, since it is neither a proposition nor a sophism. Thus, neither is it a sentence, since a sentence is defined as a conventionally significant expression, whose parts are significant separately. Therefore, when you say "This boy will be Baf tomorrow," I say that if this expression "baf" stands materially, that proposition is to be denied as false. And if it does not stand materially, then that whole expression "This boy will be Baf tomorrow" is neither true nor false, and is to be neither conceded nor denied, just as neither would it be if you were to say "Buf baf," even though part of that expression namely, this part "buf," should be a true proposition—namely, the proposition "This boy will be tomorrow." And the same sort of thing is to be said of this spoken or written expression "What is or will be Baf will be baptised."

But you may have two doubts. The first is whether this proposition "This boy is Baf" will be true tomorrow. The second is that if one says that this boy will be called "Baf" tomorrow, whether this is true.

To the first, I say that a spoken or written expression such as "This boy is Baf" will be true tomorrow if it is spoken or written, or also if what is now spoken or written remains. But it is clear that you will then take this whole expression "This boy is Baf" materially. Similarly, to the second doubt, I say that it could be called true, but also it takes this expression "baf" materially. For to say that this boy will be called Baf is to say that he will be called by his name, namely, by the word "baf." Hence, "baf" thus taken materially is indeed part of a true or false proposition.

But still you will say that Aristotle formed a syllogism concerning this in the first of the *Prior Analytics:* "Every B is A and every C is B, so every C is A." [5] So here is a valid syllogism, and consequently, there are premisses and a conclusion which are true or false propositions, although they are not significant.

It is answered that unless those letters are taken materially for themselves or for their concepts, they are not propositions, properly speaking, and there is no syllogism. But we use such letters to designate that if, in place of those letters, we should substitute significant terms which can serve as subjects and predicates—whatever those terms should be—the syllogism would be valid. And Aristotle means only this, and this is what we should mean.

(3) *This expression "A" is a proposition.*

We posit the case that, for the purpose of a disputation, we grant that this expression signifies for us absolutely and exactly whatever the proposition "A man is running" signifies for us, so that those expressions are taken as synonymous.

Then the sophism is proved: This expression "A man is running" is a proposition, so this expression "A" is a proposition. The consequent is clear, since these expressions "A" and "A man is running" are synonymous and equivalent, as is clear by the case; and whatever is truly said of one equivalent is truly said of the other.

The opposite is argued, since every proposition is a sentence, and this expression "A" is not a sentence, since it does not have separate significant parts. Therefore, it is not a proposition. Likewise, one could ask what its subject is and what its predicate is, and they could not be assigned.

I answer that this expression "A" in the case posited and agreed to could not be the subject of the proposition, just as neither could the expression "A man is running." Hence according to the grammarian, although a sentence of the infinitive mode retains the supposition of the verb exactly, even if taken significatively—as in saying that for Socrates to study is good for him—yet this is not a suitable sentence: "Socrates runs is good for him." Thus, such a sentence is neither true nor false, nor is it a proposition, unless one takes "Socrates runs" materially, in the sense that this sentence "Socrates runs" is a good [sentence]. But then it appears that in the given sophism,

[5] Aristotle, *Prior Analytics* i. 4. 25b 39–40.

"A" was not taken significatively, but materially. In the same way, if we asked whether the expression "A man is running" is a true proposition, it appears that "A man is running" would be here taken materially.

It appears to me, then, that the question concerning the given sophism is the same as if we ask whether a hoop hanging before a tavern is a true proposition. And it seems that it is, since it is equivalent in conventional signification to what is imposed on this expression "Wine is sold here," which someone announces at the door of the tavern. And this is a proposition.

I say, therefore, that if a word or other conventionally instituted sign is called a proposition because it signifies to us a mental proposition, so that nothing more is required, then in the case posited, this expression "A" or a hoop hanging before a tavern or the placing of a finger upon the brow among nuns would be a true proposition (for neither in speech nor writing do nuns communicate with each other). But it is to be said that for a spoken proposition, properly speaking, more is required, namely, that the subject of the mental proposition be signified by one spoken term and the predicate by another, and the complex concept which is the copula by a third, or at least the subject and predicate by one verb. And so I should say that this expression "A" would not be a proposition, nor also a hoop before a tavern. In the same way, although this word "vacuum" and this expression "place not filled with a body" have the same signification within the mind and also as to things conceived, still this expression "place not filled with a body" is called a sentence [6] and not this expression "vacuum."

Then concerning the argument that if expressions are synonymous, whatever is truly predicated of one is also truly predicated of the other: I agree, if they are taken significatively. But if they are taken materially, this is not necessarily true. For example, if "Marcus" and "Tullius" are taken to be synonymous, still it does not follow that if this name "Tullius" has three syllables, then "Marcus" has three syllables.

(4) *It is in our power that a man is an ass.*

It is proved, since you and I shall argue, and then we can use conventional words in whatever way we agree to, as regards their sig-

[6] *oratio.*

nifications. So the disputants often agree that "A" signifies man and "B" ass. Therefore, let us agree that in our disputation, this term "man" signifies for us what this term "whiteness" commonly signifies for others, and this term "ass" signifies for us what this term "color" commonly signifies for others, for this is in our power. Therefore, between us the proposition "A man is an ass" is synonymous with, and for us it makes the same sense as the proposition "Whiteness is a color" makes for others. But the proposition "Whiteness is a color" is for others a true proposition. Hence, the proposition "A man is an ass" is true for us. So this is in our power. But this follows: the proposition "A man is an ass" is true, so a man is an ass; hence, it is in our power that a man is an ass.

And if you say that this is true for us, but the other is true absolutely, then I posit the possible case that there are no men except those who are now in Paris, and that all others are destroyed. Then all can at once agree on the above signification and can teach their children that signification as proper. And so similarly, among all these it will be true that a man is an ass. Then it is argued concerning this as follows: this proposition "A man is an ass" is true, so it follows that a man is an ass. Thus, if it is in one's power that this proposition "A man is an ass" is true, then it is in his power that a man is an ass. But the first is in the power of us who are in Paris; hence, the second.

But the opposite is argued, because by this same argument, it would be in our power that God should not be, nor heaven nor earth, and to say this is absurd and heretical.

It is answered, according to previous statements, that the sophism is false. For when we use these terms "man" and "ass" significatively, we use them according to the significations which they now have. But according to the significations which they now have, this proposition "A man is an ass" is impossible. Hence, it is not possible that a man is an ass. But if we use these terms "man" and "ass" materially, then it is to be conceded that for us it is possible to change their significations and to make a spoken proposition such as "A man is an ass" true. And when you argue that it follows that if "A man is an ass" is true, then a man is an ass, I concede this; but the antecedent is false. But you say that if it is not true, still it could be true. I concede, then, that this is so. And you conclude: therefore, a man can be an ass, or at least this proposition "A man is an ass" is possible. I deny the consequent. For we can change the signification but not the thing signified. Hence, when I say that a man is an ass or a man can be an ass, I use those terms according to the significations which they now have, according to which these or similar propositions cannot be true. Hence, they are absolutely impossible. And although it may follow that a proposition such as "A man is an ass" is true, so a man is an ass, still it does not follow that such will be true, so a man will be an ass. For the signification is not yet changed. And [when it is true], this proposition will not be asserted as having the signification according to which this proposition "A man is an ass" or "A man will be an ass" is now asserted. Indeed, also, I do not agree that this is a good consequence: a proposition such as "A man is an ass" is true, according to the way the words are used; hence, a man is an ass, although this may be true in some other language. And yet this consequence is not valid, because the antecedent employs terms taken significatively in our language, and according to the significations which they have for us. But Aristotle in the *Categories* concedes such a consequence, assuming that the antecedent is true according to the significations according to which the consequent is taken.[7]

(5) *You are an ass or you are not a man.*

I prove this, positing the case that in whatever true proposition "A" is placed, it signifies ass, and so it stands for ass and for nothing else. And in whatever false proposition "A" is placed, it signifies man, so that it stands for man and for nothing else.

Then the sophism is apparent, because either you are A or you are not A. This division is clear by the rule of contradiction. But if you are A, it follows that the proposition "You are A" is true, so you are an ass. And if you are not A, it follows that the proposition "You are A" is false. Thus, this is false: "You are a man." Therefore, you are an ass or you are not a man. Likewise, this proposition "You are A" is either false or true. If it is true, it follows that you are an ass. If it is false, it follows that you are not a man.

The opposite is argued, for since this is a disjunctive, its contradictory is a copulative composed of the opposed contradictory categoricals, namely, "You are not an ass, and you are a man." This is true, so the sophism is false.

It is answered that the sophism is false. For proof, I say briefly

[7] Aristotle, *Categories* 12. 14b 14–22.

that the case is impossible, since it posits that the same term has one signification in one contradictory and another in the other. And this is impossible, because then the contradictories would not be contradictories. And also the case is impossible, because a proposition presupposes the signification of its terms. For it is first required that the terms be imposed to signify before any proposition is formed from them. Thus, it is impossible that due to the position of terms in one proposition or another they should have one or another signification, unless there is a new imposition or there is equivocation. And the case posits the contrary. Thus, it also follows that the sophism is false.

(6) *This can be true: "Man is non-man."*

It is proved, because this term "man" can signify all that is non-man, so that it could stand precisely for all that is non-man. This is possible, because its significations could be changed, so that it could signify precisely as this term "other than man" now signifies. Thus, it would then stand precisely for all that which is non-man, since this term "other than man" so stands. Then since this singular proposition of possibility is true, namely, "This term 'man' can stand for all that which is non-man," I assume that it will be so taken tomorrow. Then this will be true: "This term 'man' stands for all that which is non-man." Hence, taking that term significatively, this will be true: "Man is other than man," since this is affirmative. And by the case, the terms stand for the same, and so it follows that man is non-man, since it is equivalent to "Man is other than man."

The opposite is argued, since it follows: man is non-man, so man is not man, and this is impossible. Indeed, it could not be true, at least retaining the signification of the expression "not" and the expression "is," however the signification of this name "man" might be changed.

It is replied that the sophism is false, at least, that it is not true for any whole time, retaining the significations of these expressions. And now concerning the argument, I say I concede that this expression "man" can stand for all that which is non-man, by a change in its signification. And you say that this could be the case tomorrow. I agree. But I say that its being the case will not be expressed by this proposition "This term 'man' stands for all that which is non-man." For this term "man" in the predicate, taken significatively, has changed its signification. Thus, it does not stand for the same thing for which it stood in the proposition of possibility. Thus, it appears that in expressing the new case, it is necessary in the predicate to change this word "man" to one which would stand for those things for which that word "man" previously stood—for example, by saying that this term "man" stands for all that for which this term "non-man" formerly stood. Or universals could be reduced to singulars, indicating them by the term "man." And this may be sufficient on the sixth sophism.

(7) *You do not know whether a proposition such as "A man is an ass" is true.*

It is proved, because it would be possible that in another language unknown to us the vocal proposition "A man is an ass" could signify absolutely as this sentence "Whiteness is a color" signifies to us. And among them, it would be true, just as among us "Whiteness is a color" is true. Therefore, if you do not know whether it is so, then you do not know whether that is true.

The opposite is argued, for if you do not know whether that is true, you ought not to deny it, but to doubt. And then for the same reason, you ought to deny nothing which is inconsistent.[8]

It is answered briefly that the sophism is true, speaking in such a way. Nevertheless, I do indeed know that this proposition "A man is an ass," when it is stated among us, is false and impossible and not true. For we state it according to a signification such that no such proposition, according to such a signification, can be true. Thus, we ought not to deny this other one proposed to us, but we ought to doubt whether that proposition containing those same words "A man is an ass" is true.

[8] *inconveniens.*

CHAPTER VII
TIME AND TRUTH

The seventh chapter will be about standards by which a proposition is to be understood as true or false. And there are stated some sophisms.

SOPHISMS

(1) *No spoken proposition is true.*

It is proved, because whenever a proposition is not, it is not true; but one never is; hence, one is never true. The minor is proved, because there is never a proposition without a subject, or also without a predicate. Thus, one never is except when its subject and predicate are. But they never are, because when the subject is, the predicate is not yet, and when the predicate is, the subject is no more but has passed; therefore, etc.

The opposite is simply to be conceded.

It is to be noted that Aristotle makes a similar argument in the sixth of the *Physics*, arguing that time is not, since future time is not yet and past time is no more and present time, since there is no indivisible instant, is composed of a past part and a future part, which, as was said, are not.[1] But a whole whose parts are not is not, hence, there is no time. And the Philosopher responds that time is, but not the whole at once, rather in succession, one part after another. And when it is argued that the past is not, nor also the future, I concede, speaking of absolutely past or future time. But the present time is, and it is composed of parts which also are, but not simultaneously, but one first and the other later. Nor is any part of the present time simply past or future, simply speaking of past or future. Rather each

[1] Aristotle, *Physics* vi. 3. 234a 10–25.

part is present, although one is prior and the other posterior. But you will ask how much is, then, the present time, since there is no indivisible instant, according as this is to be supposed and to be declared in the sixth of the *Physics*.[2]

And I say that it is not determined for us how much is the present time which we ought to use as the present. But we are allowed to use as much as we wish, for we call this year present and this day present and this hour present. And if we use this day as the present, then the first hour is and the noon hour is and the vesper hour is, but successively. However, if we use only the noon hour as the present, then we say that the first hour is past and is no more, and the vesper hour is future and is not yet. And this should be more fully explained in the fourth and sixth of the *Physics*.[3]

Therefore, having noted this, it is to be said that the sophism is false. Rather, a spoken proposition and its parts are, but not simultaneously, but the subject first and the predicate later. But if you object that when the subject is the predicate is not, I agree. But it is also true that when the subject is the predicate also is. For here this term "when" is taken indefinitely, and in some time, namely, in this hour, both the subject and the predicate are. Thus, we truly say that when the subject is, the predicate is. But also there is some small part of this hour in which there is the subject and not the predicate. Thus, it is true that when the subject is, the predicate is not. For an indefinite affirmative and an indefinite negative may be true simultaneously. But these universals are denied: "Whenever the subject is not, the predicate is not" and also "Whenever the subject is, the predicate is."

(2) *No one can contradict me concerning any spoken proposition of mine.*

It is proved, because if I say "Socrates is running," you do not know what propostion I shall say until I have spoken. So you do not know how to contradict me as long as I am speaking. Hence, you cannot contradict me until I have spoken, and then you cannot contradict me, because the time is not the same, which is required for contradiction. Indeed, if you say, wishing to contradict me, that Socrates is not running, it may be that I spoke the truth and that you

[2] Aristotle, *Physics* vi. 1. 231b 15–18.
[3] Aristotle, *Physics* vi. 3. 233b 33–234a 5; and *Physics* iv. 13. 222a 10–24.

also speak the truth, since when I spoke, he was running, and when you spoke, he was not running. But a true proposition never contradicts a true one.

The opposite is argued, because to [assert the opposite] would be to affirm the method of refutation.

I say that the sophism is false. And it is not necessary to respond to the argument, as some have said, namely, that you do not contradict in saying that Socrates was not running, but in saying that Socrates was not running when you said he was running. This is not the proper response. For contradictories ought to be of the same subject and of the same predicate and of similar circumstances, both according to the words and according to intent.[4] Thus, it is to be said that according to the intent, I ought to refer the verb of my proposition to the same time to which you referred the verb of your proposition, so that the intent is to deny for the same time for which you affirmed (or conversely), even though that time should coexist with your proposition and not with mine. For I speak according to the intent. And if I should speak of the same time, this is also permissible, since we can agree to the same intent. For so it is often in holy scripture. For we say that Christ is born today or will be born tomorrow, speaking according to intent as if we were in that time in which He was born.

(3) *The proposition "Socrates is sitting" is true at some time, during which entire time, Socrates does not sit.*

This is proved by the determination of the preceding sophism. For I posit the case that you say "Socrates is not sitting" and that you use as the present only that time which coexists with your proposition, and that at that time he was sitting, so that your proposition is false. And that time is called A, and the time immediately following in which I can contradict you is called B. And [I posit] that Socrates exists in that time B and he is not sitting. Thus, I am then contradicting you in that time B. I say that Socrates is sitting, and it is agreed that my proposition is true, since it contradicts yours, which is false. And yet it is true only when it is, and it is in B and not in A. Therefore, in time B, it is true. And yet Socrates is posited to be standing, not sitting, in that entire time B. Thus, the sophism was true.

[4] *intentionem.*

The opposite is argued, because then it would not be a valid consequence that the proposition "Socrates is sitting" is true, so Socrates is sitting. Aristotle states the opposite of this in the chapter of the *Categories* on priorities.[5]

I answer briefly that the sophism is true and well proved. And concerning the authority of Aristotle, I say that it indeed follows that if the proposition "Socrates is sitting" is true, then Socrates is sitting. And yet in the consequent "Socrates is sitting," we take the time consignified by this verb "is sitting" for that time for which the proposition is true and not for that in which it is, unless the former and the latter are the same. Hence, one allows this proposition " 'Socrates is sitting' is true" in time B, yet it was for time A.

(4) *This copulative "Socrates sits and Socrates does not sit" is true.*

It is proved from the preceding, because whenever Socrates stands, he does not then sit. Thus, if this is true: "Socrates sits and Socrates stands," then this is also true: "Socrates sits and Socrates does not sit." But this is true: "Socrates sits and Socrates stands," because since the time which we use for the present is divisible, Socrates sits in the first part of the time and in the latter part he stands. Therefore, he sits and he stands, although earlier and later. Likewise, this is true: "Socrates is sitting and Socrates is non-sitting," although earlier and later. But from the proposition "Socrates is non-sitting," which is affirmative with an infinite predicate, there follows a negative with a finite predicate, namely, "Socrates is not sitting," as is said in the *De Interpretatione*.[6] And this is true: "Socrates is sitting and Socrates is not sitting," which is equivalent to the sophism.

The opposite is argued, because no copulative composed of contradictory categoricals is true, since it is required for one contradictory to be false. But the sophism is of this kind. Hence, it is false.

I say briefly that this is true: "Socrates sits and Socrates stands" and also "Socrates is sitting and Socrates is non-sitting," as is well proved. Indeed, it is necessary so to describe this verb "to be changed," namely, that to be changed is to be one way earlier and another later. For it does not suffice [to say] that is other than it was, since this could signify not to be changed, but to have been changed, nor [to say]

[5] Aristotle, *Categories* 12. 14b 14–18.
[6] Aristotle, *De Interpretatione* 10. 19b 25–29.

that it is other than it will be, since this would signify not to be changed, but to be going to be changed. And yet I say that the sophism is false and impossible.

And I answer the arguments. To the first, I would concede that when Socrates stands he does not sit, because here "when" is taken indefinitely, and so that proposition is the equivalent of "Socrates stands in some time, in which he does not sit," and this is true. But this is to be denied: "Whenever Socrates stands, he does not sit," for it is equivalent to this: "Every time in which Socrates stands, in that [time] he does not sit," and this is false in the case in which we use the entire time as present. Since in the first half he stands, and in the second he sits, there is a certain time in which he sits and he stands. Hence, it does not follow that if he stands, then he does not sit, or also that if he is white, then he is not black or that if a horse is dead, then it is not living. And the reason is that in an affirmative proposition, the verb, with respect to the time which it consignifies, is taken indefinitely. Thus, if in one part of the present time, Socrates sits or is white or is dead, it is simply true to say that he stands or is white or is dead. But in a negative, the verb, with respect to the time it consignifies, is distributed. Thus, if for some part of the present time, someone sits or is black or is alive, then it is false that he does not sit or is not black or is not alive.

In the same way, due to the divisibility of the future, it is true that A will stand and that A will sit, that it will be white and it will be black, that it will be alive and it will be dead. To the other, it is said that it is simply not a good formal consequence [to move] from an affirmative proposition with an infinite predicate to a negative proposition with a finite predicate. For it is manifest that due to the divisibility of the past or the future, it would not hold for things of past or future times; hence, neither would it hold for those of the present, for the same reason. But Aristotle's meaning is that a consequence is valid, whether in things of present time or in those of past or future, on the assumption that that affirmative is true for every time consignified by the verb; otherwise, [it is] not [valid].

(5) *This copulative is true: "Aristotle disputes and Antichrist preaches."*

I prove it, because it is said that we are allowed to use for the present time whatever time we wish. And this is apparent, for since we suppose there to be no indivisible instants, it is clear that it is necessary to use a divisible time as the present, and not the least time according to the sense, as some have said. For then a long proposition would never be true, since it is never wholly in that time, although some small part of it is. Nor is it necessary to use as the present only that time which coexists with the proposition which we utter, for often our propositions are true for a greater or lesser length of time than is the length of time of our utterances, even though our utterances or propositions are of the present. And also in an earlier sophism it was said that we are allowed to use as the present a time other than that in which our proposition is stated. And it is absolutely clear that everyone speaks always using a greater time as present, for we say that one mass is long and another is short, and that summer days are longer than winter days. And Aristotle holds that heavenly motion is perpetual. Thus, if one is so allowed to use a long time as the present, there is no reason why one should not use whatever time one wishes. Therefore, if this is assumed, I posit the case that we wish to use a hundred or a thousand years as the present. And then, according to the aforesaid, each part of it is present. So also, everything is said to be present with which any part of that time coexists. But Aristotle's disputing coexists with one part and Antichrist's preaching with another. Therefore, Aristotle presently disputes and Antichrist presently preaches.

The opposite is argued, because Aristotle does not exist, indeed, he died a long time ago. Hence, how could he dispute? And Antichrist is not yet generated, so how could he preach? For he has neither a tongue to speak nor a voice to shout.

I answer that the sophism is to be conceded, in the case in which we wish to use so much time as the present, which we can reasonably do, as was well argued. But still it is true that, generally speaking, in our daily practice we do not usually use a large time as the present, but a small one, in order to state better the difference between an earlier and a later action, with regard to time. Thus, because of the habit of viewing a short time as the present, it seems to us, at first glance, unnatural to say that Aristotle disputes. Still, using the argument and deciding to use so much time as the present, we ought to concede the sophism and to say also that Aristotle is dead and that he is alive. And so of Antichrist, according to earlier and later. And it is false concerning Antichrist to say that he is not yet generated, that he does not have a tongue. But it is true that he is not generated and does not have a tongue, according to the way he is viewed apart from this sophism.

(6) *In every time Socrates runs.*

I prove it, because only this hour is used as the present. And I posit that in this whole [time] Socrates runs. Then it is argued, because in every present time Socrates runs, so in every time Socrates runs. The antecedent is clear by the case. The consequent is also apparent, because in the given proposition there are given no ampliative terms, so in the given proposition there was not supposition or ampliation except for the present time. Hence, these are equivalent: "In every time Socrates runs" and "In every present time, Socrates runs." Likewise, this sophism is apparent by induction, since in no time which is is an exception found and, according to our purpose, nothing is the case concerning those men who are not. For example, if I say that every man is running, nothing would be the case, according to the purpose, concerning those who have been or will be, if they are not.

The opposite is argued, because it is the same to say that in every time Socrates runs and that Socrates always runs, because this expression "always" does not distribute more than "in every time." But it is not true to say that Socrates always runs, since then both Socrates and his running would be everlasting. Indeed, using only this day for the present, everything which would be for this whole day would be everlasting, for something is called everlasting from its always being. And this seems to be absurd.

I answer that the sophism is true and well proved, in the case posited. But concerning the argument in opposition, it appears to me that we must return to the voluntary signification of this term "always" and this name "everlasting," since names signify by convention. Therefore, if I say that these expressions "in every time" and "always" are synonymous, then it may be conceded that Socrates always runs. But it seems to me that according to common usage, this expression "always" has been imposed to be distributive for every time, present, past, and future, and so the term is ampliative. And it would be the same to say "[something] always runs" as to say "at every time, past, present and future [something] runs, or ran or will run." Or perhaps it can be said that this expression "always" is imposed to be distributive for every time which it is permissible to use for the present time, if the verb is of present tense; and for the past if the verb is of past tense; and so of the future. Or also, [it is distributive] for every time, present, past, or future or possible, if the verb requires this—as for instance, if it is said that something is always known or that God always knows and is known.[7] So that I reduce the whole to the conventional signification of this term "always" and of this term "everlasting."

(7) *The same spoken or written proposition is true or false to all men of the same language, and without any new imposition or requirement.*

I prove it, since I posit that the proposition is written or spoken that Robert is not running. And I posit that Robert at the first hour of this day is not running, but at every other hour of this day, he is running. Also I posit that Socrates uses only the first hour of this day as the present, and Plato uses the whole day as the present. Therefore, that proposition is true according to the use of Socrates and false according to the use of Plato. Hence, it is true and false, since either sense is suitable and neither violates the proper way of speaking.

The opposite is argued, because if any proposition is true, its contradictory is false, and conversely. Hence, if something is true and false, it is necessary that its contradictory be true and false, and consequently, both contradictories would be simultaneously true and false, which is impossible and against the law of contradiction.

I answer briefly that the sophism is true and well proved. And concerning the argument, I say that all contradictory propositions ought to differ in affirmation and negation and in the distribution and non-distribution of common terms. And so if some propositions are contradictories, they ought to be similar also in other respects, and not according to words only, but also more according to intent. And then I say that in the posited case, those propositions "Robert is running" and "Robert is not running" are contradictory for Socrates, and one is true and the other false. Also, they are contradictory for Plato, and one is true and the other false. But the affirmative with Socrates and the negative with Plato are not contradictories, since they differ in

[7] On "to know" as an ampliative verb, see above p. 33.

intent. Thus, it is not inconsistent that an affirmative spoken proposition for this one and a negative for that one are simultaneously true.

(8) *All which is moved was moved previously.*

It is proved by the authority of Aristotle in the sixth of the *Physics*, where it is expressly declared.[8] Indeed, it is also declared that it is necessary for all which is changed to have been changed previously, and for what is to have been made previously, etc.

The opposite is argued by our previous determination, since if this whole day is used as the present, we say that each part of this day is to be called the present and none past or future. But this verb "was moved" is of past tense, and similarly "to have been moved" is of past tense. Thus, concerning none is it true to say that it was moved or has been moved, unless it should be moved in the past. Let us posit, therefore, that A never has been before this day, indeed, it will be generated at the first hour, and also that it will not be after this day, indeed, at the vesper hour, it will be corrupted. And in the noon hour, it is moved. It appears that A is moved and yet it was never moved nor will it be moved, since it never has been and never will be, because by the case, it has been in no past time. And yet it has not been, unless it should have been in past time. And in the same way, it would be argued, since whatever little time we should use as the present, I posit that A could be moved in no such precise time.

The solution seems to me that these names "past" and "future" standing for times are taken sometimes simply and absolutely and other times relatively. Therefore, if it is taken absolutely, then no part of the time which is used as the present should be said to be past or future. For thus no past time is, but it has been and no future is, but it will be. And according to this way of taking "past" and "future," the sophism is false and well disproved. But in another way, "past" and "future" are taken relatively, so that the earlier part of the present time is called past with respect to the later, and the later part is called future with respect to the earlier. This way of taking the terms is customary. For if only the earlier part is used as the present, then the later part will truly be called future, and conversely, the earlier part would be truly called past. And according to this way of taking the terms relatively, the sophism must be conceded, since all

[8] Aristotle, *Physics* vi. 6. 236b 33–34.

which is moved in some whole time is moved also in each of its parts. And so insofar as it is moved in the earlier part, we say that it was moved, and insofar as it is moved in the later part, we say that it will be moved. Thus, all which is moved has been moved previously and will be moved later. And this is what Aristotle intended. And according to this way of taking the terms, these are not denied: "The past is" and "Future time is." And so one usually says that present time is composed of past and future, that is of earlier and later.

(9) *No change is instantaneous.*

I prove it, because every change is either in an indivisible instant or it is in a divisible time. But none is in an indivisible instant, since an indivisible instant cannot be given in time, as is always supposed. Hence, every change is in a divisible time, and every such must be called temporal and not instantaneous.

The opposite is argued, because at least the creation of our intellective soul is instantaneous. For since it is indivisible, it must be made altogether at once, not one part after another. And such creation we call instantaneous. Therefore.

It is to be noted that it does not belong to the logician to determine whether an instant is something and if it is, what thing it is. But we suppose only that there is no indivisible thing in a continuum, which would be the end-point of the continuum, as many have imagined concerning points in lines and instants in times. But still we say that to be instantly created which, after nothing of it was, is altogether at once, so that no part of it is prior to another part in time. And of this sort, the creation of the rational soul is called creation, or instantaneous change. Thus, since our intellective soul is made in this way and every indivisible thing which is made, it is manifest that there is indeed some instantaneous change. So the sophism is false.

But then someone can ask when there is any change and what thing it is. To which I answer, as it pertains to the present business, that such a change is the thing itself which is said to be created. Nor is [what is] to be made [9] other than the making [10] and [what is] made.[11]

[9] *fieri.*
[10] *factio.*
[11] *factum.*

Nor is [what is] to be created [12] other than the creation [13] and [what is] created.[14] Nor in exactly the same way is [what is] to be changed [15] other than the change [16] or [what is] changed.[17] And thus what is to be changed or the change is when something is changed, and the change never is except when something is changed. But indeed, the changed is when the change is not. For these names "changed" and "change" agree in this, that both connote two times—one as that in which a thing is or has been and another as that in which a thing is not or has not been. But they connote these times differently. For the change which is called making connotes both its times by a present mode. Hence, this kind of making is described by this, that there is earlier non-being and later being. But "made" connotes the time in which previously it is not or was not by a past mode. For something is said to be made, because earlier it was not or is not and later it is or will be. Thus, if we use as the present no time in which the thing earlier was not or is not, but only some succeeding time, then we do not say the thing to be made but to have been made. And also if we use only the time preceding the being of the thing as the present, then we say that thing neither to be made nor to have been made, but to be going to be made.[18] And if we use as the present some time composed of that in which it earlier is not and that in which it later is, then we say that thing to be made and also to have been made,[19] by reason of the posteriority of the time, with respect to which we can call the present the past, although absolutely both are called present.

And so this is the end of the seventh chapter.

[12] *creari.*
[13] *creatio.*
[14] *creatum.*
[15] *mutari.*
[16] *mutatio.*
[17] *mutatum.*
[18] *fiendam.*
[19] *factam esse.*

CHAPTER VIII
INSOLUBLES

The eighth chapter will be about propositions having reflection on themselves, due to the significations of their terms, in which chapter are contained the so-called insolubles.[1] And starting from the easier, this sophism is stated:

A. Sophism

(1) *Every proposition is affirmative, so none is negative.*

It is proved, first, by the argument from contraries, for just as it follows that if every man is ill, then no man is healthy, because it is impossible for the same person to be both healthy and ill, so it follows in the proposed [case] that it is impossible for the same proposition to be both affirmative and negative at once.

Likewise, an enthymematic consequence is valid if by the addition of a necessary proposition, one could complete a syllogism of valid form. For by such additions are we accustomed to prove our enthymematic consequences. For example, we say that this consequence is valid: the ass flies, so the ass has wings, because this [proposition] is necessary: "Every flying [thing] has wings." And if it is made the major premiss, the syllogism will be valid in the third mood of the first figure. But so also in the proposed [case], this is necessary: "No affirmative proposition is negative." And if this is made the major premiss in the preceding enthymeme, it will be a valid syllogism in the second mood of the first figure.

Again, from the opposite of the consequent, there follows the opposite of the antecedent. Therefore, the consequence is valid. This rule is not common to every valid consequence. But the antecedent is

[1] On insolubles, see above pp. 49–60.

clear, since it manifestly follows that if a certain proposition is negative, then not every proposition is affirmative.

The opposite is argued, because from a possible proposition there does not follow an impossible. And yet the first proposition is possible, namely, "Every proposition is affirmative." For God could destroy all negatives, leaving the affirmatives. Thus, every proposition would be affirmative. But the other is impossible, namely, "None is negative," for in no case could it be true. For whenever it is not, it is neither true nor false, and whenever it is, then some [proposition] is negative, namely, it. Hence, it is false to say that none is negative.

Likewise, a consequence is not valid, if the antecedent could be true without the truth of the consequent. But so it is in the proposed case, since from the fact that the antecedent could be true and the consequent could not be true, it is apparent that the antecedent could be true without the truth of the consequent. And this is clear also because this is true: "Every proposition is affirmative," granting that God should destroy negatives. And then that consequent would not be true, because it would not be. Hence, it is manifest that the antecedent could be true without the consequent. So the consequence is not valid.

But I answer that a consequence is not said to be valid because the antecedent could not be true without the consequent or without the necessity of the consequent, but because it could not be true without the truth of the consequent formed at the same time as [the antecedent]. But this is not the case in the proposed consequence.

The contrary is argued, because if a consequence were called valid for this reason, it would follow that this consequence would be valid: No proposition is affirmative, so a stick is in the corner, since it is impossible for the antecedent, formed at the same time as the consequent, to be true. And if it could not be true, it follows that it could not be true without the consequent.

Likewise, those are not good consequences in which the consequent, if it should be stated with a true antecedent, would falsify that antecedent. For such a consequent seems to have more conflict,[2] than agreement[3] with such an antecedent. And yet this is so in the proposed case. For positing that this is true: "Every proposition is affirma-

[2] *repugnantiam.*
[3] *convenientiam.*

tive," then if this: "No proposition is negative" should be stated with it, it will be false. Hence, it is not a valid consequence.

I answer that the consequence is valid, as is well proved. But then it is difficult to say whence the consequent ought to be called true or false. And concerning this, I posit briefly some conclusions.

B. Conclusions

(1) The *first conclusion* is that a consequence is valid of which the antecedent could be true without the truth of the consequent and without the consequent. For this consequence is valid: a man runs, so an animal runs, and yet the first could be true although the second should not be true and should be destroyed.

(2) The *second conclusion* is that in a valid consequence, the antecedent could be true and the consequent could be not true. This is clear in the proposed case, for this could be true: "Every proposition is affirmative," and this could not be true: "No proposition is negative." And yet the latter follows from the former. And it must be similar in many other [cases], such as: every syllable is of many letters, so no syllable is of one letter.[4]

(3) The *third conclusion* is that some proposition is possible which could not be true. It is proved, because from a possible antecedent, there never follows an impossible consequent, as I suppose from the first book of the *Prior Analytics*.[5] And yet from this which is possible: "Every proposition is affirmative," there follows this: "No proposition is negative." Hence, this is possible, and yet it could not be true. And so it is manifest that a proposition is not called possible because it can be true, nor impossible because it cannot be true. But it is called possible because as it signifies, so it can be, taking these words in a good sense, according to that use which they were said to have in the second chapter, and impossible when it could not be so, etc.

(4) The *fourth conclusion* is that it is impossible for the antecedent of a valid consequence to be true and the consequent to be false. For thus ought to be understood the statement that a false

[4] *omnis syllaba est plures littere, ergo nulla syllaba est unica littera.*

[5] Aristotle, *Prior Analytics* i. 13. 32a 17–27.

statement cannot follow from a true, as is said in the *Prior Analytics*.[6] And so indeed it is true that of every valid consequence, it is impossible for the antecedent to be true without the truth of the consequent formed at the same time as it. Hence, without denying this, it is to be conceded that from a true proposition, there can follow a false. For we could posit that this proposition is true: "Every proposition is affirmative." Then there could follow from this a false proposition, namely, "None is negative." But when this is concluded, namely, "None is negative," then the first is no longer true, but false.

(5) The *fifth conclusion* is that it is not sufficient for a consequence to be valid that it is impossible for the antecedent to be true without the consequent formed at the same time as it, as has been well argued previously, concerning a stick in the corner. And this is apparent in another example, for it does not follow that no proposition is negative, so no proposition is affirmative. Which should be clear, because from the opposite of the consequent, there does not follow the opposite of the antecedent. And yet the first could not be true without the truth of the second, which could not be true. So more is required, namely, that it could not be as the antecedent signifies, unless it were as is signified by the consequent. But concerning this conclusion, it has been said earlier that these words are not proper, but we use them to convey the meanings otherwise given. For we cannot express in one general statement, concerning all true propositions, why they are true, nor concerning false ones, why they are false, as has been said elsewhere.

C. Solution of Sophism

(1) And by these remarks are solved the arguments refuting the sophism. To the first argument, it is said that this is possible: "No proposition is negative," although it could not be true. To the second, it is clear from the preceding what the answer is. To the third, it is to be said that those propositions are indeed in conflict with regard to being true, but they are not in conflict with regard to the case being as they signify, speaking always in the proper sense. Rather, they are in this way in agreement. For it is necessary that if the case is as the first signifies, so also it is as the second signifies.

[6] Aristotle, *Prior Analytics* ii. 2. 53b 7–8.

D. Sophisms

(2) *No proposition is negative; hence, a certain proposition is negative.*

I prove it, assuming that from any proposition it follows that it is true. This seems to be expressed by Aristotle in the chapter of the *Categories* on the term "prior." [7] For it follows that if man is, then this is true: "Man is," and conversely. And he says the same of others. Then it is argued: it follows that if no proposition is negative, then this is true: "No proposition is negative." And it follows that if this is true, then it is. And it follows that if it is, then some proposition is negative. Hence, it follows, from the first to the last, that if no proposition is negative, then a certain proposition is negative.

Likewise, it is not possible for it to be as the first signifies, unless it is as the second signifies. Hence, the consequence is valid. The consequence seems manifest, because in the preceding sophism, we said a consequence to be valid for this reason, and no other reason could be given why a consequence is called valid. But I prove the antecedent, because it follows that if it is as it signifies, then it signifies, and it follows that if it signifies, then it is; and if it is, then it is as the second proposition signifies.

The opposite is argued by that which was said in the preceding sophism, for it could be as it is signified to be by the first and yet not be as the second signifies. For it could be thus if every negative proposition should be destroyed. Hence, the consequence is not valid.

Likewise, from a possible proposition, its contradictory does not follow. But the first is possible, and its contradictory is the second. Therefore, etc.

I say briefly that the sophism is false, for that was not a valid consequence, as was well proved. And I answer to the first argument that the second proposition, as it is stated, is not true, properly speaking,[8] namely, that from any proposition, it follows that it is true. Thus, it does not follow: man is, so this is true: "Man is." For a man could be, even if there were no proposition. For it is possible for it to be as this proposition "Man is" signifies or could signify, even if the case

[7] Aristotle, *Categories* 12. 14b 14–16.
[8] *de virtute sermonis.*

stated by this proposition "This is true: 'Man is'" were without existence. For it could be as the first signifies, if a man should be and no proposition should be. But you could ask how that rule of Aristotle should be understood. I say that it should be understood as assuming the existence of the proposition, so that from every conjunction composed of some proposition and the statement that it is, it follows that it is true. For example, it follows that if man is and the proposition "Man is" is, then that proposition is true. For it could not be as that copulative signifies unless it were as is signified by the conclusion, speaking always in the proper sense.

Concerning the second argument, which seems to be difficult, I say, first, that a conclusion is never either true or false unless it is. And in order for the conclusion to be valid or true, it is necessary that both its antecedent and consequent are. And then, this rule is given, that the consequence is valid if it is impossible for it to be as is signified by the antecedent, unless it is as is signified by the consequent.

And this rule can be understood in two ways. One way is that it is a proposition of impossibility in the composite sense, in which way it is commonly stated. And the sense is that a consequence is valid if it is impossible to say "It is as is signified by an existing antecedent, and it is not as is signified by an existing consequent." And this rule is not valid, since according to this rule, it would follow that the sophism is true. And the argument proceeded according to this false rule.

In another way, it is understood that it is a proposition of impossibility in the divided sense, so that it has the sense that a consequence is valid if howsoever it is signified by the antecedent, it is impossible that it is so unless howsoever the consequent signifies, so it is. And it appears that it could not be argued by this rule that the sophism is true. For howsoever this signifies: "No proposition is negative," it is possible that it is so, even though it is not as the other signifies, because it would be thus, if, affirmatives remaining, every negative should be destroyed, which is possible.

(3) *If every man runs, then an ass runs.*

The third sophism is determined from the following. And it is this: I posit that every man is an ass. It follows that if every man runs, then an ass runs.

This is proved by syllogizing in the first mood of the first figure, as follows: every man runs, every ass is a man, by the case; hence, an ass runs. Hence, a syllogism to an impossible conclusion could be thus, namely, by taking the position of the opponent with some true proposition. And so we could infer the conclusion by a valid consequence, although that conclusion should be impossible. Thus also, in the proposed case, the consequence is valid. Likewise, as it is stated, it could not be as that antecedent signifies, unless it were as that consequent signifies. Therefore, from that antecedent, with another assumption, there follows that consequent.

The opposite is argued, for the rule is posited in logic that every false consequence is impossible, and every true consequence is necessary. But an impossible proposition cannot be made necessary by positing any case. Hence, whatever case is posited or removed, conceded or not conceded, a false consequence cannot be made true. But it is certain that this consequence is false, for it is not necessary, namely, this: every man runs, so every ass runs. Hence, whatever case is posited, it never follows that every man runs, so an ass runs.

The solution to this sophism is easy. For you voluntarily say or posit or assert whatever proposition you please. And never because of such an act could a necessary consequence be made not necessary, or conversely. Thus, as the sophism is stated, it is false. But still because of the arguments, it is to be known that some proposition can be uttered or posited or conceded simply as a proposition taken by itself. And then nothing follows from this proposition concerning other propositions or consequences, whether they are true or false. In another way, one might posit a proposition as the antecedent or a part of the antecedent, in order to infer something. And then it is indeed necessary to see whether or not the proposed conclusion follows from that statement, together with other statements. For example, in positing, if you should posit simply that every man is an ass, the consequence stated in the sophism is not made better or worse because of this. But if you posit in the manner of an antecedent, in order to infer some other conclusion, that every man is an ass, immediately I say that it does indeed follow that every man is an ass. And if you should propose the aforesaid proposition in the manner of a part of the antecedent, together with this other part "Every man runs," then I say that it does indeed follow: "Hence, an ass runs." And so the arguments proceed.

(4) *I say that a man is an ass.*

And it is asked concerning this sophism whether, in so speaking, one speaks truly or falsely.

And it is argued that one speaks falsely, for one says that a man is an ass and this is false; hence, etc.

But it is argued that he speaks truly, for his whole proposition was this: "I say that a man is an ass," and that was true, since he actually uttered that whole. Likewise, his proposition was affirmative, so it was true, because the subject and the predicate stood for the same thing. Hence, his proposition which he uttered was true. But that the subject and predicate stood for the same thing is clear, for if the copula is explicated, the proposition will be this: "I am saying that a man is an ass," and it is manifest that the term "I" and the term "saying that a man is an ass" stand for the same.

Concerning this sophism, many answer that he speaks both truly and falsely, since he utters the whole proposition "I say that a man is an ass" and this is true; hence, he speaks truly. But in so uttering that whole proposition, he utters each part of it. Hence, he says that a man is an ass, and in this he speaks falsely.

But this solution seems to me very dubious, for this solution supposes that a part of a proposition is a proposition, which I do not believe. The psalmist David, in speaking prophetically by the Holy Spirit, says nothing false, and yet he utters this whole proposition "He begins to say in his heart that God is not." Therefore, the psalmist utters the expression "God is not," and if this should be a proposition, he would be speaking falsely and heretically. Hence, it was not a proposition so expressed, but a part of this proposition. But that foolish one sinned who uttered such an expression alone as a proposition. And similarly, the half of a worm is not an animal, as long as it is part of an animal. But separated from the other part, it is an animal.

And concerning this proposition, I have said enough in the first chapter of the first tract of the *Summula de dialectica*. Therefore, it seems to me that in saying "I say that a man is an ass," one speaks truly, properly speaking. It is to be said also that he does not speak falsely. And when it is objected that he says that a man is an ass, I say that he does indeed utter such an expression, but not alone, as a proposition. Thus, that expression was neither true nor false.

But you reply strongly that from this position, it would follow that one would lie who said that this proposition "A man is an animal" is true. It is proved because his whole proposition is affirmative, and the subject stands for nothing. For this expression "A man is an animal" is not a proposition, but part of a proposition. And so that whole subject "this proposition 'Man is an animal' " stands for nothing, just as it would be if, pointing at a stone, I should say "This man is a substance." The subject would stand for nothing and the proposition would be false.

I answer that one must know what you indicate by the pronoun "this." For if you are indicating this expression "A man is an animal," which you say in your proposition, I say that your proposition is false, as was well argued. But if you should indicate another similar expression, taken and stated in itself, then the proposition would be true and its subject would stand for something, namely, for that expression which is by itself a false proposition. So in this sense, such propositions ought to be understood and conceded, and not in the other sense, except perhaps conditionally, namely, that proposition "Man is an animal" is true, that is, this expression "Man is an animal," if it should be stated by itself, would be a true proposition. And it appears that the whole thing is resolved in the same way.

The fifth sophism is solved in a similar way.

(5) *Whatever Socrates hears Plato says.*

The case is posited that Plato says this proposition "No man is an ass," and Socrates does not hear the first word but hears the rest, namely, "Man is an ass," and he hears nothing else.

Then the sophism is proved, for Socrates hears this expression "Man is an ass" and nothing else. And Plato utters that expression with another expression. Hence, whatever Socrates hears Plato says.

The opposite is argued, for Plato did not speak falsely, but truly. But Socrates heard a false proposition, namely, "Man is an ass." Hence, he hears what Plato does not say.

Likewise, by a syllogism with an impossible conclusion, it is argued thus: whatever Socrates hears Plato says, and Socrates hears a false proposition; hence, Plato says a false proposition. But this conclusion is false, for Plato says a most true proposition, namely, "No man is an ass," and it can be condemned for no falsity.

I answer that the sophism is true. Concerning the arguments for the opposite, I say that Socrates does not hear a true proposition or a false proposition, for he hears no proposition, but he hears only a part of a true proposition. Indeed, I believe that Plato said nothing false, but something true which implies no falsity. Yet he did indeed say something which was not true, namely, part of a true proposition.

But you will say against this that that expression is false which, when heard, causes a false mental proposition in the mind. But that expression which Socrates hears causes in Socrates a false mental proposition, whence Socrates, in the given case, believes that Plato is speaking falsely. Therefore, that expression is false.

I answer that he who speaks truly speaks neither badly nor falsely because of those badly hearing and receiving his proposition. Hence, it is certain that often someone utters a proposition, and another hearing it badly, believes that he utters another. And then that proposition causes in the hearer not the mental proposition which it signifies, but the mental proposition which that proposition which one believes he hears would signify. And in such a case, the spoken proposition is not false for the hearer. But that would be false which he believes he hears. But every proposition would be false to a hearer which, when perfectly heard by one who also perfectly understands its signification, causes, according to those significations, a false mental proposition in the hearer.

So in our case, Socrates does not hear any proposition. But he believes that he hears one. Hence, that expression which Socrates hears does not make in him the sense which it signifies, for that is not the sense of the proposition, but it makes in him the sense which that proposition makes which he believes himself to hear. And from this it follows only that that proposition which he believes himself to hear would be false.

(6) *It is true to say a man to be animal.*

It is asked concerning this sophism whether in saying a proposition such as "It is true to say a man to be an animal," one speaks the truth. I posit that it is said. And I note that in these sophisms, I intend to speak of absolutely nothing as true or false, except as they pertain to differences in propositions. For I do not intend to ask whether God is true and the first truth, and whether man is false or a coin is false. But I want to speak of true and false according as they establish contradictions, as is said in the sixth of the *Metaphysics*,[9] for the logician is not concerned about the true and the false.

Therefore, I argue that one does not speak the truth in that. For this predicate "to say a man to be an animal" is taken either materially or significatively. If significatively, then to say a man to be an animal is the same as saying a man to be an animal, as I suppose from the *Metaphysics*.[10] And saying man to be an animal is one which is neither true nor false, because it is not a proposition nor a part of a contradiction. And if it is taken materially, it appears that it does not stand for any proposition. For if it should stand for itself or for something similar in expression, it is manifest that this expression "to say a man to be an animal" or something similar is not a proposition nor a complete sentence. Thus, it is neither true nor false. And if it is said that it does not stand for itself nor for any similar expression, but for another sentence formed under the indicative mood—just as this expression "man to run" ordinarily stands for an expression such as "Man runs," which is a proposition—then it is manifest that it does not stand for a proposition, but for a part of a proposition. For although "man to be good" could stand for that proposition "Man is good," still "to be good" does not stand for that proposition, but for an expression such as "is good," which is not a proposition. And so it is in this case. For although this expression "someone to say a man to be an animal" should stand for an expression such as "Someone says that a man is an animal," still this expression "to say a man to be an animal" could stand only for an expression such as "says a man to be an animal," which is not a proposition, nor is it either true or false. Thus, the sophism was false, but it is true to say "man to be animal."

The opposite is argued, because it is true that a man is an animal, and yet this expression "a man to be an animal" and this expression "A man is an animal" are materially equivalent, and one is taken for the other. Therefore, it is true to say a man to be an animal.

Likewise, to affirm a true proposition is true, just as to deny a true proposition is false. But to say a man to be an animal is to affirm a true proposition, namely, "A man is an animal." Therefore, to say a man to be an animal is true. And then the proposition may be converted, and it is the sophism.

[9] *Cf.*, Aristotle, *Metaphysics* vi. 4. 1027b 17–25.
[10] Aristotle, *Metaphysics* v. 7. 1017a 25–30.

I answer that the sophism is false, properly speaking. Yet some, speaking properly, substitute such expressions for others which could be true. For example, this is true: "One speaks the truth saying 'a man to be an animal,'" *i.e.*, saying such an expression itself as "A man is an animal." Similarly, this is true: "To say 'a man to be an animal' is to say the truth." Similarly, this is true: "It is true 'man to be an animal.'" And yet the sophism, properly speaking, was false, as was well proved.

Then concerning the arguments. To the first, I say that this is false: "true to say that man is an animal." But this is true: "It is true that man is an animal." But "a man to be an animal" and "to say a man to be an animal" are greatly different.

To the second, I deny that to affirm or to deny any proposition is true or false. For to affirm or to deny is nothing other than the one affirming or denying. And this is a man, who is neither true nor false. And if "to affirm a proposition" should stand materially, then it is the same to say "to affirm a proposition" and to say "affirms a proposition," and this not a proposition but an incomplete sentence, as Vergil reads.[11]

(7) *Every proposition is false.*

The seventh sophism is this so-called insoluble: "Every proposition is false."

I posit the case that all true propositions should be destroyed and false ones remain. And then Socrates utters only this proposition: "Every proposition is false." Then it is asked whether his proposition is true or false.

And it is argued that it is not true, for I assume that it is impossible for the same proposition to be both true and false at the same time stated in the same language and received by all hearers. Thus if the proposition is true, it follows that not every proposition is false, for a certain one is true, and this contradicts that proposition. Hence, it is false, indeed, impossible, for every proposition is impossible from which its contradictory follows.

Furthermore, it is proved that it is not false, but true, for it is a universal proposition having no exception, neither in itself nor in another, according to the case. Therefore, it is true.

[11] This appears to be only a point of grammar, but it is interesting to note that Buridan was familiar with Vergil and assumed that his readers were as well.

Likewise, if it is false, its subject and predicate do not stand for the same universally. Thus, since it is affirmative, it follows that it is true.

Again, if it is false, then howsoever it signifies, so it is. For it signifies only that every proposition is false, and so it is. Therefore, it is true.

Concerning this sophism, there are difficult doubts to be considered. The first is whether this proposition, in the given case, is true or false. The second is how it is possible to assign to it a contradictory or an equivalent.

And to the first, I say that retaining and conceding the aforesaid case, still with that it can be posited that it is true, which is apparent by what was said in the second sophism and in the third sophism of the seventh chapter, where it was said that we can use one time for another time. For we say truly in some time that Socrates sits, in which time he does not sit. For by the time known and by this verb "sits," we do not understand the time which now coexists with the proposition, but another time. And so generally the case is conceded that for the whole first hour of this day, no proposition is true, but every one is false. And let us posit that after the end of that hour Socrates says that every proposition is false, and that he speaks not for the time at which he speaks, but for the time of that first hour. Thus, his proposition would be true, for an induction would be sufficient which would take account of the propositions of the first hour.

But this solution, although it is true in that case, still does not remove the difficulty of the sophism in another case, namely, that he speaks for that time in which he speaks. And some, wanting to escape, say that terms which are of a nature to stand for propositions are not placed in propositions to stand for those propositions in which they are placed, but for others. Thus, they say that Socrates' proposition was true, because that term "proposition" in Socrates' proposition did not stand for that proposition, but for all others, and all those were false.

But it is clear that this solution is not correct. For one can speak of what one understands but by the concept from which this name "proposition" is taken, one understands indifferently every proposition, present, past, and future, his as well as another. Thus, he can speak of all propositions. So, it is manifest that I can say that the proposition which I now actually utter is affirmative, and it can be my intention to speak of it. Thus, that term stood for that proposition in which it was placed.

Likewise, in no way does this evasion avoid the difficulty, for I state that Socrates utters that proposition, and similarly Plato utters another similar proposition. And then by what reason one could call one true, by the same reason the other. And so of the false. Thus, either one should call both true or one should call both false. I ask then whether Socrates speaks the truth. If you say he does, then, since he speaks of the proposition of Plato, although not of his own, it follows that Plato's proposition is false. And consequently, for the same reason, Socrates' proposition is false. And if one says that either is false, it follows that both are true, for the case is as they assert it to be. For they assert that every proposition is false, and it is so. And because also, if they are false, then their subjects and predicates stand for the same. Hence, they are true, because they are affirmative, and also because they are universal propositions, among the singulars of which there is no exception.

Others have said that such a proposition is both true and false at once. But this is unsuitable, as is clear; for if its contradictory were true, both contradictories would be true. And if it were false, both would be false, and each of these is impossible. Therefore.

Then also there is a doubt how a contradictory can be given. I posit the case that there are only two propositions, one that a man is an ass, and the other the aforesaid proposition of Socrates. Then, I show that a contradictory cannot be given. For the terms of the contradictories ought to stand for the same thing or things, not in one contradictory for more than in the other. Now in the proposition of Socrates, the subject stands for two propositions, namely, for itself, according to the case, and for this proposition "A man is an ass." Now if you wish to give the contradictory, namely, "Some proposition is not false," immediately in that, the subject would stand for more, namely, for three—itself, and the other two. Therefore, it could not contradict that proposition of Socrates.

But this doubt is solved by that which was said in the second and third sophisms of the seventh chapter. For that proposition contradicting the proposition of Socrates could be formed and not for the time in which it is formed, but for the time in which the proposition of Socrates was made. Thus, that third proposition would stand only for those for which Socrates' proposition would stand, and it would not stand for itself, since it was not of this time.

Now we must look into the truth and falsity of these propositions. And briefly, I believe that that proposition would be false. For it would be either false or not false. If it is false, I have my conclusion, and if it is not false, it follows that it is true, from which also it is. And if it is true, it follows also that it is false, as was previously argued. Hence, I have my conclusion, namely, that it is false.

But then it is difficult to respond to the sophism. For concerning the arguments, some have said, and so it formerly seemed to me, that although the proposition, according to the significations of its terms, signifies or affirms only that every proposition is false, still since every proposition, because of its form, signifies or asserts itself to be true, so every proposition asserting itself to be false, whether directly or indirectly, is false. For although howsoever it signifies the case to be, so it is, insofar as it signifies itself to be false, still it is not the case that how it signifies to be, so it is, insofar as it signifies itself to be true. Thus, it is false and not true, because for its truth, it is required, not only that how it signifies the case to be, so it is, but howsoever it signifies the case to be, so it is.

This response does not seem to me to be valid, properly speaking. And I do not object for now to this way of speaking: howsoever it signifies the case to be, so it is. For enough has been said about this. But I show that that which was said is not true, namely, that every proposition signifies or asserts itself to be true. For you take that expression "itself to be true" either significatively or materially. If materially, then this proposition "A man is an animal" does not assert itself or signify itself to be true, for its sense would be that it would signify this proposition " 'A man is an animal' is true," which is false. For that second proposition is of second intention, and the first, since it is of first intention, could not signify these second intentions. But if someone should say that that expression "itself to be true" is taken significatively, then that proposition "A man is an ass" does not signify itself to be true. For just as man-being-ass is nothing, since man could not be an ass, so this proposition " 'Man is an ass' to be true" is nothing, nor could it be, since it could not be true. Now concerning that which could not be or is not, it is not true to say that it is signified or understood or asserted, as has been sufficiently said elsewhere. For if you say this proposition " 'A man is an ass' being true" is signified or understood or asserted, then you speak falsely, since the proposition is false, for it is affirmative and its subject stands for nothing. And so it is in the proposed case, that a proposition such as "Every proposition is false" cannot be true, so it-being-true neither is nor could be. Thus, it is not signified or understood. So it does not signify itself to be true.

Thus, it is otherwise said, nearer the truth, that every proposition virtually implies another proposition, so that of the subject standing for it, there is affirmed this predicate "true." I say it implies virtually just as an antecedent implies that which follows from it. Thus, any proposition is not true, if in this consequent affirmation, the subject and predicate do not stand for the same. For example, we could posit that this proposition of Socrates "No proposition is true" is properly called by the name "C." And then it follows that no proposition is true; therefore, C is not true. And thus, unless it is as is signified by this consequent, it follows that the predicate in the given proposition was virtually implied in that proposition. The proposition is not true. For it does not suffice for a proposition to be true that it is as it signifies according to formal significations. Rather, it is required that it is as is signified by the consequent which was virtually implied. Hence, because of this, it will be said that when a proposition has or can have reflection on itself, it does not suffice for the truth of an affirmative that the terms stand for the same, as is said elsewhere. But it is required that in such a consequent, the terms stand for the same. And then it is necessary, given this, for the proposition to be true. And by this the arguments are easily solved.

To the first argument, it could be said that it is indeed universal, but the objection is not in itself against its formal signification, but against that which it implies as consequent.

To the other, it could be said that the subject and predicate of the said consequence do not stand for the same, that, however, for the truth of a proposition, this is required, whatever that proposition should be. To the last, it could be said similarly that it is not howsoever that implied consequent signifies, even if this way of speaking is employed in the proper sense.

But this solution, although it is near the truth, as I think, yet is still not complete. For it assumes falsely that from any proposition that consequent follows. For given that this proposition "A horse runs" is properly called by the name "B," then it does not follow that a horse runs, so B is true, as was said in the second sophism of this chapter. And so for completing this solution, we ought to say that from every proposition, together with the condition that it is, there follows the conclusion that it is true. So in the aforesaid case, namely, that this proposition "A horse runs" is properly called by the name "B," it follows that a horse runs and B is, so B is true.

Now in our proposition which is the present sophism, it seems that this proposition is added by the case. For it was stated that Socrates uttered this proposition "No proposition is true." Hence, it is posited that it is true, and so from this proposition and the case, or from a proposition explaining the case, it follows that it is true, which is false. Therefore, either it is false or the case is false. Hence, if the case is taken as true, it is necessary to say that this proposition is false.

But then, it is necessary to solve the arguments.

The first argument, even with that addition, has not been sufficiently solved. For when it is said that it is a universal having no exceptions, I say also that although there is not an exception opposed to it according to its precise formal significations, still there would be opposed that exception which is implied by way of the consequent in it, together with the case. And this suffices to falsify it, if the posited case is true. And so are solved the other arguments.

But then it is doubted whether such a proposition is possible, namely, "Every proposition is false." And I say that it is possible, although it could not be true. For it could be as it signifies if God should destroy all propositions except these two: "God is an ass" and "A horse is a goat." For then every proposition would be false. And I would say that the copulative from this and the case would be impossible. For an impossible proposition would follow, namely, that it is both true and false.

(8) *Plato speaks falsely*.

There is an eighth sophism and it seems more difficult. And it is this: "Plato speaks falsely."

I posit the case that Socrates utters this proposition "Plato speaks falsely" and he utters no other. And conversely, Plato utters this proposition "Socrates speaks falsely," and not another. Then it is asked whether Socrates' proposition, which is the sophism is true or false.

And it is argued that it is true, for there is no reason why Socrates' proposition should be more true or false than Plato's proposition, or conversely. For they are related to each other in exactly the same way. Thus, if one is true, the other is true. And if one is false, the other is false. This I assume. So if you say that Socrates' proposition is not true but false, then also Plato speaks falsely for the same reason. And Socrates affirms this and nothing else. So he affirms what is, so his proposition is true. Also his proposition is affirmative and the terms stand for the same, namely, Plato and the one speaking falsely. From which we assert that Plato speaks falsely. Hence, it is a true proposition.

Likewise, I posit that with Socrates, Robert also says that Plato speaks falsely. And I posit also that Socrates and Robert utter these propositions according to similar intentions, and they believe that they speak the truth, because they believe that Plato utters the proposition "God is not." Hence, it appears that Socrates' proposition and Robert's proposition are absolutely similar in sound and intention, to the hearer as well as to the speaker. And yet Robert's proposition is true, because we posit that Plato speaks falsely. Hence, similarly, Socrates' proposition is true.

Again, we posit that Robert wants to contradict Socrates, by saying that Plato does not speak falsely. Then it appears that this proposition is false, because we posit that Plato speaks falsely; hence, only Socrates' proposition was true, unless you say that both contradictories are at once false, which is impossible.

The opposite is argued, because if Socrates speaks truly, then for the same reason, Plato speaks truly. And if Plato speaks truly, since he says that Socrates speaks falsely, it follows that Socrates speaks falsely. Thus, the proposition of Socrates is false and not true.

It is to be said briefly that Socrates' proposition is false and not true, because every proposition is false, from which, together with some true proposition, there follows a false one. But from this, together with a true proposition, there follows a false one. Hence, it is false. The major is an infallible rule. And the minor is proved, for since the case is possible, I suppose the positing of the case to be true. Now from the case and the proposition of Socrates, it follows that Socrates' proposition is true and that it is false. And consequently, the whole is false and impossible. Hence, it appears that from Socrates' proposition, together with a true proposition, there follows a false one.

Now, therefore, it remains to show in what way from the proposition of Socrates and the case, it follows that that proposition is both true and false. And first it is proved that it is true, because the case posits that that proposition of Socrates is. And yet it has been said that from any proposition, together with the statement that it is, it follows that it is true. But also it appears that it is false, as was argued. For if it were true, it would be necessary for Plato's proposition to be true, from which it would follow that Socrates' proposition would be false. And similarly, for the same reason, it is to be said that Plato's proposition is false.

Thus, it is necessary only to answer the arguments that are very difficult, and the reader is referred to that which was said in the preceding sophism.

To the first, it is said that although it is as Socrates' proposition signifies according to its formal signification, still it is not as the proposition following from it and the case signifies. For it follows that it is true, and it is not so.

Similarly, concerning the second, it is said that when a proposition can have reflection on itself, whether mediately or immediately, according to which reflection it follows that it is false, it is not sufficient for the truth of an affirmative that the subject and predicate stand for the same. But it is also necessary that the subject and predicate of that consequent, namely, that it is true, stand for the same, as was said earlier.

But the third and fourth arguments are difficult. And I say, concerning the third without doubt that Socrates' proposition and Robert's proposition are consimilar, according to expression and intention, of the speakers as well as the hearers. But they are not equivalent, because Plato's proposition, concerning which both spoke, has reflection on Socrates' proposition and not on Robert's proposition. Thus, from the propositions of Socrates and Plato, together with the case, it follows that Socrates' proposition is false. And this does not follow from Robert's proposition. Rather, it is true.

Then it is doubted how one can take equivalent propositions in another than the aforesaid way. Concerning this, I say that if a proposition is of a nature to reflect on itself because its terms stand for propositions, then it is also required that an equivalent proposition be of a nature to reflect on it. For example, there is first a proposition A, and secondly B. And if B should be equivalent to A, it is necessary that in whatever case A reflects on itself, so B reflects on A, since it is necessary in every case that if one is true, then the other is true. Now the second does not have reflection on the first except in asserting that consequent which is implied by asserting the first, namely, that A is true. But if this second is posited, then it is equivalent to the first. Thus should it be the proposition of Socrates that Plato speaks falsely, then Robert's proposition will be equivalent to "Plato speaks falsely and A is true," positing that Socrates' proposition is called A. For this proposition of Robert's adds nothing which is not implied indirectly in the case in which the proposition of Socrates is. And we posit this case in positing that they are equivalent or not contradictory. For if they are not, then they are neither equivalent nor contradictory. And generally, from every proposition and the statement of its existence, there can be taken an equivalence, for example, that if those statements exist, then they are equivalent. Namely, Socrates' proposition, which is properly named B, could be that a man runs, and Robert's equivalent proposition could be that a man runs and B is true. But it is not necessary to add the other statement when the proposition is not of a nature to reflect on itself. But when it can, it is necessary to add this. For if there is reflection on the first, then there is reflection on the second.

And something similar, I believe, must be said about the fourth argument. For Socrates' proposition and Robert's proposition are both false and do not contradict. For it is possible for there to be reflection on one, from which it follows that it is false, although there be no reflection on the other, as it is in the case posited. Thus, in contradicting Socrates' proposition, it is necessary to contradict the copulative composed of it and the consequent implied in it, namely, that which was stated to be equivalent to it. For example, Robert may say that Plato does not speak falsely or A is not true. For in no way could those two be at the same time either true or false. Nor also is it hostile if more of other terms are applied in one than in the other. For whatever terms are explicitly expressed in one are implicitly and equivalently contained in the other.

But again, it is doubted, for if those propositions of Socrates and Robert were contradictories, then positing that they would always remain by divine power, it is certain that never by a change in other things could they be at the same time true or false. Then I posit that the case concerning Plato is changed, so that Plato does not utter the proposition "Socrates speaks falsely," but he utters the proposition "Robert speaks falsely." Then it is asked concerning each of those propositions, namely, Socrates', Robert's, and Plato's, which is true or false. And I say that Plato's proposition is false, because it follows from it immediately and according to the case that it is false. For if it should be held to be true, it would follow that Robert's proposition is false. And if Robert's proposition is false, this is either because Plato speaks falsely or because Socrates' proposition is true. And from both it follows that Plato's proposition is false. And then, it likewise follows that Robert's proposition is false and Socrates' proposition is true. For Socrates asserts only that Plato speaks falsely, and so it is. Nor is there reflection from Plato to Socrates, because of which it does not follow that Socrates' proposition is false. Thus, it is true, and Robert's proposition contradicting it is false, because it is a disjunctive of which each part is false.

(9) *Socrates speaks truly.*

The ninth sophism is related to the preceding, namely, "Socrates speaks truly."

The case may be posited that Socrates utters only this [proposition] "Plato speaks falsely" and Plato, conversely, only this proposition "Socrates speaks truly." Then it is asked whether that proposition of Plato is true or false. And similarly also, it could be asked concerning Socrates' proposition.

It is argued that Plato speaks truly, because he speaks either falsely or truly. If truly, we have the conclusion. If falsely, still it follows that he speaks truly. Hence, whatever is given, it follows that he speaks truly. Then I demonstrate the assumption, that is, the antecedent, namely, that if Plato speaks falsely, then he speaks truly. And if he speaks falsely, then Socrates does not speak truly. And if Socrates does not speak truly, then Plato speaks truly, and so we have the conclusion as it was proved above, namely, that Socrates speaks truly.

Next, it is disproved similarly. For either Plato speaks truly or he speaks falsely. If he speaks falsely, I have the conclusion. If he speaks truly, still it follows that he speaks falsely, and again I have the statement. I prove, then, the assumption, namely, that it follows that if Plato speaks truly, Socrates speaks falsely. For if he speaks truly, it follows that Socrates speaks truly. And if Socrates speaks truly, it follows that Plato speaks falsely.

It is to be said briefly, as before, that each proposition is false, because I assume it to be as it is supposed to be in the case, since this is possible, and so the proposition expressing the case is true. Hence, every proposition is false from which, together with the statement given in the case, a falsehood follows, since the false does not follow from the true. But from each, together with the case, the false follows. Therefore, etc.

I prove that from each, together with the case, the false follows. For it follows that the same proposition is both true and false without equivocation, and this is false. First, therefore, it is demonstrated that from Plato's proposition, together with the case, it follows that the same proposition, namely, itself, is both true and false. For it is posited in the case that it is, and it has been said earlier that from every proposition, together with another stating that it is, it follows that it is true. And yet it follows finally, that if it is true, then it is false. Therefore, it follows that it is false. And so it would be argued concerning the other.

But then it is doubted whether these are impossible. It seems that they are, for from a possible there follows only a possible. And yet from these there follows an impossible, namely, that the same is both true and false.

The contrary is stated, because a proposition is possible which, when it is true, could be false, because of a change in the things signified. But Plato's proposition, namely, that Socrates speaks truly, could be true if we posit that Socrates says that proposition "God is." Hence, it is possible or not impossible. And so it is argued that Socrates' proposition could be possible, for it could be true if Plato should say that a man is an ass.

Concerning the argument, I say that an impossible follows from neither, but from each and the case posited, an impossible follows. Thus, I concede that the copulative constituted of these and the case is impossible. And this is often the case, namely, that a copulative is impossible of which each part is possible. For instance, if I say "Every running thing is a horse and a man is running," there follows from this an impossible, namely, that a man is a horse. So also, this is impossible: "Socrates runs and Socrates does not run," although either part is possible.

Then it is answered concerning the argument which held that Plato's proposition could be true. When it is asked whether it is true or false, I agree that it is false. And when it is said that if it is false, then it is true, I deny the consequent. And when it is proved because if Plato speaks falsely, it follows that Socrates does not speak truly, I concede. And when it is further said that if Socrates speaks falsely, it follows that Plato speaks truly, I deny the consequent. For Socrates' proposition is not said to be false because it is other than it signifies according to its formal significations, for thus it signifies that Plato speaks falsely and so it is. But it is called false because the consequent implied by it and the case, which is true, is false. Thus, it is consistent that A is a true proposition, for it is posited that Socrates' proposition is properly named A. And it is not the case that it is not true because it is not true.

And if it is argued that Socrates' proposition, stating that Plato speaks falsely is true, because the terms stand for the same, and because howsoever it signifies, so it is, and because its equivalent, which Robert utters, is true, or because its contradictory, which John utters, is false, it is to be replied to all these arguments as we did in the preceding sophism.

(10) *There are just as many true propositions as there are false propositions.*

There is a tenth sophism, and it is similar in force, namely, "There are just as many true propositions as there are false propositions."

The case may be posited that there are only four propositions. The first is "God is," the second "A man is an animal," the third "A horse is a goat," the fourth the stated sophism. With it so being, I ask whether the sophism is true or false.

It is argued first that it is not true, for then it would not be as it signifies, rather, there would be more true than false, since there would be three true and one false.

Next, it is argued that it is not false, for if it were false, then it would be as it signifies, since with two true and two false, it is true.

I say that the sophism is false, because from it and the case, it follows that it is false and that it is true. And the argument for the opposite is answered, since it is not false because it is other than it signifies according to formal significations, but because it is not as that proposition signifies which is virtually implied by it and the case, as the consequent [is implied] by its antecedent. For this is implied by it: "A is true," positing the case that that sophism is properly named A. And it is not as this signifies: "A is true."

But it is asked whether the sophism is possible and whether it could be true. And I immediately answer that it is possible, since it could be that there were as many true as there were false as for instance, if there were only these four: "God is," "God is good," "A man is an ass," and "A horse is a goat." I say also that it could be true in the case that we do not take the time consignified by the verb for the present time in which we form it, but for the time in which there were only those four immediately aforesaid. Indeed, also, in this way, this could be true: "Every proposition is negative," but it could not be true if we take the time consignified by the verb for the time in which it is formed. Nor also could the present sophism be true, but still if the case posited in the sophism is as it is posited, some man, coming in, could truly say that for the time of this case, precisely as many were true as were false. But for a verb of the present, some man could not truly say this, except as was said, namely, using the time of the verb for a time other than that which precisely coexists with his proposition.

(11) *I speak falsely.*

The eleventh sophism is of similar force—"I speak falsely."

It is posited that I say nothing except this proposition "I speak falsely." Then, it is asked whether my proposition is true or false.

If you say that it is true, then it is not as my proposition signifies. Thus, it follows that it is not true but false.

And if you say that it is false, then it follows that it is as it signifies. Hence, it is true.

Also, since then the terms stand for the same and it is affirmative, it follows clearly that if it is false, it is true. And then from this, it follows that it is necessary to concede that it is true and false, since whoever concedes the antecedent ought to concede the consequent. And it is necessary to concede either that it was true or that it was false. And then it follows that if it is true, it is false, and if it is false, it is true. Hence, it is necessary to concede both. But again, to concede this is inconsistent, since then its contradictory would be true, and so two contradictories would be true at the same time. And if it is false, then the two contradictories would be false at the same time. And all these are impossible.

Next, also, it is doubted in what way the contradictory of the sophism is to be taken and whether it is possible or impossible.

I answer that the sophism is false, because from it and the proposition expressing the case, a false proposition follows. Yet since this proposition expressing the case is said to be true, and that false, what thus follows is that the sophism is both true and false at once. But a proposition is false, from which, together with its truth, a false proposition follows.

And the arguments for the opposite are answered, according to what was said earlier. For it is said that if it were false, it would follow that it is true. I deny that consequent. And you prove it because if it is false, then it is as it signifies. I agree, with respect to the formal signification. But this is not sufficient because it reflects on itself. For because of this it is not true, for it is not as the consequent of it and of the case signifies. For that consequent is that A is true, positing that my proposition is properly named A. And it is not as this signifies: "A is true." And similarly, it is said, concerning this, that the terms stand for the same.

But still you can object, arguing that it follows that if it is false, then it is true, because if it is false, it follows that it is, and so it is. And from its being so and the fact that it is, it follows that it is true. Hence, it follows that if it is false, then it is true. And whoever concedes the antecedent ought to concede the consequent. Therefore, we ought to concede that it is true.

I answer that it does not follow that if it is false, then it is true. But I do indeed agree that it follows that if it is false, then it is. I concede also that from it and the fact that it is, it follows that it is true. But I do not concede the antecedent. Rather, I deny the antecedent, because the antecedent was composed of it and its being. And I deny it, so I also deny the consequent, namely, that it is true.

But there is a doubt in what way you can contradict me. Hence, if you speak negatively concerning a similar subject, according to expression, as by saying "I do not speak falsely," you do not contradict me, because in a contradiction, the terms of one ought to stand for the same things as the terms of the other. And this would not be here, for in my proposition, this term "I" stands for me, but in yours it stands for you. And if you say negatively, changing that term "I" to that term "you," namely, saying to me "You do not speak falsely," it is apparent that you do not indeed contradict me. For a contradictory ought to be of the same subject and predicate, and it is not sufficient that there are different predicates standing for the same. Likewise, my proposition is false, and yours is also false. Therefore, they do not contradict.

For solution, I say that it is not necessary for contradictories to be exactly alike in words. For first it is necessary for them to be dissimilar according to affirmation and negation. Secondly, they can be dissimilar according to what they signify or according to their manners [of supposition]. For instance, these contradict: "Every man runs" and "Some man does not run." And similarly these two: "It is possible that Socrates runs" and "It is necessary that Socrates does not run." But also sometimes, we can change the verbal predicate, on account of relative terms. For instance, if you say "Every man having a horse sees that [horse]," if we should have to contradict that other than by asserting the negation of the whole proposition, it will be necessary to change the wording of the predicate. For this is not its contradictory: "Some man having a horse does not see that [horse]," since both can be true at once in the case in which every man should have one horse which he sees and another which he does not see. Hence, it seems that its contradictory is this: "Some man having a horse does not see the horse which he has." But this, will be discussed in particular elsewhere.

But still, just as was said in the eighth sophism, because of the reflection which a proposition has on itself, or is of a nature to have, it is necessary in contradicting it to express it in other words, in accordance with the sense of the consequent implied by the first proposition.

And also if someone speaks of himself in the first person, it will be necessary for another, in contradicting him, to speak in the second person and not in the first. For instance, if Socrates says "I am running," Plato does not contradict him by saying "I am not running," but by saying "You are not running." It is necessary, therefore, principally to inspect the intention, since we use words only to express intentions. Thus, if we cannot express a mental contradictory without changing the words, it is necessary to change them. So, therefore, it seems that you contradict me in saying "You are not speaking falsely," yet with the additions mentioned in the prior sophisms. Hence, if you wish to state a proposition equivalent to mine, you say "You are speaking falsely, and A is true," positing the case that my proposition is properly named A. And then the contradictory would be "You are not speaking falsely, or A is not true," and this disjunctive is true.

(12) *God is and some copulative is false.*

Let us posit that that proposition is written on a wall, and that there is no proposition besides it and its parts. Then it is asked whether it is true or false.

And it is argued as before. For if it is true, it follows that it is false. And if it is false, it seems to follow that it is true, for it would be as it signifies, since its contradictory would be false, namely, this: "God is not or no copulative is false."

It is to be said that it is false. And the arguments are solved as before. Granted that it would be as it signifies according to its formal signification, still it would not be as would be signified by the consequent implied in it and the case posited. I assume that it is properly named A, and its contradictory would be "No God is, or no copulative is false, or A is not true." Similarly also, sophisms can be made from disjunctive propositions, such as "A man is an ass, or a disjunctive is false," positing that there is no other disjunctive. Similarly also, concerning exceptives, such as "Every proposition except an exceptive is true," positing that there are no other propositions except the aforesaid exceptive and two others, namely, "God is" and "A man is an animal." So also concerning an exclusive, such as if Socrates says "God is" and Plato says "Only Socrates speaks truly," and no one else says anything.

Other sophisms can also be formed from that which is a proposition of doubt or no doubt, of knowing or not knowing, of belief or unbelief.

(13) *Socrates knows the proposition written on the wall to be doubted by him.*

I posit the case that only the aforesaid proposition is written on the wall, and that Socrates sees it, examines it, and doubts whether it is true or false, and that he knows himself to doubt it. It is asked whether it is true or false.

And it is argued that it is true. For the case is posited that Socrates truly knows that proposition to be doubted by him, and this is what the proposition signifies. Hence, it is true. Likewise, of similar propositions, if one is true, the other is true. But whoever should utter a proposition similar to this one would speak the truth. Hence, it is true.

The opposite is argued. A proposition is false from which an impossible follows, namely, that Socrates knows and doubts the same proposition. For according to the case, he doubts it, and yet he knows it, because he knows it to be as it signifies, since he knows that it is doubted by him. Indeed, it is also possible that he knows himself to know that it is doubted by him. And that proposition signifies nothing more. But to know that it is as a proposition signifies is to know the proposition. For you know the proposition "A man is an animal," from the fact that you know that it is indeed so.

It is confirmed that if he gives it heed, he knows that proposition to be true, since if you should utter a similar one, he will know that you are speaking the truth. Hence, for the same reason, he would know it to be true.

And similarly, if you utter the contradictory, he will know that you speak falsely. But whoever knows one contradictory to be false knows the other to be true, if he gives it attention, and he knows those to be contradictories. Therefore, etc.

Some people respond concerning that sophism that there is a twofold proposition written on the wall, according to the case, namely, one whole one, that Socrates knows that the proposition written on the wall is doubted by him. And there is another partial one, which is a part of that, namely, that the proposition written on the wall is doubted by him. Now, therefore, Socrates indeed knows this partial one, namely, that the proposition written on the wall is doubted by him, but he does not know the whole, rather, that is doubted by him. And this is not impossible, so it is conceded that the proposition is true.

But this solution does not appear to me to remove the doubt. First, because it is not true according to the case that there is a twofold proposition written on the wall, because it was said elsewhere that no part of a proposition is a proposition, as long as it is a part of a proposition. And likewise, the case did not posit a proposition concerning which it was asserted that it was written on the wall, but a proposition such as "Socrates knows the proposition written on the wall to be doubted by him." But that expression of the infinitive mood "proposition written, etc." is not a proposition. And even if it should stand for a proposition, still it would be only for this whole, since nothing else is written on the wall. Thus, if he knows the proposition written on the wall, he knows this whole.

Likewise, it was posited that he not only knows that it is doubted by him, but rather he knows himself to know this. We could posit, therefore, that it is possible. So Socrates knows not only that that proposition is doubted by him, but he knows that Socrates knows that proposition to be doubted by him. And so it seems to follow that he knows a whole proposition and not only a partial one. Thus, I say otherwise, conceding that that written on the wall is doubted by him and that he knows with certainty that it is doubted by him, indeed, he knows that he knows this. And then there is a doubt whether he knows that proposition.

For the purpose of resolving these doubts, it is to be noted that the concept is in more than knowledge.[12] For the concept can be without complexion and it can be without enunciation.[13] And it is required for knowledge that a man assents to a true enunciation. And this kind of enunciation, to which we thus assent with certitude and evidence, we say to be known, and that we have knowledge of it. Indeed also, concerning things themselves signified by terms, we thus distinguish a twofold knowledge, namely, one primary and immediate which is that enunciation, to which we assent in the aforesaid way. The other is a remotely known thing or remotely known things,

[12] *conceptus est in plus quam scientia.*

[13] See above p. 45.

namely, the things signified by the terms of the enunciation known in the first way.

But it is impossible that a proposition is doubted by you and known by you as a thing primarily known. For you do not assent with certitude and evidence to a proposition doubted by you. And yet you assent to the proposition thus primarily known. Hence, it is necessary that that proposition written on the wall is not known by Socrates by the primary way of knowing, since it is doubted by him, and he does not know whether it is true or false. But I say that it is known by Socrates by the remote way of knowing, since Socrates forms in his mind a mental proposition such as "The proposition written on the wall is doubted by me." And he assents to that mental proposition with certitude and evidence, because of which that mental proposition is known by him by the primary way of knowing. And since the subject of that mental proposition stands for the proposition written on the wall, it follows that Socrates has knowledge of that proposition written on the wall as a remotely known thing.

But again, I say that if Plato should utter the proposition "Socrates knows the proposition written on the wall to be doubted by him," and if Socrates should hear and understand Plato well, immediately Socrates will know Plato's proposition also by the primary way of knowing. For Socrates would assent to Plato's proposition with certitude and evidence as true and not doubted by him. Indeed also, if on a paper is written a proposition exactly like the one written on the wall, Socrates, seeing and reading it, would know it to be true, nor will he have doubt concerning it.

Then it will be doubted how this is possible, namely, that there are two absolutely consimilar propositions and that a man is certain of one and doubts the other, since he still notices them and knows them to be consimilar. And I say that this is indeed possible, since one observes that that which is written on the wall reflects on itself. Thus, the doubt is that because of this reflection it could be false, as happened in the preceding sophisms. But also he observes that Plato's proposition or also that written on paper does not reflect on itself, so there is no doubt whether it is true. But also, when it is argued that if Plato utters the contradictory, namely, this: "Socrates does not know the proposition written on the wall to be doubted by him," immediately Socrates knows that Plato's proposition is false, I agree.

And you conclude, therefore, he should know that that proposition written on the wall is true, since it is its contradictory. I say that this does not follow, for he does not know that they are contradictories. For one could doubt whether the reflection which the proposition written on the wall has on itself impedes the contradiction.

Finally, it is doubted whether this proposition written on the wall is true or false. And I say that it is true, since the reflection which it has on itself does not determine that it is false, but only that it is doubted, from which it does not follow that it is false. And when it is argued that from it an impossible follows, I deny it, for it does not follow that it is known except by the remote way of knowing. But you prove that Socrates knows it to be as it signifies. This is conceded. And you conclude, therefore, that there is no doubt whether it is true, if one heeds this. I say that this does not follow. For Socrates sees in the solution of the preceding sophisms that many propositions were false by the reflection which they had on themselves, although it was as they signified. Thus, because of this ignorance, it is necessary to opine that this is also false, because it is seen to reflect on itself, or at least he may have doubt concerning it.

But still there is a doubt concerning that sophism, whether that proposition is true or false, adding to the case posited before that Socrates is most wise. And I say that the case is impossible, since because Socrates is most learned in the art and he observes as far as he can concerning that proposition, it follows that if it is true, then he knows it to be true, and if it is false, then he knows it to be false. And yet with neither of these is it consistent that it is doubted by him. But if that clause is removed from the case, namely, that it is doubted by him, it is asked whether it is true or false for him. And I say that it is false, and that Socrates knows it to be false, and not to be doubted by him.

(14) *Socrates sits, or the disjunctive written on the wall is doubted by Plato.*

Let us posit the case that this proposition is written on the wall and that Plato sees it and gives full consideration to whether it is true or false. And I posit also that that Plato is in every art most trained and most learned in knowledge, but yet that Plato does not see Socrates and does not know whether he stands or sits. And so he doubts that proposition "Socrates sits." Then, therefore, it is asked how Plato is related to that whole proposition, which is a disjunctive, namely, whether he knows it to be true or he knows it to be false or he doubts it.

And it is argued first that Plato does not know it to be true, for he must know either part to be true, since it is required for the truth of a disjunctive that either part be true. But yet by the case, he does not know the first part to be true, namely, that Socrates sits. And similarly, he does not know the second part to be true, since from this it would follow that that second part would be true and false, which is impossible. I prove the conclusion. For first it would follow that that could be true, since nothing is known to be true except the true. Secondly, it would also follow that it would be false, since if he should know it to be true, he would know the disjunctive to be true, since for the truth of a disjunctive, it suffices that one part is true. Therefore, he would not doubt it, and consequently, that second part would be false, since it says that disjunctive to be doubted by Plato.

Next, it is also argued that Plato does not know that disjunctive to be false, since in order to know a disjunctive to be false, one must know each part to be false. And it is posited that Plato does not know whether the first is true or false. Likewise, if he should know the disjunctive to be false, he would know its contradictory to be true, if he should pay it heed. For he is stated to be most learned in every art. But the consequent is false, for its contradictory is this: "Socrates does not sit, and no disjunctive written on the wall is doubted by Plato." But this copulative Plato does not know to be true, for he does not know concerning the first part whether it is true or false. For he doubts it.

Next, it is argued that this disjunctive is not doubted by Plato, for if it is doubted by him, he knows it. Indeed, even if a person with little learning should attend to any proposition, he would know well whether he doubts it. But if he knows that to be doubted by him, he knows the second of its parts to be true, which says this. And if he knows that second part to be true, he knows the disjunctive to be true, from which it follows that he does not doubt it.

I answer that Plato does not know that disjunctive to be true and that he does not know it to be false, as the reasons concerning this argued. Thus, it remains that he doubts it, and he knows that he doubts it. Which is also proved. For the second part of that disjunctive is false, as is proved. And Plato well knows this, since he is posited to be most learned in every art. Thus, he knows that the disjunctive is false if the first part is false, and that it is true if the first part is true. Since he thus knows that he doubts the first part, he knows that he doubts the whole disjunctive.

Now, therefore, it is necessary to show that this second part of the disjunctive is false. This is proved thus: since that proposition is false from which, together with some true proposition, a false one follows. But so it is concerning this. So it is false. Then I prove the minor, because since the whole case is possible, I suppose that the proposition stating the case is true; and because from the case and the second part, a false proposition follows, indeed an impossible proposition. For it follows that that disjunctive is doubted by Plato and not doubted. First, that it is doubted, because this is stated by the second part. Second, that it is not doubted, as was earlier argued. This is clear also, because from the second part and the case, it follows that it is both true and false. First, that it is true, because by the case it is posited to be, and it was often said that from any proposition and another stating that it is, it follows that it is true. But again, also, it follows that it is false, because if it is true, then Plato knows this, since he is assumed to be most learned, and who knows the truth either doubts concerning that disjunctive or not. And if he knows it to be true, then he does not doubt. And consequently, that second part is false.

Then, it is responded concerning the arguments in opposition that although Plato knows it to be as it is signified by that second part according to formal significations, still he does not know it to be true, but false, for he knows that it reflects on itself, from which it follows, together with the statement that the case is true, that it is false. And he also knows every such proposition to be false.

But perhaps there is a reply against the statement, since if that disjunctive is doubted by Plato,[14] it is necessary that its contradictory also be doubted, and yet this is false. For the contradictory is that Socrates does not sit and no proposition written on the wall is doubted by Plato. And Plato does not doubt that, since he knows it to be false, for it is a copulative whose second part is false. It follows, therefore,

[14] Reading *Platoni* instead of *Sorti*.

that Plato ought not to doubt the proposition written on the wall, but to know it to be true.

For solution, I say that the contradictory is not sufficiently taken, because it reflects on itself. Thus, it is necessary to explain the consequent implied by the second disjunct and the case. So that if that disjunctive written on the wall is properly named A, the equivalent of it will be this: "Socrates sits, or the disjunctive written on the wall is doubted by Plato, and A is true." And then the contradictory will be this: "Socrates does not sit, and no disjunctive written on the wall is doubted by Plato, or A is not true." And then I say that this is doubted by Plato, since it is a disjunctive composed of a copulative which is known to be false and a categorical which is doubted. Thus, the whole is doubted.

(15) *To someone is proposed a proposition doubted by him.*

And I posit the case that only the aforesaid proposition is proposed to you and that you do not know that any other is proposed to someone else. And I posit also that you are most learned in the art and that you seek, as far as you can, to discover whether that proposition is true or false. And then it is asked whether you know it to be true, or you know it to be false, or it is doubted by you.

It is argued first that you do not know it to be false, since you could not know that to be false, unless you know that to no man is proposed a proposition which he doubts. For it is known that it could be true if in Rome a proposition were proposed to Robert that was doubted by him. And you could not know whether it is so, so you could not know it to be false. Or it is argued thus: if you knew it to be false, you would also know its contradictory to be true, if it should be proposed to you, since you are most learned in the art. But this is impossible, namely, that you should know this to be true: "No doubted proposition is proposed to anybody." Therefore, etc.

Next, it is argued that you do not know that to be true. For you do not know concerning other men whether or not any proposition which is doubted is proposed to anybody. Hence, you do not know that there is proposed any proposition which is doubted by someone, unless you know this one which is proposed to you to be doubted by you. But it is impossible that you know that to be true and that you know it to be doubted by you. For it would follow that that would not be doubted by you, because you know it to be doubted by you.

Next, it is argued that this could not be doubted by you, for if it were doubted by you, then you would know that it was doubted by you. Then, you would know that to someone is proposed a proposition doubted by him, namely, you. And so you would know it to be as that proposition signifies. Thus, you would know that to be true for you, from which it follows that it would not be doubted by you. It follows, therefore, that that would neither be known by you to be true, nor known to be false nor doubted by you. And this is impossible in the case posited, namely, that you should consider it as far as you can and that you should be sufficiently learned for the consideration.

I say that this proposition could be doubted by you and that you could know it to be doubted by you, since you could not know that it would be false, as was well argued. Nor could you know that it would be true, as was also well argued. Thus, it remains that you doubt it. And the cause of this is that if to someone else is proposed another proposition doubted by him, then it is simply true. If, however, to no one else is proposed a proposition doubted by him, it will be false; which I prove, because that is false from which, together with a true, a false follows. And so it would be in the given case. I prove this, because I suppose the aforesaid case to be true, for it is possible. And yet from that proposition and the case, it follows that that is both true and false, which is impossible. I assert, first, that from it and the case, it follows that it is true. For the case posits that it is and yet it has often been said that from any proposition, together with another stating that it is, it follows that it is true. Next, it is shown that from it and the case, it follows that it is false. For you know that it is doubted by you, and you know that this is signified by its formal significations. Hence, you know that it is as it signifies, with regard to its formal significations. Now you who are most learned know well that every proposition is true if it is as it signifies in its formal significations, unless it has reflection on itself, because of which it follows that it is false. Therefore, you ought to conclude that you know this disjunctive: "Either it is true or it has reflection on itself, because of which it is false." Now, finally, you who are most learned should know whether in any such case a proposition can reflect on itself or not. And if you know that it cannot, then you know it to be true, which is false, as has been said. Therefore, you know that in some case, it can have such reflection, and yet you well know that this could not be if to another should be proposed a proposition doubted by him. For you know that in some case it would be true. Hence, it remains that you know that the reflection would be such that from it, it follows that it is false, if no other doubted proposition should be stated. Therefore, it would be false. And so it is clear that from it and the true case posited earlier, namely, that no other doubted proposition is proposed, it follows that it is false. And this is what we wanted to prove. So, therefore, it has been explained that it is true if to another should be proposed a doubted proposition, and that it is false if to no other should be proposed another doubted proposition. And you do not know whether another doubted proposition is proposed to another person or not. So it is necessary that you doubt whether it is true or false.

Concerning the arguments in opposition, it is to be said that you do indeed know that it is doubted by you and that it is as it signifies according to formal significations. But from this it does not follow that you know it to be true nor that it is true. For it can have reflection on itself such that it is false, and you do not know whether it has.

However, someone replies that of contradictory propositions proposed to you, if one is known by you to be false, it is necessary if you give heed and are learned, that you know the other to be true. But it is established that if the contradictory of the sophism is stated, namely, this: "No proposition doubted by him is proposed to anybody," you know that it will be false. For you know that there is an exception in your case, since you know that a proposition doubted by you has been proposed to you. Hence, it follows that you know the sophism to be true. Again, more strongly, it is argued that you do not doubt this sophism. Indeed, you know it to be true, since I could argue thus: a proposition doubted by you is proposed to you, and you are someone; hence, a proposition doubted by someone is proposed to him. This syllogism is valid and formal, because it is expository. And yet, you know the premisses to be true, and hence, if you pay heed and are learned, you know the conclusion [15] to be true, since you well know that a false proposition does not follow from a true. And yet that conclusion is the sophism. Therefore, you know it to be true. So it was badly said that it was doubted by you.

Concerning the first of these objections, it seems that the con-

[15] Reading *conclusionem* instead of *contradictionem*.

tradictory was not sufficiently taken, because it can have reflection on itself, from which it follows that it is false. The contradictory is to be taken from a copulative composed of it and that which is implied in it and the case, namely, that it is true. So that if the given proposition is properly named A, it will be equivalent to this affirmative proposition "To someone is proposed a proposition doubted by him, and A is true." Thus, the contradictory will be "No proposition doubted by him is proposed to anybody, or A is not true." And it is clear that this would be doubted by you, just as would the preceding. For the first part of this disjunctive you know to be false. And concerning the second part, you do not know whether it is true or false.

Concerning the second objection, I say that that argument was valid: to you is proposed a proposition doubted by you, and you are someone; hence, to someone is proposed a proposition doubted by him. And I say that you know the argument is valid and that the premisses are true, and consequently, that you know that the conclusion is true. But the conclusion is not the sophism. Rather it is another similar to it, which is known to be true, because its terms stand for a sophism which you know to be doubted. Nor is it equivalent to the sophism, as it was earlier stated to be. Rather, to make it equivalent, it would be necessary to say that to someone is proposed a doubted proposition, and A is true, positing as before that the sophism is properly named A. But then, this does not follow from those given premisses.

Therefore, it is to be noted well that if someone first proposes this to you: "A doubted proposition is proposed to you," you will doubt it and you will consider whether it is true or false. But granting this, whoever, coming in, should say to you that to someone is proposed a doubted proposition, you will know that he speaks truly and that his proposition is true, not for itself, but for that first one.

But then you will posit another case, namely, that Socrates and Plato are coming at the same time, and each utters a proposition such as "A doubted proposition is proposed to someone," and one does not speak sooner than the other, and you give heed equally to them. Then [it is asked] whether both propositions will be doubted by you or one doubted and the other known to be true.

I say that both will be doubted by you, because you could know neither to be true for the other. Because for the same reason that you would know one to be true for the other, for the same reason conversely. And so you would know both to be true, which is false. For they are perhaps false in the case in which to no one is proposed a proposition doubted by him. For in that case, if you should know them to be true, you would not doubt them. Thus, nothing would be doubted by anybody, of which the opposite would be signified by those propositions. Thus, they would be false. But doubts not existing, whatever doubtful proposition comes to you, signifying something to be doubted by someone, it would be known by you to be true, not for itself, but for that which you then doubted.

Finally, concerning this sophism, someone can ask how it would be if it should not be posited in the case that you should be learned. And I say that perhaps because of your ignorance you would indeed not doubt. Rather, perhaps because of some reasons, you could believe it to be true without doubt, although it should perhaps be false. Or perhaps, because of other reasons, you will believe it to be false, also without any doubt. For it happens that one doubts nothing concerning that which he falsely opines. Hence, Aristotle says in the seventh of the *Ethics* that some, in a state of opinion, do not doubt, but opine.[16] Certainly, some believe in what they opine no less than others in what they know.

(16) *You will answer negatively.*

The sixteenth sophism concerning combinations of answers to questions is this: "You will answer negatively."

And this is proposed to you, and you are obligated that concerning what is proposed to you, you ought to respond directly that it is so or that it is not so. For you ought to admit this obligation, since whatever proposition is proposed is either true or not true, and since by "to be so" we signify that it is true and by "not to be so" we signify that it is not true. Therefore, concerning any, we can truly answer either that it is so or that it is not so. Hence, you ought to accept the obligation that you will so respond. Then, therefore, I ask that you respond to the stated proposition which is proposed to you, namely, this: "You will answer negatively."

If then, you respond that it is so, I shall argue against you, since you respond falsely. For you concede that you respond negatively and yet it is not so, for you respond affirmatively. But if you respond that

[16] Aristotle, *Nicomachean Ethics* vii. 3. 1146b 25–36.

it is not so, again I shall argue against you, that you answer falsely. For you deny that you respond negatively, and yet, as a matter of fact, you do respond negatively. Therefore, etc.

I say that according to the aforesaid obligation, you could not respond truly. But without that obligation, you could respond well, saying to him who proposes that he proposes falsely, or that his proposition was false. Or also, you can truly respond saying that he does not propose falsely to you. Hence, I say that you ought not to admit that obligation except under the condition that a proposition proposed to you could not consignify your response, because of which signification, your response would reflect on itself, from which it follows that it is false.

When, therefore, it is argued that you ought to admit the obligation because whatever proposition is proposed to you, it will be either true or false, I agree. But that proposition which was proposed to you was either true or false, since if you respond nothing, it was false. And if you respond that it is so, it was also false. And also your response was false, because it affirms that which was false to be true. But if you answer that it is not so, then that is true and your response is false, since it denies that which is true. Therefore, when it is said that concerning every true proposition, we ought to answer that it is so, and concerning every false proposition that it is not so, I concede, unless the response should have reflection on itself, because of which it would follow that it is false. But in this case, one ought to change the response.

In the same way, if someone wishes to obligate you to respond precisely concerning a proposition which he proposes to you, that it is true or it is not, you ought not to accept the obligation. First, because you do not know whether a proposition doubted by you will be proposed. But also, if one wishes to obligate you to respond either that it is true or that it is false or doubtful, still you ought not to accept the obligation, unless under the aforesaid condition. Hence, to that proposition "You will respond negatively," you ought not to respond that it is true, nor that it is not true, nor that you doubt it. But you could respond that it is false.

But someone has replied that these are contradictories: "You have spoken truly" and "You have not spoken truly." But to whichever of these you should respond to him who proposes to you the given sophism, your response will be false. Therefore, both contradictories will be false, which is impossible.

To this, I say that to whichever of these you respond without the other, it will be false. Nor from this does it follow that the two contradictories are at the same time false, since they are not at the same time. But if you should respond to both at once, then you will respond negatively and affirmatively at once. And if you should respond negatively and verify the sophism, then your affirmative response would be true, and the negative false. Thus, both contradictories would still not be false at the same time. It would be the same, if we should posit that A signifies every man responding or going to respond negatively and nothing else, just as "man" signifies every man and nothing else, and that an opponent proposes to you that you are A. And then he asks whether it is so or is not so, for this is similar as to a proposal that you will answer or are going to answer negatively. And then it could be asked whether it is so or not so. Thus, you could not answer well by saying directly that it is so or not so, because of reflection. But you could truly answer, saying that the proposition was false, or answering that the proposition was not false but true.

(17) *You will throw me in the water.*

The seventeenth sophism is about some conditional promises or vows. And this is the sophism: "You will throw me in the water."

I posit the case that Plato guards a bridge with much assistance, so that none can cross without his assent. And then Socrates comes asking Plato with great supplication that he allow him to cross. Then Plato angrily vows and swears, saying "Surely, Socrates, if in the first proposition which you utter, you speak the truth, I will permit you to cross. But surely, if you speak falsely, I shall throw you in the water." Then Socrates will say to Plato the aforesaid sophism, namely, "You will throw me in the water." Thus, it is asked then what Plato ought to do, according to his promise.

If you say that he will throw Socrates in the water, this is against the promise, since then Socrates spoke truly. Thus, Plato ought to allow him to cross. And if you say that he will allow him to cross, it appears that this is again against the promise and the oath, since then Socrates speaks falsely, in which case Plato ought to throw him in the water.

It is to be answered that concerning this sophism, many questions can be raised. The first is whether Socrates' proposition is true, which was stated for the sophism. The second is whether Plato's proposition, which was the promise or vow, was true or false. The third is what Plato ought to do, keeping the promise or the vow.

Concerning the first, I say that Socrates' proposition is about a future contingent. Thus, I cannot determinately know whether it is true or false, until I see what will be concerning that future act. Hence, it is in Plato's power whether it is true or false. For if he throws him in the water, the proposition is true, and if he permits him to cross, it is false.

Concerning the second question, I say that Plato's proposition was a conditional, which according to the proper sense, could not be true. For the antecedent could be true without the consequent. For it was possible that Socrates should have said a great truth, as that God is, and that Plato yet should not have permitted him to cross. But still a promissive conditional in a less proper sense is conceded in the case that, the condition being fulfilled, the promise is fulfilled. For instance, if I say "If you will come to me, I will give you a horse," then if, you coming to me, I give you a horse, all would believe that I had spoken truly. And so speaking, I say that Plato does not speak truly, since Socrates has not fulfilled the condition. For he utters a proposition which had to be true or false, although not determinately true or determinately false, until the future act has followed, as ought to be seen in the *De Interpretatione*.[17] And yet, given this, Plato cannot fulfill the promise, since because of Socrates' proposition, Plato's promise reflects on itself, from which it follows that it is false.

When, therefore, it was asked on the third question what Plato ought to do, keeping the promise, I say that he ought not to keep the promise, for he could not or ought not so to promise except with an exception, namely, unless Socrates should utter a proposition having reflection on the promise, because of which it would follow that the promise could not be verified.

(18) *Socrates wishes to eat.*

The case may be posited that Socrates wishes to eat if Plato wishes to eat and not otherwise, for men often wish so to have company in eating, so that without company, they do not wish to eat.

[17] Aristotle, *De Interpretatione* 9. 19a 27–29.

Next, it may also be posited, conversely, that Plato does not wish to eat if Socrates wishes to eat. For he is angry with Socrates, so he does not wish to eat with him. Then it is asked whether the sophism is true or false. For these are contradictories: "Socrates wishes to eat" and "Socrates does not wish to eat." So it is necessary for one to be true and the other false, whatever case is posited.

Thus, if you say that Socrates wishes to eat, the opposite follows, since it follows that Plato does not wish to eat, from which it also follows that Socrates does not wish to eat.

And if you say that Socrates does not wish to eat, the opposite follows. For it follows that Plato wishes to eat, from which it also follows that Socrates wishes to eat.

I respond that the case, as it is posited, is impossible, properly speaking. For this is a conditional: "Socrates wishes to eat if Plato wishes to eat," and it is not a valid consequence from the antecedent to the consequent. For it is possible that when Plato wishes to eat, Socrates does not wish to eat. But still, as conditionals are usually conceded in our promissive acts or vows or desires, this case is possible: Socrates desires to make true this proposition (or desires it to be as it signifies): "If Plato eats here, I will eat with him, and if not neither will I." And Plato, conversely, desires to verify this: "If Socrates eats here, I will not eat, and if he does not eat, I will eat." But I say that it is impossible for both to fulfill their wishes. But you ask whether, therefore, Socrates wishes to eat or not. I say unless Socrates and Plato have other acts of willing than the preceding, neither wishes to eat here, since the will is determined to that which one wills. And the will of neither of them is determined to eating. Hence, it does not follow: I wish to go to Rome if Socrates goes; hence, I wish to go to Rome. But you say it follows that if Socrates does not wish to eat here, then Plato wishes to eat here. I deny it, because that conditional was false and not to be admitted. But that categorical is indeed to be admitted, that Socrates desires the case to be as is signified by this proposition "If Plato eats here, I will eat with him." And Plato has an aversion to this being the case, so he intends the contrary. And from this, nothing impossible follows.

(19) *Socrates curses Plato.*

The case may be posited that Socrates says "Plato should be cursed if he curses me, and not otherwise." And Plato says, on the contrary, "Socrates should be cursed if he does not curse me, and not otherwise." Then it is asked concerning the truth of the sophism, whether Socrates curses Plato.

If you say that he does, there follows an inconsistency, namely, that Plato curses Socrates and does not curse Socrates. And if you say that he does not, the opposite follows, since it follows that Plato curses Socrates, and consequently Socrates curses Plato.

I say that you posit here, to express the case, a proposition such as "Socrates says that Plato should be cursed if he curses Socrates." I say that that proposition can be understood as a conditional, namely, in a sense such as "If Plato curses Socrates, Socrates says that Plato should be cursed." And that proposition is false and impossible and not to be admitted. For it does not follow that if Plato curses Socrates, then Socrates says Plato should be cursed. Rather, whether Plato curses Socrates or not, Socrates says what he says, or also, does not say what he does not say.

In another way, it can be understood that that proposition is a categorical in this sense: "Socrates utters a sentence such as 'Plato should be cursed, if, etc.'" And this ought to be conceded. For it is possible that Socrates utters such a proposition.

In the same way ought to be distinguished the proposition which the case posits, that if Plato says, etc.

Then a question is asked, whether thus speaking, Socrates and Plato curse each other. And I answer that to curse someone is to say, under a verb of the optative mode, that that person should come by some evil. Hence, I understand the same in saying "Plato should be cursed" as in saying "Plato should come by evil." And then, furthermore, I say that such cursing sentences are absolute curses without the addition of a condition, as if I say "Plato should be cursed." And sometimes there are conditioned curses, as if I say "Plato should be cursed if he goes into the fields." And then since names can signify conventionally, if you wish to call both simply curses, I say both cursed each other, although not absolutely.

But you argue against this, since it follows that if Socrates curses Plato, then Plato does not curse Socrates. I deny this consequence for I did not admit the proposition directly as a conditional. But granting that Plato uttered such a proposition, and that it is true that he uttered it, then he cursed Socrates by a conditioned curse, whether

Socrates cursed or not. However, if you do not wish to call a conditioned curse simply a curse, then I say that neither curses the other. Nor does it follow that if Socrates does not curse Plato, then Plato curses him. For it follows only that Plato says that he said it, and this was only a conditioned curse.

In order to fill out more the preceding sophism, because verbal abuse is seen to designate a desire that someone come to evil, there is still one sophism posited.

(20) *Socrates wishes Plato evil.*

I posit that Socrates conditionally wishes Plato evil, namely, if Plato wishes Socrates evil. And conversely, Plato wishes Socrates evil, if Socrates does not wish Plato evil. Then it is asked concerning this sophism whether Socrates wishes Plato evil or not.

And it could be argued as it was argued concerning curses.

And I answer as before, that the propositions expressing the case can be taken as conditionals. And then they are not to be admitted, since it does not follow that if Plato wishes Socrates evil, then Socrates wishes Plato evil.

In another way, they can be taken and received as categoricals, so that Socrates wishes it to be as is signified by this sentence "May Plato come to evil if he wishes Socrates evil." And then when it is asked whether Socrates wishes Plato evil, I say that he does, according to a conditional wish, but not absolutely.

And so leaving the curses behind, may God, who is praised through all time, bless us.

AMEN